D0782440

OXFORD STUDIES IN
SOCIAL AND CULTURAL ANTHROPOLOGY

Editorial Board

JOHN DAVIS LUC DE HEUSCH CAROLINE HUMPHREY
EMILY MARTIN PETER RIVIÈRE MARILYN STRATHERN

A PLACE APART

OXFORD STUDIES IN SOCIAL AND CULTURAL ANTHROPOLOGY

Oxford Studies in Social and Cultural Anthropology represents the work of authors, new and established, which will set the criteria of excellence in ethnographic description and innovation in analysis. The series serves as an essential source of information about the world and the discipline.

A Place Apart

*An Anthropological Study of
the Icelandic World*

KIRSTEN HASTRUP

CLARENDON PRESS · OXFORD
1998

RARITAN VALLEY COMMUNITY COLLEGE
EVELYN S. FIELD LIBRARY

Oxford University Press, Great Clarendon Street, Oxford OX2 6DP

Oxford New York

Athens Auckland Bangkok Bogota Bombay Buenos Aires
Calcutta Cape Town Dar es Salaam Delhi Florence Hong Kong Istanbul
Karachi Kuala Lumpur Madras Madrid Melbourne Mexico City
Nairobi Paris Singapore Taipei Tokyo Toronto Warsaw
and associated companies in
Berlin Ibadan

Oxford is a registered trade mark of Oxford University Press

Published in the United States
by Oxford University Press Inc., New York

© *Kirsten Hastrup 1998*
The moral rights of the author have been asserted

First published 1998

All rights reserved. No part of this publication may be reproduced,
stored in a retrieval system, or transmitted, in any form or by any means,
without the prior permission in writing of Oxford University Press.
Within the UK, exceptions are allowed in respect of any fair dealing for the
purpose of research or private study, or criticism or review, as permitted
under the Copyright, Designs and Patents Act, 1988, or in the case of
reprographic reproduction in accordance with the terms of the licences
issued by the Copyright Licensing Agency. Enquiries concerning
reproduction outside these terms and in other countries should be
sent to the Rights Department, Oxford University Press,
at the address above

British Library Cataloguing in Publication Data
Data available

Library of Congress Cataloging in Publication Data
Hastrup, Kirsten.
A place apart: an anthropological study of the Icelandic world /
Kirsten Hastrup.
(Oxford studies in social and
cultural anthropology)
Includes bibliographical references and index.
1. Iceland–Civilization–20th century. 2. Iceland–Social life
and customs. 3. Anthropology–Iceland. I. Title. II. Series.
DL375.H37 1998 949.12–dc21 97-39269
ISBN 0-19-823380-9

1 3 5 7 9 10 8 6 4 2

Typeset by Best-set Typesetter Ltd., Hong Kong
Printed in Great Britain
on acid-free paper by
Biddles Ltd., Guildford and King's Lynn

PREFACE AND ACKNOWLEDGEMENTS

This book has been in the making for a long time. Since my fieldwork in the 1980s I have moved towards it mainly by way of sidetracks. In a decade of profound changes within and around anthropology, the canons of writing ethnography have dissolved. The present attempt to describe the Icelandic world, therefore, follows no strict rule and has no clear precedent, except in the general and well-established imaginative attention to ethnographic detail. The future will show by which standard it is judged. The inherent propensity to generalization is not an attempt to measure the Icelanders by the lowest common denominator, but an ambition to show how this world is comprehensible and interesting at a general level of understanding.

The work is a sequel to my two previous monographs on Iceland. The first, *Culture and History in Medieval Iceland. An Anthropological Analysis of Structure and Change* (Oxford 1985) was an attempt to identify the dynamic points in the historical development of the Icelandic Commonwealth (930–1262). The second, *Nature and Policy in Iceland 1400–1800. An Anthropological Analysis of History and Mentality* (Oxford 1990) dealt with four centuries of disintegration, and the book was an exertion in comprehending the reasons for what seemed to be an inexplicable decline, by comparison with the well-structured and highly literate medieval society. Both books were works of historical anthropology, dealing as much with process and dynamisms as with culture and patterns.

The present work brings history up-to-date, as it were. In articles and collected works, I have dealt with the periods in between, but in this book the perspective is contemporary. As we shall see, history is still very much part of this perspective, and there is a sense in which, therefore, the book incorporates previous periods and closes my historical anthropological work on Iceland.

I would like to thank Curtis Brown, Ltd and Princeton University Press for permission to reproduce poems from W. H. Auden and Louis MacNeice, *Letters from Iceland* © 1937 by W. H. Auden and Louis MacNeice, one of which appeared in *The Complete Works of W. H. Auden: Prose and Travel Books in Prose and Verse*, vol. i 1926–1938, published by Princeton University Press © 1996 by The Estate of W. H. Auden.

During the years, I have incurred a number of debts to people and institutions without whom this work would never have seen light. The Danish Research Council for the Humanities funded part of my fieldwork and long periods of research time since then. The Icelandic Ministry of Education funded that part of my research in Iceland which took place at the Manuscript Institute of the University of Iceland. Professor Jónas Kristjánsson, then Director of the Institute, welcomed me into an extraordinary scholarly environment for seven months. The erudition and learning of the place was extended to me by all members of the Institute, but I want to mention Stefán Karlsson in particular for his friendship and philological patience, and Hallfreður Örn Eiriksson for his interest and his help in finding the right places for subsequent fieldwork elsewhere in Iceland. At the Institute of Anthropology of the University of Iceland, I profited much from conversations with Gísli Pálsson whenever we had an opportunity to talk on matters Icelandic. More recently, Gísli read the first draft of this book, and made a number of critical and constructive comments, which helped me improve the book in important ways. Similarly, David Koester and Finnur Magnússon both read and commented constructively on my draft. To these three scholars with firsthand research experience in Iceland I remain grateful. At the last stage, Anthony Cohen once again extended his friendship and his learning to my work in reading the draft and making important suggestions, without which the work would have been less readable. My thanks are sincere. As will be understood, the shortcomings that remain in the book are owed less to a lack of intelligent advice than to a failure always to follow it on my own part.

In the Icelandic countryside, I had the invaluable fortune to be welcomed at the farm of Hali in Suðursveit. The wise and lively extended family of Hali were my prime interlocutors in the Icelandic countryside, and through them I got to know life and people in Suðursveit in a more comprehensive way than would otherwise have been possible. I thank them all from the bottom of my heart; Fjölnir, Þorbjörg, Kristinn, Arnór, and Vésteinn are especially remembered for allowing me to live in their house, for their patience in teaching me Icelandic ways, and for letting me return as often as I could.

In the fishing village of Hellisandur I found much comfort in the friendship of Smári, Auður, and Hildigunnur. At moments of exceeding cold, they provided warmth and made me experience the life and hospitality of an Icelandic family, also at later occasions, and with them I share many fond memories. Many other people contributed in other ways during fieldwork. I cannot mention them all, but I do hope none of them will feel let down by the present book, which can only in a very modest way reflect their rich reality, and which by any standard is overdue.

At home, my mother, Else, and my four sisters, Karen, Lisbet, Anne, and Helene (and their families), provided almost limitless support during years of hard work and frequent travel; with four children I would not have been able to get very far without this female network. My children, Rasmus, Simon, Anders, and Frida, are likewise gratefully remembered for their sharing with me so many experiences, Icelandic and others—and in such good ethnographic spirit. Mogens encouraged me to finally make this book happen, and commented wisely on parts of it. To him I extend my affectionate thanks for his taking an interest.

Kirsten Hastrup

Copenhagen
July 1996

CONTENTS

LIST OF ILLUSTRATIONS

JOURNEY TO ICELAND

And each traveller hopes: 'Let me be far from any
Physician.' And each port has a name for the sea,
    The citiless, the corroding, the sorrow.
    And North means to all: 'Reject!'

The great plains are for ever where the cold fish are hunted
And everywhere. Light birds flicker and flaunt:
    Under a scolding flag the lover
    Of islands may see at last,

Faintly, his limited hope, as he nears the glitter
Of glaciers, the outlines of sterile mountains, intense
    In the abnormal day of this world, and a river's
    Fan-like polyp of sand.

Then let the good citizen find here natural marvels:
A horse-shoe ravine, the issue of steam from a cleft
    In the rock, and rocks, and waterfall brushing the
    Rocks, and, among the rocks, birds.

The student of prose and conduct find places to visit:
The site of a church where a bishop was put in a bag,
    The bath of a great historian, the rock where
    An outlaw dreaded the dark.

Remember the doomed man thrown by his horse and crying:
'Beautiful is the hillside, I will not go';
    The old woman confessing: 'He that I loved the
    Best, to him I was worst.'

Islands are places apart where Europe is absent.
Are they? The world still is, the present, the lie,
    And the narrow bridge over a torrent
    Or the small farm under a crag

Are natural settings for the jealousies of a province:
A weak vow of fidelity is sworn by the cairn,
    And within the indigenous figure on horseback
    On the bridle-path down by the lake

The blood moves also by crooked and furtive inches,
Asks all our questions: 'Where is the homage? When
 Shall justice be done? O who is against me?
 Why am I always alone?'

For our time has no favourite suburb: no local features
Are those of the young for whom all wish to care:
 The promise is only a promise, the fabulous
 Country impartially far.

Tears fall in all the rivers. Again a driver
Pulls on his gloves and in a blinding snowstorm starts
 Upon his deadly journey: again some writer
 Runs howling to his art.

       W. H. Auden, 1936

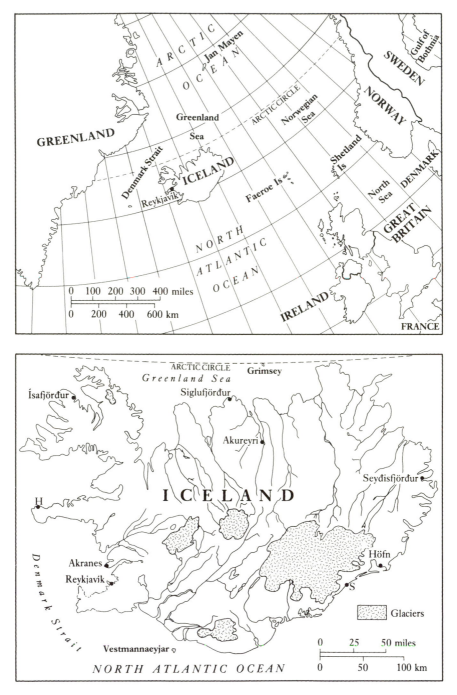

Maps of Iceland.

Showing Hellisandur on Snæfellsnes (H) and Suðursveit (S)—where fieldwork took place.

Prelude

Prelude

Imagine yourself suddenly set down surrounded by all your gear, alone on a subarctic coast, while the bus which has dropped you drives away on the dirt road out of sight, and you stand there like a misplaced Malinowski, whose 'arrival story' from tropical Trobrianders (1922: 4) I am here adapting to my own experience of arriving at one of my Icelandic fieldsites, a farm situated on a narrow strip of farm land on the south-eastern coast of Iceland. 'Imagine further that you are a beginner, without previous experience, with nothing to guide you and no one to help you,' as Malinowski had it. And there you are, in the field, hoping for the best and fearing the worst. The fear has nothing to do with a fear of the as-yet-unknown people; it is a fear of your own shortcomings in relating to people you do not know but through whom you are supposed to understand the human condition better than before. The fear is also a fear of yourself, however, or—more accurately—a fear of the other in yourself, whom you may not be able to control. Today we have openly acknowledged what Malinowski privately sensed, and as his diary revealed, that living another culture brings a different side of yourself to the fore, which will be your constant companion in the field, your counterpart and trickster whom you will come to know only gradually through the reflection in the new people's behaviour towards you. Although alone and possibly isolated on arrival in the field, the ethnographer's task implicates her deeply in a world of intersubjectivity. With time, the arrival belongs to a past, and becomes the beginning—of a new story: an ethnography.

A Story of Cows

The weather is rough and reminds one of the approaching winter. The country is shrouded in fog, wind, rain, and cold, and here on the coastal lands between the roaring North Atlantic sea and the rocky mountains and glaciers, preparations for winter have long since begun. Sheep must be collected from the mountain pastures, some of which are distant and accessible only with difficulty. One has to sell the sheep for meat and wool, slaughter some of them for home consumption, cut them up, singe the heads, and smoke other parts. Sausages have to be made from liver and blood, and rams' testicles are to be preserved in *sýra*, that is sour whey which has always served as the principal means of preservation in this country so short of salt. There are potatoes to be dug out of the stony ground, rhubarb to be preserved,

Fɪɢ. 1. Rounding up the cows.

and berries to be collected from the mountains. It is a busy season, and the maid Kristín is very preoccupied.

Right now she is on her way to the pasture to collect the cows for the evening milking. She shares the milking job with one of the young farmers of the farm, but she is alone in collecting the cattle. She feels cold in the wind to which one is always exposed here, but she likes the landscape and enjoys the sight of the huge glacier close to the farm site. In this thinly populated country, one is quickly absorbed by the landscape when leaving the farm, and the feeling of being at one with the vastness is exhilarating. Kristín reaches the mobile electric fence, which is moved and reset every day, calls for the cows and opens the wire-gate. The cows are restless, and Frekja and Skotta in particular seem agitated. As usual, the silly Rökk is difficult to attract. Kristín yells and gesticulates and works hard to keep the flock of twenty-eight brindled cows together. In this landscape it is very important that the herdswoman can manage this, because there are no boundaries other than the mobile fence to keep the cows from scattering in the vast and barren wilderness. And wilderness it is: mountains, slopes, rivers, and sands all around, with few traces of people.

Today, everything goes wrong for Kristín. A couple of cows leave the flock and go off their own way. In the attempt to get them back, Kristín must overtake the main herd, but the cows seem to sense her panic and start running in all directions. Each new attempt to overrule them makes matters worse. It is cold and windy, and the rubber boots don't make running in the rocky area any easier. The situation is hopeless and she trots back to the farm to get help. Eventually, two men on horseback get the flock together, and with some delay the evening milking can begin. Kristín is rather embarrassed by the incident but the young farmer laughs and says that cows are stupid. She silently agrees and laughs with him. They milk together and change into the usual gear of small talk and silent acknowledgement of each other's contribution to the work. There are two milking machines and they have one each; before and after the machine is used, the udder must be thoroughly worked through by hand, to 'prepare' it and, afterwards, to make sure it is empty. This brings Kristín in close physical contact with the cows, whose characters she has gradually got to know. Apart from milking, Kristín also cleans out the cowshed and swings huge 50-kilo sacks of supplementary fodder from the stack in the storeroom and into the shed, where the contents must be distributed. The farmer often smiles when seeing her efforts, and she smiles back at him.

Later she reads more about the local view of cows in a book written by the farmer's kinsman, describing life and livelihood on the same farm some fifty years earlier. They only had two cows then, because the milk was only for home consumption, there being no roads, no dairies, and no notion of commercial cattle-breeding. Then, it had been the youngster's task to take the cows to pasture every day, away from the precious *tún*, or infield, where hay was grown for winter storage. Even with only two cows, the task could be a tricky one, and not altogether pleasant. The relative writes:

Aldrei voru kýrnar skemmtilegar. Þær virtust vera alveg húmorslausar. Það var eins og það lægi alltaf illa á þeim, varu jafnvel oft í vondi skapi. Þegar þær brugðu sér á leik, þá var eins og þær gerðu það í illu. Maður sá aldrei lífsgleði eða spaugsemi í hreyfingum þeirra og heyrði aldrei þessa skemmtilegu blessbresti aftan í þeim eins og hestunum, þegar þær ruku á sprett frá manni. (Þórbergur Þórðarson 1981: 59)

(The cows were never enjoyable. They were regarded as completely humourless. It was as if they were always sad, still they were often in bad temper. When they moved to play, it was as if they did it out of malice. One never saw cheerfulness or jocularity in their movements and never heard this amusing windsmack from behind as with the horses when they jerked to jump from man.)

Apparently, young Þórbergur had as ambivalent an attitude to the cows as Kristín now has. As stated, Kristín is milkmaid on an Icelandic farm, but she is also an anthropologist doing fieldwork—me. At home I am Kirsten, but in Iceland I was translated to Kristín; it was not only my name that was translated but also my identity. I could not take the cows seriously as a practical task from any other position than the milkmaid's. Who would be able to yell at them, to milk them, to let oneself be annoyed by the impudent and pleased by the easy ones from the exclusive position of a scholar? To become immersed in the world of the Icelanders,

I had to find a local position for myself, which made me an 'other'. It was a shift from a first person 'I' to a third-person 'she', who was objectified in the local discourse, and who in turn came to see herself as such. While obviously the same individual, my 'self' was different in world of the Icelanders of which I was temporarily a member. Within such worlds one cannot separate materiality from meaning, or event from classification (cf. Hastrup 1995*a*: 18–19). When oneself is another, experiences are different. This is the basis of anthropological fieldwork—such as my fieldwork in Iceland upon which this work builds.

Fieldwork means living another world, and getting to know it by way of a process of (secondary) enculturation, that is a process of incorporating tacit local knowledge as based in experience. As related elsewhere (Hastrup 1995*a*: 18), I incorporated at least part of the Icelandic world to the point where I was ready to accuse myself of something like 'witchcraft' when one of my cows dropped dead after my having cursed it. My work with the cows was a shortcut to the main street of local *experience* and thus to the implicit sensations of the world of Icelanders.

It was my privilege to live at a farm where I was transformed into an almost useful member of the family. In previous generations, when cows had lived under the same roof as people at the farm where they had given warmth to each other, cows had also been part of the family. Again Þórbergur writes *þær vore partur af fjölskyldunni, ennþá nákomnari henni andlega og líkamlega en hestarnir og kindurnar* (Þórbergur Þórðarson 1981: 56–7) ('they were part of the family, spiritually and bodily even closer to it than the horses and the sheep'). The cows were further praised because they gave milk, 'the healthiest food in the home'. By their association with milk and hearth, cows were always associated with the female domain, and although they now had their own shed, they were still part of the domestic space, to which women had immediate access (Hastrup 1985*b*). My tending the cows thus gave me a truly localized position to act from. It also connected me to age-old practices, and therefore to history, in a very direct sense.

The point of opening my account of the world of the Icelanders by this impressionistic sketch of my life with the cows is to stress the nature of this world, not simply as a place in which Icelanders live their individual lives—men, women and children, farmers, fishermen, philologists, and many more—but as a 'space' which I could only know by becoming part of it. Spaces are practised places; autumn slaughter, story-telling, passing judgements on cows, laughing together and so forth are social practices which make the space materialize. What you should imagine, then, is not simply the faraway beaches of a subarctic island, which you have come to study with the outsider's clear gaze, but the shores of a distinct world that cannot simply be seen or told, but must be perceived by all the senses and recalled in a language that will allow us to feel the sensational depth of reality beyond the words. What I am after is not the Icelandic culture in the old sense of pattern and wholeness, but the 'contexture' of the Icelandic world, contexture being 'both the texture that surrounds and the texture that constitutes' (Daniel and

Peck 1996: 1). Part of my feel for the Icelandic contexture is owing to my position in the Icelandic cowshed and in the vast wilderness herding my flock.

As Kristín, I could not always keep my flock together, and without pushing the analogy into absurdity, all ethnographers also know that they cannot 'capture' the reality of the people they work with. What I myself found was that, conversely, 'I' was captured by the Icelandic world; in being absorbed by the landscape I also found myself embraced by people who were warm and generous enough to make room for an other, and show her their selves. This book has no pretence of covering that world in full, but to render a feel for its distinction within a shared global reality, and a feel for the particular sense of time and history that qualifies it, and not least a sense of the particular rhythm which beats beneath the surface saliences of the contexture. In the process, I hope to show how action and understanding are grounded—and how they may also shift the ground.

The Poetics of Space

The above preamble points to the poetical nature of the ethnographic enterprise. It is not that ethnography *is* poetry, or that we have to write in particular metres to convey the truth about other realities. It is rather that the ethnographic—like the poetical—image is a sudden salience on the linguistic surface, which because of its newness makes us sense, and maybe 'recognize', what we did not know or only dimly knew before. Like the poem, the unprecedented ethnography extends our feeling of a shared humanity, and like the poet, the ethnographer is present as author, yet her 'self' is not simply premissed by her willing pen but also by her embodied experience as another. There are other parallels, as recently suggested by Valentine Daniel, quoting William Pritchard, who writing about poetry said:

'Poetry will continue to count as a living force insofar as we keep the poems open, prevent them hardening into meanings which make them easier to handle only because they are no longer fluid, problematic and alive.' Substitute 'ethnography' and 'ethnographers' for 'poetry' and 'poems', and you have the means for judging good ethnography. (Daniel 1996*a*: 8)

No master narrative here, as Daniel points out, but a significant echo of Evans-Pritchard's classic claim that anthropology is a philosophy of art rather than a natural science of society (Evans-Pritchard 1962: 152).

In the poem prefacing this book, W. H. Auden gives voice to a complex sentiment about Iceland where the poem was originally written. The experience of the landscape and its people is transformed into words rendering shadows of a history which is inscribed in nature, and in sensations of separation and sadness. There is also vastness and fear of being englobed by this place apart. The reason I have chosen this poem to preface this work is its resonance with my own feeling, not only about Iceland, but also with the task that lies ahead: the encircling of the Icelandic world in words that can only present language shadows of life. However, I cannot but run howling to my art—the art of anthropology. The tension of the not-yet written has forced me to my pen after years of silence on matters Icelandic.

The silence may need some explanation; it is partly owing to inherent difficulties in writing ethnography in this challenging age of dissolved canons, and partly to a rather stark criticism of some of my work from within the field of Icelandic anthropology, mainly a few articles dealing with contemporary issues. Having had time to reflect upon the criticism, I now read part of it as an expression of disagreement on the epistemological foundation of our discipline. This is why I will have to make a brief detour around some general matters concerning the practice of anthropology.

Just as poetry makes a voice out of those voices that surround it (Geertz 1983: 117), ethnography makes an image of a people out of those images that surround it. In this case, the images stem from both local and foreign visions of the Icelandic world, visions that are inferred from complex situations and interpretations rather than observed ready-made. My fieldwork encounters blend with Auden's and other literary reflections, produced by the indigenous figure on horseback and the outlaw who dreaded the dark as well as other people, each of them carrying forward their own vision of Iceland. In ethnography, there are points of view and crossing perspectives that will for ever prevent any single representation from taking power. Life unfolds where language cannot but infold and give passing judgement of the world. In the process, the verbal statements made become part of the context within which life continues to challenge whatever images are held accountable for reality. If history-making transforms experience into narrative, the narrating itself becomes part of lived experience, not something apart from it (Dening 1993: 73–4). Text and context are mutually implicated.

In this work ethnography also blends with history, not only in its objective but also in the method. The distinct form of understanding that it might claim presupposes an ethnographic gaze upon the world, and it requires a particular historical imagination—the imagination, that is, of both those who make history and those who write it (Comaroff and Comaroff 1992: p. xi). In a previous work of mine (Hastrup 1995a) I claimed that the ambition of anthropology was theoretical, and as such it had to transcend the ethnographic instance. 'Ethnography, in any case, does not speak *for* others, but *about* them. Neither imaginatively nor empirically can it ever "capture" their reality' (Comaroff and Comaroff 1992: 9). Ethnographic comprehension is a historically situated mode of understanding historically situated contexts that everywhere leave room for ambivalence and indeterminacy. Theories are not prescriptive realities; they are sentences proposing particular connections between moments of history, events, institutions, images, categories, motivation, and action. As such they point to an area of generalization which on the face of it may have little bearing on the practical lives of people, but which on closer inspection may enter into their self-understanding—from which it was originally inferred. Theorizing in this sense is a practice (Hastrup 1996). What is more, anthropological theory is a practising of place which makes a space.

Phrased differently, the only logic which anthropological theory may purport to render is not an *in*herent logic of culture, it is a logic of theoretical *co*herence. Theories are suggestions of possible coherences; their long-term value of course must be contested in the scholarly community of possible dissenters as well as in the conversational community from which they first sprang. They have to be in some sense consistent with the experiences of these communities, but they will by their very nature also pose a challenge to previous understandings of such experience—if they aim beyond reproduction. The inherent intersubjectivity and intertextuality in anthropological practice has all the features of tension that are part of any dialogue, which far from being a phatic communion resolving difference rests upon distinction and opposed points of view (Crapanzano 1992: 188ff.). Anthropological, theoretical understanding develops from this tension. We should not bemoan, therefore, that ethnographies are always written from particular points of view and that truth is contestable. There is no knowledge without a knower. This does not reduce all knowledge to autobiography, of course; there is still an anthropological project to pursue even if we have to acknowledge the position of the author in ethnographic writing as subjectively situated. The world is no less real for our being part of it—as milkmaid or anthropologist—and our knowledge is not invalidated a priori by being open for inspection and dissent.

This notwithstanding, it actually has become increasingly difficult to write ethnographically about other people. Not that it was ever easy to write, as the amount of non-written ethnography bears witness. How many fieldworks have not been properly 'written up'? Today, towards the end of the century in which anthropology was born as an empirical science, in Europe not least due to Malinowski, the difficulty presents itself differently; it has taken the shape of a true dilemma of writing within what seems an inevitable performative paradox (Fabian 1991). A performative paradox is found where an act brings about what it seeks to overcome, and cannot do otherwise; in ethnography the 'objectification' of others is paradoxically inherent in the written acknowledgement of their selves. The new self-consciousness of anthropology (Cohen 1994), is connected also to a shift from an experimental mode to an experiential one; the whole procedure of 'writing up' has lost appeal as well as epistemological backing in the process. Much has been said about the transformative and creative aspects of ethnographic knowledge, and of the anthropologist as author (Clifford and Marcus 1986; Geertz 1988; Hastrup 1992*c*). Similarly, some acknowledgement of writing as an instrument of oppression of the others has been noted. To stop writing about anyone but oneself seems a logical conclusion, and one which has been tried out by a number of anthropologists. Non-writing about others could become a pleasant refuge for compassionate anthropologists.

As convincingly said by Johannes Fabian, there is less need for that kind of demonstration than for a thorough subversion of a 'stubborn residue of positivity in conceptions of anthropological writing' (Fabian 1996: 220). Positivity both in the sense of an evaluation, and in the sense of positivist thinking. Ethnographies are still to a large extent evaluated as if they were representations, allegedly produced to report on the field of study. Non-writing, accordingly, has been a matter of *not* producing the standard monograph about the 'others'. This is what must be revalued. First, we should acknowledge that the ethnographic encounter may yield reflective potential that cannot be 'written up' in the traditional ethnographic mode. Next, we have to invent modes of presenting people that will not reduce them to objects and social automatons, while still allowing for some generalization, without which anthropology cannot make claim to anything but entertainment value. Maybe we cannot safely generalize about culture, but people do live in real social spaces that account for at least part of their orientation and motivation; what we can still generalize about are different modes of attending to the world within particular spaces of orientation.

These preliminary thoughts are important to this piece of writing. It is not monographic in the traditional ethnographic sense—yet who would ever make a claim to that status at the moment of writing? What I want to impress is my fear of objectifying a social space which before anything else is constructed in practice by people who are subjects. The work derives from my experience and work in Iceland and, of course, from my reading about the experiences and works of others, be they Icelanders or foreign poets, but its ambition is of a general kind—which may be seen as just another form of objectification. The difference is maybe one of degree in that I see this book as but one textual version (among other possible ones) of the Icelandic world towards which I directed my ethnographic gaze, and an attempt to render it comprehensible within a scholarly context to which it may hopefully be seen as a contribution. It is tempting to quote Clifford Geertz where he is reflecting upon his own recent work. He says that

I, too, have stories to tell, views to unfold, images to impart, theories to argue, and I am eager to expose them to whoever might sit still and listen. To describe a culture, or as I have here, selected bits, purposively arranged and cut to fit, is not to set out some odd sort of object, a knot in hyperspace. It is to try to induce somebody somewhere to look at some things as I have been induced, by journeys, books, witnessings, and conversations, to look at them: to take an interest. (Geertz 1995: 61–2)

If anthropologists can achieve just that: make others take an interest in the story they are able to tell, and the theory they have evidence for, on the basis of their experiences in the field world, part of our collective ambition is fulfilled. By stating this, I have no intention of reducing scholarship to the telling of little stories; my aim is to stress that whatever value is to be found in anthropology it must be communicated. Silence appears counter-productive, even if fear of having misunderstood your friends makes non-writing seem peculiarly attractive, because it is so fundamentally uneventful.

Today, when we have abandoned 'the savage slot' (Trouillot 1991), the ethnographic practice is not based upon the rendering of exotic others, of strange lifeways and primitive beliefs, against which we can measure our own superiority, but rather upon the demonstration of the eccentricity of our shared world. People share at least one feature: they are imaginable to one another. By way of vicarious experience of other ways of living, ethnographic writing extends imagination and brings it back upon one's own life. Writing, therefore, consists not so much in a precise representation of the other world as in an evocative account of some ways of experiencing and defining any world. Like theatre, good ethnography should make people experience an experience; this is what the notion of vicarious experience amounts to in the present connection. Narrating is an impersonation, clustering signifying actions into recognizable roles: bard, novelist, historian, or ethnographer (Wagner 1972: 9). Here, evidently, I take the role of ethnographer, in her own way also a poet of space.

The present narrative is based on long-term research in Icelandic history and on fieldwork in Iceland in the 1980s. I make no claim to an exhaustive account of that world which may for all purposes be portrayed in a variety of ways. The individual Icelanders may each have their favourite portrait and share only the empty identity label. In present-day self-conscious anthropology we cannot rely on category labels and take the individual for granted. The others are selves, making their world up as they go along. Similarly, my discovery of the Icelandic world went by my own self, and by a particular frame of interpretation. If ethnography is a portrait of another world, however, I remain the painter not the 'sitter' for this particular portrait of Iceland. Painters may change their style of painting; what at one time were the preferred strokes of the brush may be subverted by others, just as the shades of colour and the favourite kind of light will naturally shift in the course of time. Concurrently with changes in anthropology in general, my own emphasis in the study of the world of the Icelanders has shifted from an implicit idea of representation to an explicit view of theory as a practice which cannot represent, only seek to understand. Like speaking, understanding is an active engagement with the world, not passive reception. As extensively argued by Said (1994), intellectual activity is potentially offensive since it almost by definition takes a questioning standpoint, a critical attitude to commonplaces. My own search for understanding the Icelandic world has been directed from the perspective of the intellectual exile, the restless and quizzical standpoint of the marginal observer, suspended between the private and the public worlds. Possibly, some of my suggestions about Iceland have been too quickly made, and have laid themselves open to criticism on that account as well (and I shall deal with part of it in due course), but I will defend the point made by Said, that 'least of all should an intellectual be there to make his/her audiences feel good: the whole point is to be embarrassing, contrary, even unpleasant' (Said 1994: 9–10). If anthropology is an intellectual activity, as I see it, it must embrace local knowledge while also challenging it.

Anthropology in general is based on hindsight; it comes after the fact (Geertz 1995). Any writing parts company from the events portrayed. So also for anthropological accounts because they are pieced-together presentations of particular events, experiences, reminiscences, and memories bound together by a series of interpretations, undertaken in more or less implicit dialogue with other interpretations. Like myth, anthropology describes not simply what happened, but what *generally* happens, if on a solider grounding, and with a claim to consistency with experience (ibid. 3). And like poetry, ethnography is at once 'data' for analysis and itself a body of generalizations (cf. Friedrich 1996: 39). This is one reason why the ethnographic present is still an appropriate tense in anthropology (Hastrup 1990*c*). The tense does not reflect a timeless reality of other worlds, but points to the fact that while based in concrete historical circumstances and situated experiences, ethnography is not about recording the world. It is 'radically interpreting' it (cf. Davidson 1984: 128), that is adding or supplying to the world something which is not already part of its own self-constitutive discourse. 'Records' relate to time, but radical interpretation lifts the recollection out of time and posits it in a space of timeless (if temporary) knowledge of the interplay between figure and ground, of specific social detail and the general human condition.

Evidently, my emphasis will be on the Icelandic condition but the lesson for others, if they take an interest, will be of a more general kind. They will, literally, recognize what they themselves implicitly know of their own world by similarity or difference. The ethnographer is in a position that is not radically different from that of Auden, who in 1936 had to write a travel book from Iceland, and had an idea:

In the bus today I had a bright idea about this travel book. I brought a Byron with me to Iceland, and I suddenly thought I might write him a chatty letter in light verse about anything I could think of, Europe, literature, myself. He's the right person I think, because he was a townee, a European, and disliked Wordsworth and that kind of approach to nature, and I find that very sympathetic. This letter in itself will have very little to do with Iceland, but will rather be a description of an effect of travelling in distant places which is to make one reflect on one's past and one's culture from outside. But it will form a central thread on which I shall hang other letters to different people more directly about Iceland. (Letter from W. H. Auden to E. M. A., in Auden and MacNeice 1985: 139)

I did not bring a Byron with me to Iceland, but I brought other texts, in matter or in memory, representing conversational partners during fieldwork. Apart from my anthropological readings I read Icelandic novels, grammars, and other deliberations on the world of the Icelanders most of the time. In letters to friends and relatives, Iceland was brought to bear on matters of mutual concern. The ambiance of the Icelandic experience was made manifest in such letters, while all along I knew that I was *not* writing a travel book, but had to make a systematic, scholarly account. It has proved difficult, and I admit to having been tempted to leave the Icelanders alone, thus converting my compassion for their world into non-writing. Yet for a number of years I have been unable to forget the islanders among whom I experienced such character and friendship; the tonality of their world kept coming back to my ear, refurbishing my original wish to comprehend a mode of life which made me change. Having now made more substantial explorations of the bases of anthropology (e.g. Hastrup 1995*a*), I have decided to return and to re-enter the Icelandic world once again to convey the poetics of a particular space.

The Music of Chance

I landed in Iceland by chance, even if retrospectively it seemed 'right'. This is a general feature of life; things just happen, or we make them happen, and only retrospectively may they be rationalized and woven into a larger design, by which we may then understand the happenings and identify some of them as events of significance. It is only when we allow ourselves a view of the whole, however defined, that we may perceive a design at all. In the course of daily life, the minutiae blur the vision, we are lost in detail. The music of chance is complex and accomplice to our varying senses of history.

The idea of this book, as of the original fieldwork, is to propose some connections between images of Icelandicness, that may be summarized as cultural identity and local social experience. There is no claim to representing 'Icelandic culture', there is only an attempt to reflect upon a particular, empirical space of orientation within which action is motivated, and to which it contributes practical revisions. Like music itself, my composition is non-representational. In the process of composing my own impressions of the Icelandic sound space, I hope to demonstrate how generalization about a living world is still possible by way of a concrete analysis. By generalization we do not refer to an absolute order of things, waiting to be discovered. 'It is not history one is faced with, nor biography, but a confusion of histories, a swarm of biographies. There is order in it all of some sort, but it is the order of a squall or a street market: nothing metrical' (Geertz 1995: 2). Generalizations about history and society, therefore, are pieced-together stories of patternings, experienced as such by the author. There is an element of chance in this process of collation; because it is not representation but radical interpretation, and the resulting pattern is not empirical in the old sense of the word, but it is still very real. There is no way of upholding the distinction between the real and the unreal on positivist grounds. The stories that are told by anthropologists are reflections within reality, not outside or 'upon' it. There is no way to study the world from outside it.

Stories about history naturally have a beginning, a middle, and an end, but this form has less to do with the inner direction of history than with our parenthetic experience of them, to paraphrase Geertz (1995: 11). In other words, there can be no claim to absolute objectivity, let alone to a metrical representation of history, when simple clarification is not our objective. I am not seeking out the inner nature of the Icelandic world, but delving in some general modes by which also Icelanders attend to the world. This is the main reason I have chosen the musical allegory as a key to my writing. It is a way to acknowledge the non-linearity, and the non-representation of ethnographic writing. To acknowledge the parenthesis of subjective experience makes it possible to play out ethnography in a different key, replacing the monological authority with a presentation of the orchestration of local life within the possibilities given by available instruments, musicians, sensations of harmony, and sense of direction. Far from being an essence, culture is more like the performance of a symphony, in which members of the orchestra contribute varyingly, and possibly even have completely different opinions about the music they are playing (Cohen 1994: 97). Yet for the individual members of the audience there is an experience of a unified score, a whole into which variation blends without destroying it. Writing culture, these days, therefore is neither canonical representation, nor creative fiction; it is a mode of orchestrating real experiences which brings contexture to life.

In his personal chronicle of life in Suðursveit, which I have already quoted a couple of times, Þórbergur Þórðarson introduces an image of a 'twilight opera' (*rökkurópera*) for his playful doings in the hour of twilight, when the day's work was over, and before the evening's work began. He tells: *Mig hafði oft langað til að gera solitlar óperur í kvöldrökkrum* (1981: 363), ('I had often longed to make a little opera in the evening twilight'), by which he means that he wanted to make something happen. Beyond that, the notion itself 'writes culture' in a way that resonates deeply with social experience. The twilight opera is not about singing at a particular hour, but about somehow stirring a particular moment: the still moment between the day's outside tasks and evening work in the house. It was an hour of napping, but also sometimes of storytelling, whence the word *rökkursögur*, twilight stories. The silence, the sleep, and the sonorous telling of stories within the darkening house is invoked by the twilight opera alongside the youngster's wish to crack open the surface calm. He succeeds occasionally to have the grown-ups speculate on certain occurrences, but by his choice of word Þórbergur also succeeds in rendering a feel for the compact texture of the twilight, which is deeply social. By his invocation of music, we discover a space with a extensive experiential scope. In the present book, I shall also resort to musical allegories to convey the contexture of the historical moment.

The anthropological study of history is known to have produced 'other histories' (Hastrup 1992*a*; Tonkin *et al.* 1989), precisely because the unilinearity of chronology and progress has given way to the lines of music. Reading history as a sequence of events implies a notion of direct chronological causation, in which antecedents are by force seen as causes of later events, largely by ignoring the most permanent and most necessary preconditions of the events in question (Bloch 1979: 190ff.). Reading history as one reads music, as I do here, means juxtaposing historical moments that are wide apart in chronological terms, yet which all of them inform present-day views of possible courses of action. By spanning the entire period from the early medieval time of the settlements to this day, I deliberately blur the rigid distinction between myth and history, a distinction which is one of modes of representation rather than kinds of reality (cf. Hastrup 1987*b*). The content of the two modes is reality itself, and in so far as we may separate them as distinct genres, they have always been blurred in Iceland. In the present work, therefore, I shall relate comments from both genres and discuss how they provide clues to the images of present-day Iceland, as held by contemporary Icelanders in practice. Evidently, anthropology cannot be reduced to myth even if it is not history either:

[T]he inventions of anthropological thinking must be recognized as epistemologically different from the inventiveness of myth—or the founding inventions of anthropology's subjects. Thus the invention of the Jew is believed by 'Jews'; not only that, there is a *sui generis* claim—the founding myth is an exclusive truth for them and canonicity flows from it. By contrast, Evans-Pritchard's 'belief in' *The Nuer* was not one that he lived by: *its* claim is referential. (Paine 1995: 59)

Truly, the claims made by anthropologists of the pioneer generations were referential; yet meaning always went beyond reference, and the constitutive self-understandings of Nuer and anthropologists alike are based on meanings that are always emergent. This is how we can afford to read myth itself as an allegory of ethnographic writing. With myth we are in a different mode of time, one which Lévi-Strauss analysed in terms of musical score in his *Mythologiques*. Music, again, dissolves the distinction between myth and history, subverting linearity and chronological ordering to harmony and resonance. In music there are several axes of significance, one of

successions, bien sûr, mais aussi celui de compacités relatives, qui exigeait le recours à des formes évocatrices de ce que sont, en musique, le solo et le tutti; ceux des tensions expressives et des codes de remplacement, en fonction desquels apparaissaient, au cours de la rédaction, des opposition comparables à celles entre chant et récitatif, ensemble instrumental et aria. (Lévi-Strauss 1964: 22–3)

With the musical metaphor we are thus at the heart of what I see as history; the interplay of the whole chorus and the individual voice, the movement not only in time but also along the axes. Music, and myth according to Lévi-Strauss, is a mode of expression which transcends the ordinary language of articulation. This is a major key to what I have to say about the Icelandic world. This, too, is beyond language in a very important sense. There is no way in which history, and the manifold of social experiences of which it is made, can be directly expressed in language. To express it, we have to flatten it to verbal categories, but these again must be evocative of a social, embodied experience, since this is the stuff of history. Instead of the metrical representation of history we thus aim at an evocation of the cultural orchestration of chance. The story must bring forth performance as well as information.

Music belongs to the performative domain of social life; and as other performances it is an 'extreme occasion'; the concert, big or small, is 'something beyond the everyday, something irreducibly and temporally not repeatable, something whose core is precisely what can be experienced only under relatively severe and unyielding conditions' (Said 1992: 17–18). So also for those 'mythical events' that are retrospectively constituted as history; history is not and can never be repeatable, and its core can be experienced only under relatively severe conditions. Yet the experience may be modulated and form the basis of further experiences. A musical tradition gives people certain expectations, leaves certain ways open for improvisation and transformation, while excluding others. It also opens a passageway to hidden emotions; not mainly because it is a discourse on emotion but because it is in itself an emotional discourse (cf. Lutz and Abu-Lughod 1992). Music relates to the social, therefore, in a very distinct way; it is not clarification, it is radical interpretation within a particular frame of reference. This, too, is a parallel to ethnography; it interprets life in its own way, evoking an implicit knowledge and a morphology of feeling beyond the words.

Tradition, whether in music or ethnography, relates to history in a dynamic way. It never blocks the way for improvisation, even if it tends to direct newness in a specific way. Each moment has a surplus historicity. It implies that:

a secular attitude warns us to beware of transforming the complexities of a many-stranded history into one large figure, or of elevating particular moments or monuments into universals. No social system, no historical vision, no theoretical totalization, no matter how powerful, can exhaust all the alternatives or practices that exist within its domain. There is always the possibility to transgress. (Said 1992: 55)

In the Western musical tradition, there has been a remarkable persistence of the expressive language for some centuries; in spite of the obvious differences between Haydn and Chopin, 'a learned, extremely specialized language runs right through that period of almost a century and a half. To call this a regime of police of the signifier is, I think, only little to dramatize the extraordinary extent to which such a language is maintained in place and, conversely, the equally dramatic degree to which it seems to have forbidden, or at least partially prevented, encroachment or serious, perhaps even revolutionary transformation' (Said 1992: 56). The persistence of signifiers seems to be of pertinence also to Icelandic history, at least from the point of view taken in this book. As I have argued in more detail elsewhere (Hastrup 1990a), it seems that while other people have invented traditions to discover themselves, the Icelanders through history have invented themselves to fit tradition.

Radical interpretation implies that we are beyond simple representation and classical objectivist virtue. It presents one among other versions of reality (cf. Cohen 1987: 3). In contrast to local versions the anthropological account must specify its own position; it must be inherently reflexive. Radical interpretation is not the sole basis of the ethnographic account, however; it must also be based on 'charity', in another of Donald Davidson's terms, implying basic assumptions of human intelligibility on the one hand and integrity on the other, to say it in brief (e.g. Davidson 1980: 221 and 1984: 27; Hastrup 1995a: 169). It entails that even if we acknowledge many voices, versions, and possible views on the world, we still have to assume a degree of consistency within each of them, a consistency that will somehow be premised outside the individuals in a shared world, or a common conversational community, addressed by all individuals however silently and unrecognized. There is always a self-understanding that informs history, whether persistent or turbulent—a 'tradition' that invades other areas of life at home.

In Iceland, as elsewhere, there has been a subtle interplay between the emotional and the practical sides of being at home; the spectacles that have provoked the emotional value of being an Icelander may have been small scale compared to the French National Opera and other examples cited by Said, yet for people living in small dispersed communities in the Icelandic countryside, less would have to do. We may again listen to Þórbergur Þórðarson who writes about the fireplace of the kitchen:

Eldurinn var mikill vinur allra á Hala, alveg öfugt við byljina og stórviðrin. Hann var einn af þeim hlutum í heiminum, sem voru góðir. Hann eldaði matinn og heitaði kaffið og bakaði kökurnar og brauðin, og hann tók manni alltaf hlýlega, þegar maður kom inn til hans utan úr kulda eða rigningu. Og þegar ég starði á geislaleik hans framan á taðstálinu, þá leið mér svipað í huganum, held ég nú, eins og músikelskanda, sem hlustar á mikinn meistara spila fantasíu eða fúgu eftir Mozart. Það lá snemma vel fyrir mér að finna til þess stóra í því smá. (Þórbergur Þórðarson 1981: 44)

(The fireplace was everybody's friend at Hali, in stark contrast to squalls and rainstorms. It was one of those places in the world that were good. It cooked the food and warmed the coffee and baked the cakes and the bread, and it welcomed one warmly, when one came in from outside, from cold or rain. And when I stared at its radiant play on the dung-firewood, my experience was, I believe now, like a music lover, who listens to a great master playing a fantasy or a fugue of Mozart. From early on, I was quick in finding the great in the small.)

This is very much what music is about: finding the great in the small, the sensational within the quotidian. It is not about the exceptional as separate from ordinary experience but as part of it; Þórbergur found it at the fireplace—the centre stage of homeliness; others may find it at the National Opera. People, generally, find emotional undercurrents to history in local tradition, or in those images that are collective reference points, spilling over into history and informing individual motivation and historical direction. In Iceland, tradition has fused into all domains of social life, refurbishing the image of Icelandicness with a distinct emotional value that could be transgressed only by enlargement or intensification, not by negation. This again gives substance to the musical allegory in relation to notions of 'identity'. Identities are never given, they are negotiated and relative to context. The interface between history and identity is subtly constructed. 'Newness', whether by discovery or by invention (Paine 1995), is a matter of transgression, of expanding the limits or exploding the proportions, and signalling a 'dramatically new way of understanding the importance of elaboration, its working out and filling of time and social space' (Said 1992: 64). As we shall see, in Iceland the original orchestration of society in terms of farming was transgressed by a fishing elaboration on the identity, which remained anchored, as it were, in the soil.

Music always is connected to a social space; some social spaces are even bounded by music, informing our sense of place (Stokes 1994: 3) It is tempting to add, that the reverse is possibly also true; whenever Þórbergur Þórðarson heard Beethoven's Moonlight Sonata in later life, he always recalled his childhood's moonlight, 'this beautiful piece of poetry', that had lit up the usual darkness (Þórðarson 1981: 78). In a slightly different fashion we may even say that music creates its own social space: there are performers and audience, and once upon a time there were princes who paid for it all. In this situation, music 'literally fills a social space, and it does so by elaborating the ideas of authority and social hierarchy' (Said 1992: 64). Music in this sense is instrumental (!) to the fashioning of moods, evading our notions of reference if extremely important to whatever meaning emerges from the individual orchestrations of the possible. In this way, too, music—of which we can only speak in indeterminate language—becomes a particularly apt metaphor for an ethnography which aims beyond the space of the indicative and of reference to the field of the subjunctive and of 'force' (cf. Davidson 1984: 109).

The creative moment occurs when the limits of the possible are expanded. Cultural creativity, indeed, is a matter of expanding the limits of the thinkable, sometimes individually, sometimes collectively, but always actively (cf. Hastrup 1994). There is no history without agency. History is movement created by social agents, able to attach their singularity to society. By the sheer fact that they are playing along, social agents contribute to reinterpretation.

This again likens it to music. As Said has it: 'the transgressive element in music is its nomadic ability to attach itself to, and become part of, social formations, to vary its articulations and rhetoric depending on the occasion as well as the audience, plus the power and gender situations in which it takes place' (Said 1992: 70). This could apply also to the Icelandic world, as I am going to suggest. In Iceland, instrumental musical performances were less important than poetic and other oral performances; in their own way, these were musical in that voices transform words into rhythm and sensation. The poetic indeterminacy of language and the rhythms of different genres point to the subjunctive space of moods in a way that is similar to instrumental music. As we shall see later, the emotional space created by Icelandic words is pervasive and contains forceful tropes of Icelandicness. Like Fernandez, I am interested in what tropes *do* rather than what they 'mean' in any semantic sense (Fernandez 1986: p. ix). If metaphors are the dreamwork of language (Davidson 1984: 245), the music inherent in voicing tradition is the dreamwork of a kind of performance of peculiar force through Icelandic history.

Indeed, Iceland herself has been embraced by a musical allegory before. Auden cites a certain Miss Oswald for saying in 1882:

Alone in Iceland you are alone indeed and the homeless, undisturbed wilderness gives something of its awful calm to the spirit. It was like listening to noble music, yet perplexed and difficult to follow. If the Italian landscape is like Mozart; if in Switzerland the sublimity and sweetness correspond in art to Beethoven; then we may take Iceland as the type of nature of the music of the moderns—say Schumann at his oddest and wildest. (Miss Oswald in Auden and MacNeice 1985: 59)

The keynote in the following is a search for the still point of the turning Icelandic world, the eye of the historical hurricane from where one can sense the contexture of that world. Throughout, I am working on the edge of words, and appealing more to the ear for the poetry of imagination than for the classical prose of reason. In contrast to prose, poetry's and ethnography's 'other' is radical (cf. Daniel 1996a: 7). Of course, this work is not a piece of poetry; I do not master the play of tropes nor do I see it as my purpose. But just as metaphor is the dreamwork of language, so the human and the social sciences can be seen as the dreamwork of the world, in which linkages are created by writing, overcoming an expressive inadequacy (cf. Hastrup 1995a; Tilley 1993b: 17).

An anthropological account must relate to social reality even if it cannot represent it (cf. Bourdieu 1991: 127); only therein lies its claim to truth—a claim that must be understood in the vein of Quine, arguing convincingly for the empirical *under*-determination of scientific truth (Quine 1992). The nature of the relationship between theory and practical life, therefore, must be one of linguistic indeterminacy, and therein lies the affiliation between poetry and anthropology, with which I began.

Time, Space, People

The title of this book refers to a place apart which is not, of course, outside world history, nor beyond our questions. It is Auden's Iceland and my own, but first and foremost is it the space created by Icelanders in practice. It is my contention that within this space, there are resonances across time and place, echoes of distant voices still to be heard. My ambition is to identify some of the more remarkable themes in this space, as seen from today but within the context of long-term Icelandic history.

The organization of this work is quite simple, each part being subdivided into three chapters, focusing on time, space, and people respectively. I start with an identification of some of the keys to the composition to tune the reader in, as it were. From there I proceed to the orchestration of relations within that world, reflecting upon tradition, landscape, and community as ways of thematizing time, space, and people, and showing how in each field there is an undercurrent of evaluation informing social practice, if not its 'logic' in the embodied, dynamic sense proposed by Bourdieu (1990). The last part is devoted to general theoretical propositions about the dominant themes of Icelandicness.

This way of organizing the book parts company from the traditional travel report from the territory of knowledge. The point is, that instead of seeing it as a territory which can be flattened into a map and read in a neutral fashion, I want to render the Icelandic world as a multidimensional topological space, in which present-day social agents are suspended in a web of pastness and presentness, of motivation and intention, of nature and words, of narratives and moods, and ultimately between detail and grand design, of which there are many images, varied modes of interpretation, and not least different knowledge interests. The anchor point of this work is an understanding of anthropology as an intellectual practice, a mode of theorizing which will potentially challenge pre-existing ways of (self-)understanding. The book, therefore, is an offering to the conversational communities to whom it matters—for those who take an interest. Authority and agreement subside to dialogue and resonance; if tension is inherent in dialogue it should be remembered that perhaps we will learn more from the space created *between* different points of view than from the opposed arguments themselves. Creativity resides there, along-side recognition.

PART I

Keys

1

Times Past and Present

In Icelandic, *saga* means both story and history. It is literally what is 'said' about previous events, periods, or people. Telling makes history. The Icelandic sagas are stories of different historical veracity, but the point is that in the concept of *saga*, story and history are one. In my conversations with Icelanders the notion would often be incurred in relating particular events, and although obviously the Icelanders are perfectly capable of distinguishing between truth and lie, this distinction is of less moment in the telling of the past than one would think. Knowledge (*fræði*) is neutral in relation to the distinction between truth and lie: one's learning may be somewhat wanting or wrong, but no lie; lies are made by people speaking against better knowledge (Sørensen 1993: 38). And that is the point; in telling what they know, or what they have been told, the Icelanders share what is 'said' with each other—and with the anthropologist. The story contains the knowledge of history and more often than not it is prefaced by a *sagt er* ('it is said'), or if the content is less certain: *munnmælin segja* ('legend says', or 'speech goes').

For some Icelanders, or sometimes, this is not good enough. Again, Þórbergur Þórðarson (1981: 199) provides the example; at some point in time he was desperate for precision and solid knowledge, and wished that people had written proper diaries in which they told their stories (*sögur*), instead of the eternal references in speech to *ef til vill* ('if that is so'), *gæti verið* ('could be'), *hér um bil* ('here about'), *nálægt* ('almost'), or *að haldið er* ('as is believed'), and so forth. These phrases are still much used in practical conversation, however, also on his native farm; they belong to the general register of telling the past.

The frequency of relating what is 'said' in Iceland, as prefaced by the above words or implicitly invoking them, showed me that 'history' was a vital reference point in present-day self-understanding, much more so than in my native Denmark. While not necessarily knowing the exact chronology of past events or the precise nature of particular turning points in Icelandic history most people lived by a sense of history which seemed to connect present-day identities to notions of pastness. The selves were inscribed into a historical context. History is of a complex nature; it is neither positive (or positivist) progress nor is it just social or cultural change in time. It is rather a congeries of consciousnesses about change and direction brought to bear upon contemporary action (Lyman 1978). One particular kind of consciousness is formed and transmitted in official texts, such as schoolbooks, and is often based on publicly supported research in official archives, regal courts, or tribal councils. This is the 'legitimate' history; it may still be contested but then it has to be contested from within its own paradigm. In many ways this kind of history is still based upon the 'myth of realism' (Tonkin 1990).

Alongside this we find another kind of history, which mainly exists in the consciousness of people; by consciousness I refer to an implicit knowledge of the past which lay people bring to bear on their everyday understanding of the present. The transmission of this kind of historical consciousness is largely oral and is embedded in myth and legend, folk tale and proverb, and in generally unverifiable hypotheses about the relationship between past and present. It crops up in ordinary conversation on the everyday. It is largely unofficial or unlegitimated. It stands to reason that this inauthenticated history is variable and relative to context, and highly sensitive to individual or family histories. Still, it is important to be aware of its peculiar presence in contemporary self-understanding as shaped within the local conversational community. The sense of a shared 'pastness' is an all-important parameter in the identification of a 'we', even if the stories told will always reflect the teller's own mood, and his or her own desire to impress upon the listener a particular image of the past.

The making of history through the telling of personal narratives is what gives an idea of a 'whole'; whatever else this whole is it is also a state of relatedness—a kind of conviviality in experience (cf. Fernandez 1986: 191). Narrations create a mutual tuning-in relationship, which is not exclusive to the verbal communication itself, but which is rather its foundation—and for which Schutz turned to music to comprehend (Schutz 1951). A social relationship can be understood as a making of music together. The sense of 'we' is the subtext of communication. This sense resides as much in the shared sense of pastness as in official history. In Iceland, the 'said' and retold constantly reaffirm a particular sense of contexture that is shared in the process of telling itself.

Both the officially legitimated and the inauthenticated history are forms of contemporary consciousness about the past (Lyman 1978). They are polar forms on a scale which spans a wide variety of im- or ex-plicit knowledge of previous eras, and as categories they are used mainly for shorthand. Given my own recurrent stumbling upon references to history in everyday talk and in my reading endless accounts of the meaning of history in Iceland, I have found it appropriate to start this book with a presentation of Icelandic times with which the local stories may be compared. On this largely 'official' scale of history, there have been times of feast and times of famine, times of refinement and times of roughness. Icelandic scholarship has been blessed with rich archival material and other sources, and the official history is relatively well established and widely transmitted in Iceland. This is an important basis for this chapter, which also builds upon my own extensive historical research to which I refer for general substantiation (e.g. Hastrup 1985*a*, 1990*a*, 1990*b*).

Another basis for this chapter is my experience of the presence of history in my various fieldsites (of which more in Chapter 2). While the literati with whom I worked in the Manuscript Institute largely subscribed to and produced the (ever more challenged) 'official' history, the people of the countryside and the fishing village had other ways of presenting their views. No doubt, 'history' always means different things in different settings, while historical imagination is everywhere part and parcel of present-day rationality. Taken together, they inform the generalized history I am going to present here in order to provide the reader with some preliminary sense of the pastness of the world we are going to visit. It is the framework for analyst and Icelanders alike, even if they would not use the same words or emphasize the same points. While official history is normally written according to a fixed chronological scheme, 'unofficial' history cuts across established categories and schemes. It is impossible, I would claim, to understand fully those modern voices that we are going to hear afterwards without being aware of the implicit historical reference points.

Apart from reference, the presentation of the past also carries a load of emotion, of judgement, and of directive force. In official history, such matters have more often than not had to give way to the formal chronological framework. This is slowly changing in the field of history itself, where the value of the subjective in individual testimonies is now being recognized as a challenge to the accepted categories of history, certainly also in Iceland, where the individual has never been absolutely alienated from the grand design of history. As recently stated by Raphael Samuel and Paul Thompson about this process of change taking place within the historical discipline:

We reintroduce the emotionality, the fears and fantasies carried by the metaphors of memory, which historians have been so anxious to write out of their formal accounts. And at the same time the individuality of each life story ceases to be an awkward impediment to generalization, and becomes instead a vital document of the construction of consciousness, emphasizing both the variety of experience in any social group, and also how each individual story draws on a common culture: a defiance of the rigid categorization of private and public, just as of memory and reality. (Samuel and Thompson 1990: 2)

This is where there is a profound convergence between the historical and the anthropological endeavour. Without necessarily subscribing to Samuel and Thompson's notion of culture, I would go along with the intent of their work to dissolve the dichotomies of the individual and the social, of the real and the imagined.

In this chapter I deal with the 'times' rather than the events of the Icelandic past, and my history therefore somehow finds itself in between the legitimated and the unlegitimated history. Like the former it must be based on systematic research and like the latter it must be flexible and bend received wisdom to fit experience. My interlocutors in the field taught me that Icelandic history was not seen as a series of events, organized causally and chronologically; rather it was a string of experiential spaces. In this sense they echoed the age-old notion of *aldir* (ages), being defined not only by time and space but also by quality and content. Indeed, the Old Norse notion of *veröld*, from which the English word 'world' is derived, was composed from *verr* and *öld* (the age of man), seeing the world from the perspective of the social agent, experiencing the times.

My investigations into popular notions of history yielded three such main ages: *landnámsöld* (the age of settlements), 'the old days', and 'today'. The first one was the origin of Iceland, and covered the time of the sagas as well. The next was the long and relatively nondescript time-space between the first times and these days: the 'old days' were simply seen as hard, the people as impoverished, the technological standards low, and the Danish merchants exploitative. The impression was that the old days only stopped around the Second World War; thus they were solidly within memory of the elderly. Modern society had been built since then, and had brought far-reaching changes at all levels; 'today' was seen as qualitatively different from the old days. The sentiments attached to these periods were as varied as the periods themselves; the first period, the times of the pioneers, was a time of proud memories, echoes of the sagas, heroism, and literary refinement. The next period, by contrast, was one of misery and scorn, and of a certain degree of sadness on behalf of the struggling ancestors, while recently also a site of nostalgia for the 'pure' past, stripped naked of foreign influence and alien ambitions. The modern times were seen as a period of progress, of increasing technological sophistication and wealth, which in some fishing communities gave rise to a notion of *mótorbátaöldin* (the age of motorboats) (Gísli Pálsson, pers. comm.). There was also a feeling, however slight, of an increasing social differentiation—a consequence of Iceland's transformation from an allegedly 'classless' society of independent and equally poor farmers to a fishing community, deeply embedded in the world market (see Finnur Magnússon 1990). The differentiation according to modern standards of relative wealth finds expression also in a differentiation of world-views (Wieland 1989).

The three 'ages' that we are able to generalize as operative in present-day structurings of social memory are very unevenly defined, and they are based also upon very different kinds of (implicit) sources. The first relates to the medieval literature, which is known mainly secondhand, and from oral traditions attached to place names. It is traditional knowledge, largely in the form of a myth of origin. The second kind is based on a mixture of folktale and legend, of ancestral wisdom and elderly people's reminiscences about their childhood and youth. The third is much more directly experiential; yet it is still a conglomerate of interpretations and verbalizations of a collective experience of which one only knows a small part oneself. In what follows, the historical framework of these notions of periods will be presented. Wherever we are, it should be noted that we cannot but summarize, and hence in some sense reduce, the vastness of Icelandic experience through the ages. Reduction, we know, is one of the predicaments of anthropology in the sense that only compressed images can travel from the field to the book.

The Solid Frame

'Iceland is not a myth; it is a solid portion of the earth's surface' (Pliny Miles 1854, quoted in Auden and MacNeice 1985: 58). This particular portion is situated in the

North Atlantic where it was first visited by Irish monks in the eighth century, known in Iceland (from the sagas until these days) as *papar* (popes). They were few and far between and in general Iceland was uninhabited until the ninth century, when Norse settlements began. From the early tenth until the late thirteenth century Iceland was an autonomous society with a highly developed political structure and a sophisticated literature which still captures the interest of modern readers. Prime among written texts were historical works, not least those written by Snorri Sturluson, whose hot bath is still to be seen (and used), as referred to by Auden and discovered by myself in the 1980s. From 1264 Iceland became part of the Norwegian kingdom, and as such it became part of the Danish realm in 1380, when Denmark and Norway were united. When, later, Norway was incorporated into the Swedish kingdom, Iceland remained under Danish rule, which lasted until 1918 when Iceland became independent, though still in union with Denmark. The last formal ties with Denmark were cut in 1944, when the Republic of Iceland was declared.

Compared to the popular image of the earliest times, which is probably somewhat romanticized in the literature, the period from 1400 to 1800 appears as a 'Dark Age' in Iceland. The country was not only under an increasing pressure from the foreign ruler, it was also struck by poverty and social disintegration to a point of near extinction. This process may have started earlier, back in the celebrated High Middle Ages when social inequality began to increase, but it reached bottom in the seventeenth and eighteenth centuries. In the early nineteenth century a nationalist movement sought to redress the political situation in the wake of an Enlightenment attempt to improve living conditions in general. During the nineteenth century the pendulum began to swing back towards autonomy and a more stable economy. However, Iceland remained on the margins of the modern world until after the Second World War. The economic changes following the war were remarkable, yet 'the past' is still near at hand in Icelandic self-understanding.

Today the Icelanders number about 250,000, half of whom live in the capital of Reykjavík, a town which hardly existed before 1800, and which in 1860 still only comprised 1,400 people, out of a total of *c*.67,000 Icelanders. Compared to other Nordic and European countries, urbanization and modernization came late to Iceland. Icelandic society was based on a subsistence economy, which made each household a separate unit of production and consumption. It was not until the last part of the nineteenth century that the domestic economic order gradually became supplemented by modern, capitalist enterprises, resulting in the growth of fishing villages among other things.

In what follows, this general outline will be substantiated further and analysed in anthropological terms. This means that the narrative will pay more attention to general patterns and recurrent features than to chronological events. It is a social and cultural history based on written sources that date back from *c*.1100, and whose testimony reaches back to the first settlements. Due to the isolated position of Iceland in the North Atlantic, there is a remarkable continuity in the social space within which the Icelanders orient themselves and act. This implies that the history of Iceland is the result not only of external factors and political events, but also of a set of internal images of 'Icelandicness'. In order to understand this we must start at the beginnings and attempt to grasp the structure of the Old Nordic cosmology, an influence which is still relevant in many contexts even if the myths upon which it was based have long since become obsolete.

The Mythical Beginnings

The primary source for Old Norse mythology is Snorri's *Edda*, an early thirteenth-century document of considerable importance (Einarsson 1957: 116ff.; Jónsson 1931). Snorri is one of the early Icelandic literati who through their writings have contributed immensely to our understanding of the general conditions of the Nordic world in the transitional phase between orality and literacy, and between pagan chieftaincies and Christian kingdoms.

The *Edda* is a textbook for would-be scalds designed to guide them through the metrics of classical scaldic poetry and through the elements of Old Norse mythology in increasing competition with Christian imagery but still at the core of traditional poetry. In the section *Gylfaginning*, Snorri elaborates on the ways and byways of the Norse gods, the eschatological dramas of the mythological world, and the stories of both the tragic and the comic heroes of the first times. It has often been noted that Snorri's unique achievement was to preserve extensive and systematic knowledge of the Norse world-view, otherwise prone to change and disappearance in a historical situation which increasingly integrated the Norsemen into European Christendom. His tales are generally confirmed by the scattered references to the gods and other supernatural beings in both sagas and scaldic poetry from the early Middle Ages and before.

Many attempts have been made to order the chaotic picture inherent in the narratives of gods and heroes, and many arguments about datings, source value, and so forth have been put forward and challenged (e.g. Dumézil 1957; Ellis Davidson 1964, 1967; Turville-Petre 1964). These discussions will not detain us here. Instead we shall concentrate on the general cosmological models inherent in the tales, because it was they rather than the tales themselves that survived in the Icelandic world-view almost until the present day.

There are two distinct kinds of model involved: horizontal and vertical. This means that the cosmos is organized in two dimensions, as it were. Horizontally, the cosmos was divided into Miðgarðr and Útgarðr, meaning the 'middle yard' and the 'outer yard', respectively. Miðgarðr was the central space inhabited by men and gods, while the surrounding Útgarðr was inhabited by giants and other kinds of non-humans (and non-gods). According to the myth of creation related by Snorri, this division of the cosmos was owed to the gods (the *æsir*), who subsequently built their own abode, Ásgarðr (the yard of the *æsir*), somewhere inside Miðgarðr. There is no opposition between heaven and earth in this model; topographically Ásgarðr was inseparable from Miðgarðr. Consequently, there was no absolute distinction between men and gods, but together these were firmly set apart from the inhabitants of Útgarðr (see e.g. Gurevich 1969; Hastrup 1981; Haugen 1970; Meletinskij 1973).

Separating the two cosmological domains was the sea terrorized by the Miðgarðsormr (the serpent of Miðgarðr) which the god Thorr undertook to fight. Generally speaking, the gods of the central space are constantly engaged in a battle against the evil forces from the outer space. In this sense the gods represent social order and the 'inside' (including proper human life) as opposed to the disorder and danger attributed to the 'outside'. This distinction had many parallels in the social universe of the Icelanders, notably in the distinction between *innangarðs* and *utangarðs*, meaning 'inside' and 'outside' the farm or fence. The fence not only separated the farmstead from the wilderness, and kinsmen and friends from potential enemies, but more generally also the inviolable personal social space from the uncontrolled space of spirits and evil beyond it. Each level of reality reaffirmed the others—which is probably one reason why the concentric model seems to have persisted until this century (Hastrup 1990*d*).

The vertical model fitted social experience less well and had a different fate. Originally conceived of in terms of the world-tree Yggdrasill, the vertical model embraced three separate realms. On top of the tree was the abode of the gods, Ásgarðr, and Valhöll, the upper kingdom of the dead ruled over by Odinn, and into which only glorious warriors were admitted. The humans resided on the middle of the world-ash, while at its roots we find the lower kingdom of the dead, ruled over by and named like the goddess Hel. Yggdrasill was cut down by the axe of Christianity; it fitted the Christian world-view so well that they could not coexist, but only melt into one another. Possibly, Christian Snorri was already biased towards the Christian model of heaven and earth in his exposition of the vertical model. Yet Yggdrasill was hardly his own invention; it was part of an Old Norse mythology which in subtle ways left its mark upon Iceland for a millennium.

The main point was the emphasis on real people living in the centre of the world, surrounded in two dimensions by uncontrolled forces; horizontally, evil threatened from the 'outside', and vertically, 'death' and 'fate' were governed from 'above' and 'below'. Small wonder that the boundaries around the inside, central world had to be vigorously protected if the islanders were to maintain the distinctive features of the human world—in the cosmological centre. This mythological order was (probably) shared by the Norse peoples, and as such it was part of the heavy baggage that the emigrants from the Nordic countries brought across the sea when they colonized the North Atlantic islands in a last wave of Viking expansion (cf. Foote and Wilson 1970).

The Settlements

Iceland was settled by Norsemen in the late ninth to the early tenth century. Traditionally, the 'time of settlements' has been defined as the period from 870 to 930. The dates are inferred from secondary evidence, and while for many years 870 has been accepted as the date of the first settlements (give or take a few years), recent (controversial) research has questioned this and pushed back the date by two centuries (Hermanns-Auðardóttir 1989).

The problem again is one of sources. There are no written documents on the Icelandic settlements before 1120–30, when Ari *inn fróði* (the wise) wrote his *Íslendingabók* ('Book of the Icelanders'). From his and other testimonies it can be said with reasonable certainty that the massive wave of Norse immigration began in the last third of the ninth century. This was the time when the restless Vikings of the Nordic countries were gradually settling down. Their westward emigration to the North Atlantic islands actually represents the final phase of the Viking campaigns which had successfully colonized large parts of the British Isles and caused no small stir in various southern European lands.

We know that Iceland had been discovered in the early ninth century by Irish hermits—whether or not there were already Norsemen there. These Irish *papar*, 'popes' or 'paters', of the Norse tradition had left traces of their sojourn which were later to be remarked upon by Icelandic authors like Ari *inn fróði* (Benediktsson 1968). They also left an early imprint in written sources. About 825, Iceland in all probability appears by the name of Thule in a work by the Irish monk Dicuil. Although 'Thule' was frequently used by contemporary writers with an imprecise geographical referent, being just some far northern part of the world, it has been generally accepted that Dicuil speaks of Iceland proper; if this be so, it is the first-known reference to Iceland in the literature.

The Norse settlements are documented primarily in *Landnámabók* ('The Book of Settlements'), which was compiled in the middle of the twelfth century (Benediktsson 1968). It has convincingly been suggested that *Landnámabók* served the purpose of establishing rights in land once the whole island had been effectively colonized (Rafnsson 1974). Be this as it may, the book of the settlements is of mythological proportion, lifting the history out of such mundane matters as purpose and property. It is often referred to today, not as a claim to land but as a claim to a particular quality of certain sites: places that are mentioned are invested with particular emotional value. According to this book Iceland itself received its name from one of the first would-be settlers, Flóki Vilgerðarson, *víkingr mikill* (a great viking). Flóki, arriving about 870, found the winter too hard and left again; allegedly, he named the place 'Iceland' because of the drift-ice in the fjords. Although the name changed from 'Thule' to 'Iceland' the rumour about the island was still one of northern cold. Nevertheless, in the years following Flóki's failed settlement thousands of people steered towards Iceland. In 930, when the first constitution of Icelandic society was made, the country was reported *albyggt* (fully inhabited).

Estimates about the actual number of settlers vary, but some 40,000–50,000 is probable.

An analysis of personal names and places of origin of the people named in *Landnámabók* shows a considerable preponderance of Norwegian settlers, while Danes and Swedes are far less numerous. There is also a conspicuous Celtic element, however, once the 'overcommunication' of the Nordic origin has been stripped away. The degree of influence from the Celtic world is difficult to assess from language and literature. While the language known from the first written sources is distinctly Norse, and bore the name of *dönsk tunga* (Danish tongue), like contemporary Scandinavian in general, there seems to be subtle influences in at least part of the imagery known from the early Icelandic literature as well as in personal names (Haugen 1976). There is no doubt that in the Viking period the relations between the Scandinavians and the Celts were more than accidental. For Iceland these relations became further substantiated via the immigration from the British Isles by second- or third-generation Nordic colonists there. More often than not, the actual Celts were slaves of the Norsemen, and while they thus formed two distinctive social groups, they remained 'culturally' interwoven in Iceland, which was soon defined as unified. As peoples, Norse Vikings and Celts also seem to share a feature of unrepresentationality; they seem to be always construed as myths (cf. Chapman 1992). Like beauty and pain, some people escape our words and manifest themselves between the lines. There we may meet them within their own reality.

It is impossible to give any final answer to the question of why the Norse Vikings were attracted to the arid lands of Iceland, even if they were possibly less arid at the time. It has been suggested that they were driven by the need for land and pasture, but given the sparse population of Norway at the time, this was hardly the prime motivating force. The Icelandic tradition itself insists that the settlers fled the tyranny of King Harald Fairhair, who tried to seize power over the many petty chieftaincies of Norway. To the freedom-loving Icelanders this was a major threat to their integrity. As part of the living tradition, this myth has its own reality, and as narrative it filters into present-day views of Icelandicness.

The creation of Icelandic society was very much tied into the general history of medieval Europe. Economic, religious, and social changes that affected Scandinavia at the time were related to the redefinition of the European social order in the wake of the great migrations which had come to an end in the sixth and seventh centuries, though later followed by the drift of unruly Vikings across the continent and the North Sea until the early tenth century. The new order in Europe was marked by an increase in population, in changing notions of landownership expressed in an incipient feudalism, in centralization of power, and in a process of Christianization. The particular Norwegian realization of this was Harald Fairhair's aspiration to a new kind of divinely installed kingship which certainly did not please the pagan chieftains and free farmers whose kinship-based rights to the land had roots far back in history.

Once arrived, the settlers soon defined their own world on the margins of the European order. The separate Icelandic reality was first formally expressed in an autonomous political structure, agreed upon by the first *alþingi* (general assembly), held in *c*.930. This inaugurated the first free society, most often referred to as the Commonwealth of Iceland, based on a principle of equality among free farmers, and a strong definition of 'our law'. This law was to remain in force—if not unchanged—until 1262/4, when the Icelanders swore allegiance to the Norwegian king.

The important point to be noted from the history of the settlements is that it created a myth of origin, which forever marked the Icelandic conception of their world. Motivated by a search for autonomy and an insistence upon freedom and equality, instituted through settlements, and confirmed by a law which stressed the importance of kinship, Icelandic society emerged as an alternative to the centralist and feudal kingdoms of Europe. The myth was expressed in the twelfth-century *Landnámabók* tracing the ancestors of contemporary Icelanders—now mastering their own alphabet. It is concerned with origins and beginnings: arriving in virgin land and creating their society from scratch the Icelanders were endowed with an almost autochthonous origin, as expressed also in Ari's *Íslendingabók*. Through acquiring land they were transformed from travellers to sedentary peasants; and by having their history written, the Vikings became 'Icelanders'. The aspect of sedentism and farming was to remain an important feature in the conception of Icelandicness, as was the sense of 'we' sharing a history.

Ecological Conditions

The climate of Iceland is subarctic and cold, with a high precipitation. When the first settlers arrived the climate was relatively mild, if always unstable. From the fourteenth century onwards the conditions worsened; the average temperature dropped, and a climatic pessimum was reached in 1600–1700. These conditions, noted by climatologists for all of Europe, manifested themselves in Iceland in increasingly frequent statements about drift-ice, bad harvests, and lean years. In the nineteenth century the climate gradually began to improve again.

Another feature of climate which is of importance to a seafaring nation is the prevailing direction of winds. In the period of settlements, the North Atlantic was dominated by relatively stable eastern and south-eastern winds during summer. It was these winds that brought the Vikings to the north-western Atlantic. They gradually changed during the Middle Ages, however, to far less stable westerly winds. From the annals we can infer that there were summers where no ships landed in Iceland; this had severe consequences for a people depending on foreign imports of grain. It probably also contributed to the submission to the king of Norway. In the treaty between him and the Icelanders it is stated that one of his duties was to sail six shiploads of grain to Iceland each summer (*Diplomataricum*

Islandicum, I). On the whole the changing winds at the time probably contributed to the remarkable decline in communication on the North Atlantic—including communication with the Norse colonists in Greenland who became extinct in the fifteenth century.

No doubt climate influences the course of history in a marginal agricultural area like Iceland. We must be careful, however, not to draw any monocausal links from climate to history. The human context of climatic change is an important factor in development; the social history of climate is one of adaptation rather than submission. For Europe in general it has been demonstrated how the decisive variable in the elimination of famine was not the weather (which was subject to the same oscillations between favourable and harsh) but the ability to adapt to the changes (Rotberg and Rabb 1981).

If climatic fluctuations normally result in social adaptation, this was not the case in pre-modern Iceland, where the economic security margin was so small that just one bad winter within the ordinary range of winters could be fatal. Due to technological neglect, amounting almost to a collective amnesia, this margin even decreased from the sixteenth to the eighteenth century. The results were famines and many deaths. In the late eighteenth century the Icelandic bishop Hannes Finsson compiled the internal evidence for 'the decrease of population in lean years'—as the title of his work goes. Extracting the evidence from the annals and other sources his work is a sad document about the hunger- and poverty-stricken Icelandic society during some centuries, notably the seventeenth and eighteenth centuries (Finsson 1796). When conversing with present-day Icelanders, the times of famine are often mentioned as a feature of the 'old days'; recently, it has been suggested that the emphasis on famine is somewhat exaggerated, however (Vasey 1996). This is not insignificant, of course.

Climate aside, the general ecological conditions of the island are not very benign either. Of the 103,000 sq. km., only a small proportion is arable. One-tenth of the land is covered by ice, and volcanic activities account for the vast wastelands covered in lava or ash. The primary forest of low birch that met the settlers was soon cut down and a heavy soil erosion began. Archaelogical evidence suggests that the inhabited area in the early Middle Ages was more extensive than it was to become later. Woods disappeared almost completely and large tracts were laid waste. The land was arid and fields had to be worked carefully for the yield to be optimal. As we have seen, this was not always the case.

The sea surrounding Iceland provided another vital natural resource. Towards the south the warm Gulf Stream hits the island, while the north is touched by the cold East Greenland Current. This accounts for some of the internal differences in climate and for the seasonal variations in fishing. The island comprises two more or less distinct ecological zones; due to the Gulf Stream the south and the west are characterized by relatively mild winters and cold and rainy summers, while the spell of the East Greenland Current makes the north and east suffer much greater fluctuations in temperature and precipitation. This is also where the coast is afflicted by drift ice. One of the more spectacular consequences of the climatic extreme in 1600–1700 was more frequent visits by polar bears swimming ashore from icefloes from Greenland, challenging hunters to demonstrate their manliness in battle with the starving visitors from an even more 'ultimate' Thule.

The ecological difference had great impact on the economy. The cod came to spawn in the warm waters towards the south and west in the winter season, and people living there had easier access to fishing than the northerners and easterners who had to migrate long distances to get their share. From that perspective life was easier in the southern and western regions. When offshore fishing was replaced with deep-sea fishing, and a seagoing fleet emerged in the late nineteenth century the difference was less consequential. Today it is the size of the harbour and the general landing facilities for the high-technology fishing fleet that determine the local income, as well as the local fishing quota, which has been a critical factor since 1984. There is still a degree of work migration going on; young people are attracted to the busy ports where the season is still one of much work and great economic potential.

The Economic Order

In the famous *Laxdæla saga* from mid-thirteenth century, the reason given for the emigration of Ketill *flatnefr* and his family from Norway once again is the expansionist policy of Harald Fairhair (Sveinsson 1934). The tradition of tyranny is reaffirmed, and with it another one is established. When discussing where to go, Ketill and his sons consider both the British Isles and Iceland. The sons are in favour of Iceland, because 'land is so abundant and one does not have to pay for it; there is much stranding of whales and salmon-fishing, and places to fish all the year round.' Thus there were two explicit reasons for settling in Iceland: abundance of land and abundance of fish.

Farming and fishing were to remain the basic pillars of Icelandic economy until this day. The balance between them has not always been stable, as we shall see, but together they have defined the level of Icelandic economy. Listen to the eighteenth-century reformer of Iceland, Skúli Magnússon, who observed: 'The Icelandic economy is founded on only two gifts of nature: cattle-breeding and fishing, holding out their hands towards one another, since the latter gets life and power from the former, which again is supported by the latter' (Magnússon (1786) 1944*a*,*b*: 37). The dual basis of Icelandic economy, and the lack of resources other than soil and sea have provided the framework of the economic development in Iceland through the centuries.

Another stable framework was the domestic structure of the economy. Until the rapid economic growth after the Second World War, the household, or the *bú*, was the basic unit of production and consumption. Its composition and size varied from one period to the next and between contemporary 'classes' of people, but its paramount significance persisted. There was no division of labour beyond it, no specialized tasks carried out elsewhere in urban or commercial centres. Despite the attempt at urbanization during the 'English Age' (fourteenth century), when English markets for Icelandic fish emerged, there were no permanent villages to speak of and no towns in Iceland until the late nineteenth century, and then they were very small, as they still are by comparative European standards.

The individual household was society in miniature, a microcosmos of its own. It usually consisted of parents and children, including foster children and orphaned minors of the larger family, one or more adult relatives, and one or more domestic servants and farmhands. In the so-called saga-age (which is the period depicted with greater or lesser historical accuracy in the family sagas) we have an impression of extended three-generational families where sons- or daughters-in-law were brought into the parental household. When more reliable sources appear these families seem rare. Normally the household comprised only one married couple and a number of single relatives. The point is that households were established through marriage. From the beginnings of history in Iceland there had been a ban on marriage between those who did not own land, because they were not believed to be able to sustain an independent household. When the first complete census for Iceland was made in 1703—comprising a total of 50,358 named Icelanders—the marriage ratio was staggeringly low in comparison with other European countries at the time. Among the women in the fertile age (15–49) a mere 27.8 per cent were married. Small wonder that the Icelanders barely reproduced themselves.

The point here is to note that there was an intimate link between marrying and establishing a household, and that the requirements for both prevented a varying proportion of Icelanders from entering into matrimony. This feature is important for understanding the household composition. The amount of unmarried relatives and servants varied, but they were always part of the household, as were a certain number of paupers who were circulated among the more prosperous farmsteads. We see how 'society' was concretized in the household. There was hardly any structure beyond it of immediate social relevance, except a system of *hreppir* (counties), that linked the individual households to the larger society by claiming taxes and keeping track of the population, and which formally distributed paupers among the farmers (Björnsson 1972, 1979). Yet in everyday life, the 'practised' space was firmly grounded in the *bú*.

The *bú* was the centre of the universe for individual Icelanders, conflating society and nature. It structured social experience as well as economy. In principle it was self-sufficient even if it always had to barter or trade part of its production for grain, timber, and other imported necessities brought to the island during a short summer period by foreign merchants. Essentially, the Icelandic economy was a subsistence economy with little surplus production, although woollens were made for export in exchange for grain. In each household subsistence was based on the complementary strategies of farming and fishing.

Farming mainly implied cattle- and sheep-rearing in the subarctic environment. There was a small amount of barley-growing in the early Middle Ages, a practice which the Norsemen brought with them from Scandinavia. It soon declined, however, and is heard of for the last time in 1589, and then as somewhat of an oddity. Hay was always the main agricultural resource. Natural grazing was (and is) adequate only from June to September. For the rest of the year the animals had to be kept at the farmstead on stored hay.

Hay was grown in tilled and manured infields, which were always part of the farmstead proper. Fields were fenced and individually owned. Beyond the fence were outfields and meadows where the Icelanders would occasionally cut a small amount of grass for storage, and which served as supplementary grazing. In the earlier part of Icelandic history some of these outfields served as 'saeters', the summer shielings that are widely known from the Nordic economy and which implied that a few shepherdesses moved to the saeter during summer, preparing milk produce on the spot.

Further afield—mentally if not necessarily geographically—were the common pastures where the sheep spent summer without much surveillance. Sheep were earmarked and were let out shortly after the lambing season in early June, and were rounded up communally in September. This is still the dominant seasonal rhythm in present-day Iceland. Apart from meat and milk they also provided wool and hides that were used for dozens of domestic necessities, as well as a means of exchange. The wool was never cut, but left to fall off on its own. When collected it was spun and woven into coarse cloth, that was for a long time used as a general standard of value in Iceland.

Each household had one or perhaps a few more cows for milk, which was used for immediate consumption or, more frequently, for the production of butter and sour whey. The latter was diluted with water and served as the ordinary drink with meals; in addition to that it served as a means for preservation. Due to a permanent shortage of salt, meat produce of various kinds were either smoked or preserved in whey. This is still widely practised in the Icelandic countryside, where the sour taste of liver- and blood-sausages and other things is a delicacy along with smoked or singed meat.

While farming certainly was the primary occupation in the mental image of the local economy, because it sustained the traditional conceptions of the world as centralized around the household, fishing played an equally important role, economically speaking. Part of the attraction of Iceland was the fishing possibilities, but these were not quite evenly distributed, however. The movements of the cod in particular resulted in abundant catches in the western and southern parts of Iceland compared to the north and east. During the fishing season, January–May, fishermen (and some women) came to temporary fishing places along the western and southern coasts from all over the island. The fishermen were not a specialized group, but were smallholders and farmhands working for a vital supplement to the household economy. Most of the fish was dried for storage and later domestic consumption, while some was exchanged for grain.

Both external and internal exchange took place without the use of money, although woollens and fish served as rather generalized means of exchange in different periods. Thus, in 1640 a German traveller noted that the Icelanders 'need no money to buy or sell but receive one thing for another' (Vetter (1640) 1931: 172); a century later another German observed that all payments were made in goods (Anderson 1746: 130); and in a travelogue from 1780 the Englishman von Troil wrote that due to the mountainous nature of the country 'there is no agriculture, and no commerce, except that carried on by bartering of the various commodities on the arrival of Danish ships' (von Troil 1980: 56). From his and other observations we get a clear picture of a small-scale barter economy. Even when fishing became a large-scale full-time occupation money was of limited circulation. Fish that was not used for personal consumption and storage was exchanged for credit with the local merchant. In this way, the up-and-coming local merchant replaced the landlord as the fishermen's patron, and workers were never really identified as such until the industrialization process speeded up after the Second World War. In a recent analysis of the conditions of the 'hidden' working class and its relation to the commercial conditions, Finnur Magnússon shows how this class was in fact relatively discrete (Magnússon 1990).

Fishing was generally small-scale and was conducted from small open boats by means of hooks and lines. The boats were made from planks, which made access to timber a vital problem for the Icelanders. When the Vikings first came to Iceland they had a large seagoing fleet of boats with twelve or more oars, but as time wore on the fleet could not be restored on home ground due to lack of timber, and boats became smaller; two-oar boats made the largest contingent, while four to eight oars were also quite common. This is interesting when seen against the background of the deep-sea fishing fleets from continental Europe that exploited the Icelandic waters from the fifteenth century onwards with a much more sophisticated technology.

As noted, farming and fishing coexisted in a dual economic system; the Icelandic annals give plenty of evidence for both modes of livelihood being absolutely vital. If failure occurred in one of the domains, hunger was likely to follow even if the other was of ordinary yield. If both failed, catastrophe was likely. Annalists have noted how people starved to death one year after another. Although recognized as complementary at the level of consumption, farming and fishing did not occupy equal positions in the minds of the Icelanders until recently; if a choice had to be made farming would be favoured. Thus, when in 1404, *fiskimenn* (fishermen), appear for the first time in the documents, significantly it is also the last. The Black Death had ravaged Iceland from 1402 to 1404, reducing the population by some 40 per cent (Bjarnadóttir 1986). Farm labour had become scarce. This was the reason behind a law of compulsory farm service being passed in 1402, obliging *fiskimenn* and workers to settle at a farm and work for a landowner. If they refused, they were to be exiled (*Lovsamling for Island*, I: 34–5). Thus, when fishermen are first mentioned as a distinct group, they are immediately subsumed under the farming structure. This is actually one of the first hints about the conceptual asymmetry between farming and fishing in the local definition of Icelandicness.

Fishing continued, of course, out of sheer necessity, but fishermen vanished from the records. They became subsumed under the general category of *vinnuhjú* (servants) defined by their position within a *bú* (household) headed by a landowner or a well-to-do tenant on Church or Crown property. Generally, fishing and fishing rights were defined in terms of land rights that were apparently always given conceptual priority. This can be inferred also from the fact that farmhands engaging in seasonal fishing were to return for the hay harvest at the latest, quite irrespective of the catch at the shore. During the fifteenth century, when the Icelanders still had a clear recollection of the potential surplus created by fishing, the local court passed one law after another that was designed to make fishing less attractive for people. Thus, fishing with more than one hook on the line was banned, explicitly on account of the farmers who feared that fishing, if returns increased, would be too attractive to their servants (*Alþingisbækur Íslands*, I: 432–4; V: 122). Sinker lines were likewise banned, and a prohibition on using worms as bait was issued. It was not until 1699 that part of these restrictions were lifted, when sinker lines with several hooks were again allowed, but still only during the season: outside this period it was prohibited because of its allegedly damaging effects on farming (*Lovsamling for Island*, I: 564–7). By then, the Icelanders seemed to have lost the motivation, however; a century later, in 1785, Skúli Magnússon noted how lines with just one hook almost reigned supreme, and he made a strong case for the reintroduction of sinker lines with up to thirty hooks, giving a detailed description of how to make them (Magnússon 1944a: 55–6). Generally, he complains about the conspicuous deterioration of Icelandic fishing (Magnússon 1944b).

Thus, in the fifteenth century when there was a growing interest in and need for fishing, it was publicly restricted. On behalf of society, legal representatives made fishing a marginal activity in the economic cycle of the year. While temporary migrations into the natural wilderness of the island were an absolute economic necessity, the image of Icelandicness required that the migrants return to the farm. They could not remain on the 'outside' without throwing their human identity in jeopardy, it seems. One of the results was that the fishing potential was not fully exploited in spite of the overall importance of fish in the subsistence economy. Declining technologies, such as smaller boats, fewer hooks on the line, and the prohibition of sinker lines contributed to the diminishing of the catch, while the Icelanders starved. The deliberate aim of the decision-makers, who were themselves farmers, was to redirect people towards farming where there was felt to be a more or less permanent shortage of labour.

The development in the domain of farming was no less problematic, however. Icelandic society was based on large farms and a relatively sophisticated soil technology in the early Middle Ages. At that time the soil was thoroughly prepared by plough and manure, fences were kept up to protect the infields from stray animals. Also, saeters were used to lift the pressure on the home fields, which therefore had a greater yield, and hay was stored in hay-barns that were part of the elaborate farm structure. Gradually, all this deteriorated. Grain-growing was completely abandoned, and soon the plough fell into disuse. To make matters worse, the fences separating the infields from the wilderness disintegrated. From earliest times, fences had been compulsory to protect the precious infields against stray animals; the laws of fencing had always reflected the farming interests, but the peasants nevertheless failed to keep up with the requirements. In the eighteenth century this became a major issue in the redressment of the Icelandic conditions of living, having reached their absolute rock-bottom by then. In 1776 an ordinance was issued by the Danish king demanding of the Icelanders that they reconstruct their fences, offering the threat of fines and also a promise of rewards (*Lovsamling for Island*, IV: 278ff.). Judging from later decrees it was not an easy task to convince the Icelanders of the necessity of the restoration. It was even suggested that exemplary fences be built in all regions for the people to study (ibid. IV: 426). The old technology was apparently forgotten, while the material (stone) remained plentiful. During the period, hay-barns also went out of use. In medieval Icelandic society, hay was stored in barns, as archaeological evidence shows. In the later period, hay was just stacked out-of-doors and subject to rather moist conditions. The result of these developments was a smaller yield from the scarce fields, and a greater vulnerability to just one bad winter; in more analytic terms, we could say that the 'inside', or the controlled space, diminished dramatically. The net result was an often fatally small security margin. An absolute low-water mark was reached in the seventeenth and eighteenth centuries when mass death from starvation was a recurrent phenomenon.

Poverty had reached a level which was unheard of in the other Nordic countries. With much the same ecological conditions, the population of Norway increased tenfold in the period 1500–1800, from 150,000 to 1.5 millions (Dyrvik *et al.* 1979). The Icelanders, in contrast, could barely reproduce themselves. Reformers had much to do in the late eighteenth century, when the Enlightenment reached the North Atlantic community. One of the first tasks was to re-educate the Icelanders in forgotten fishing and farming technologies. Development was very slow, however. Many reformers complained about the resistance towards absolutely basic changes. It was not until well into the nineteenth century that the 'medieval level' of technology and population was reached again, and a new trend could be seen.

With the expanding fishing and growing yields of hay, Icelandic society was finally set in motion towards the modern market-oriented economy.

Socio-political Integration

Iceland has been subject to three different socio-political structures that have influenced her history; they are the Crown, the Church, and the commercial order.

These structures have been external to Icelandic society, while at the same time integrating the island into a larger order of power and powerless-ness. Crown, Church, and commerce have been intertwined to varying degrees at different times.

Constitutionally, Iceland was a self-governing society from 930 when her first constitution was made, laying down the principles for a 'democratic' State. The Althing (*alþingi* or people's assembly) was to meet once a year, confirm the laws, and judge in cases that were brought before the court. At a lower level, local Spring assemblies headed by secular chiefs dealt with lesser issues. All farmers had to affiliate themselves to a chief.

In the year 1000 the Icelanders converted to Christianity by a communal decision made at the Althing—if not without serious difficulties. The Church gradually gained power, and came to influence decisions. Besides the secular laws, framing the political structure and social relationships, a Christian law emerged. They were certainly not always in agreement. While the traditional law permitted blood-revenge, concubinage, and women's rights, the Christian law changed all this, in principle if not always in practice. Gradually this paved the way for the idea of a kingdom based on the ruler's divine power, an idea that was foreign to the original Icelandic idea of rulership and secular power. In 1262 the Icelanders swore allegiance to the Norwegian king, and promised to pay taxes to the Crown's representatives in Iceland.

In spite of the submission, the Althing continued to function in all internal affairs. This was also true when in 1380 Iceland was transferred to the joint kingdom of Norway and Denmark. In the early centuries, the incorporation into a foreign kingdom did not make much difference, because the kings apparently had little interest in this far northern region. When the Reformation occurred in Denmark in 1536, things began to change; the king now took a stronger moral interest in his North Atlantic subjects and imposed the Reformation upon them. For the northern part of the country this could not happen without serious conflict, terminating in 1550 with the decapitation of the bishop and his sons. Apart from the changes in liturgy and law, one of the consequences of the Reformation was the sequestration of lands from the Church. After that the Crown was a major land-owner, leasing land to tenants.

A century later the absolutist State emerged in Denmark (1660). Again this had consequences for the Icelanders who had to subject themselves to more scrutiny than before. The Althing became increasingly powerless; while court functions were upheld to a certain degree the legislative functions were undermined. In 1800 it was completely abolished, only to be re-established in 1843 as a consequence of the first wave of nationalism in Iceland. After that it gradually regained power and remained the centre of the political organization of the Republic of Iceland when declared in 1944.

As mentioned, the Icelanders became Christian by a legislative act in the year 1000. The story of the conversion was first told by the aforementioned Ari *inn fróði* in 1120, according to whom the meeting at the Althing was quite dramatic and at the point of disrupting the Icelandic community, which had first been founded by pagan Norsemen and based on age-old pagan institutions of Nordic heritage. The event was not only a local one, however, but signalled Iceland's entry into the larger scene of European Christendom. The Church represented a 'centre' outside Iceland, and the conflict of values between the Althing and Rome was a contributing factor in the fall of the Commonwealth.

The conversion symbolized far-ranging social changes in Iceland. First of all, the very concept of society as coterminous with the law became replaced by a concept of society as defined by a 'divine' kingdom. This paved the way for a new concept of hierarchy in social relations, and for the Norwegian king's seizure of power in 1262. The discrepancy between the 'old' and the 'new' ideas was to remain a source of conflict for centuries in matters of property, beliefs, and practice. In 1056 the first Icelandic bishop was appointed to be supplemented by a second diocese in 1106. A Christian law was first adopted in the early twelfth century to supplement the secular laws of the Commonwealth. The two sets of laws were to some degree contradictory, and in 1253 the primacy of Christian law was affirmed at the Althing.

While the real king was distant, the two bishops of Iceland aspired to local power on an almost royal scale. The Icelandic peasants often complained about the usurpation on the part of the bishops, and tried to incur the king's sympathy. He was ready to sympathize because of an increasing conflict of interest between Crown and Church over the peasants' taxes and tithes. By the Reformation Crown and Church became united into one structure of external origin. After the Reformation this external power intensified its interest in Iceland. The people were to be morally educated and civilized. Like many other peasant populations the Icelanders had mixed feelings towards religion and towards the external rulers, and when the first wave of the Enlightenment occurred in the late eighteenth century many of the foreign observers noted how in Iceland people had retained more ancient Nordic customs and beliefs than elsewhere because of an extremely low degree of external communication apart from the one mediated by the rulers.

Until the Reformation almost all education had been in the hands of the Church and the monasteries. Reading and writing were spread from these centres of learning as well as theological and other learning. Often theology merged with magic, and as far as the sources reveal these things, it seems that the episcopal schools were permeated with magic until the Reformation, when by royal decree a different kind of cathedral school was established, often preparing young men for further education in Copenhagen.

These centres of learning were not the sole instrument used in the civilization of the Icelanders, who from the sixteenth century were compelled by law to verse themselves in the catechism, and to read aloud from the Bible every evening. If no one at the farm could read and the neighbouring farm was too distant, the people were expected to memorize psalms and biblical stories. According to a forceful 1746 ordinance about domestic discipline, it was the responsibility of the household head to see to his children's and servants' education, while it was left to the local priest to examine them at regular intervals. A result of this was that there was a high degree of literacy by the eighteenth century (Guttormsson 1983).

If royal and ecclesiastical structures of external origin integrated Iceland into the larger world by tying it to centres elsewhere, this is also true of the pattern of commerce. In Europe the wheels of commerce propelled a particular development of capitalism during the centuries from 1400 to 1800 which also affected the marginal North Atlantic community, though at a much slower pace than the rest of Europe.

Iceland was dependent on long-distance sea trade which was subject to serious physical limitations. We have seen how changes in winds and currents made communication problematic, at least until the age of steam. Navigation and trade were difficult in these circumstances, and the Icelanders were at the mercy of seagoing fleets from elsewhere. While in the early Middle Ages the Icelanders had boats that made them masters of North Atlantic trade, by 1300 their fleet had dwindled and their commerce had been taken over by Norwegian and Hanseatic merchants. In the period 1400–1500 the English dominated trade, while the Danes took over from *c.*1550 until Icelandic independence. From 1601 to 1787 the Danish king imposed a trade monopoly on Iceland, which was then leased out to various merchant agencies (Gunnarsson 1983). This paved the way for a commercial exploitation of the Icelanders whose need for grain, timber, and iron was exploited by merchants exchanging these items for fish and woollens at the lowest possible rate.

The merchants were not always completely free to set the terms of trade. The Danish King Christian IV imposed a scale of relative pricing in 1619, which is given here because it gives a vivid impression of the import needs of the Icelanders:

Commodity	Price in pounds of fish
Barrel of grain	50
Barrel of good ale	50
Barrel of salt	40
Unit of iron	10
Set of horseshoes	5
Half a pot of spirits	2
12 marks of tar	10
One ell of linen	6
Handaxe	15
Keel timber, 12 ells	60
Keel timber, 8 ells	40
Oar, 10 ellens	12
Oar, 6 ellens	6
Good knife	8

(*Lovsamling for Island*, I: 187–90)

In the seventeenth century fish had replaced *álnir*, ells (of homespun), as the general standard of value. Also, if one were able to pay in dried fish instead of butter, cloth, or socks (the knitting of which had been introduced from Denmark in the sixteenth century), one got more value for money.

In spite of the fact that Iceland was in many ways a highly commercial society, in the sense of being heavily dependent on foreign trade, its internal economic structure remained archaic. It was founded in the medieval subsistence economy to which external trade had to adapt, rather than the other way round. This is a symptom of the paradox inherent in all the domains in which Iceland was integrated into the larger socio-political organization of Crown, Church, and commerce. While certainly influenced (and to some extent exploited) by the foreign centres, the Icelanders continually stressed their own local centres—the autonomous households 'at home'.

The Nationalist Movement

The nationalist movement in Iceland was spurred by the Romanticist ideas prevailing elsewhere in Europe after 1800 (Hastrup 1990*b*: 103ff.). Its precondition, however, was the Enlightenment which in the last decades of the eighteenth century had prepared the Icelanders for some idea of change. Iceland was hit by a major disaster in the 1780s; a volcanic eruption and subseqent ash-falls had laid vast areas waste, and a period of famine and death followed. One-third of the population succumbed. Partly as a consequence of this, the trade monopoly was abolished in 1787 due in particular to the effort of the Enlightenment reformer Skúli Magnússon. The liberation of trade was not effected in one stroke, however. It took another sixty years before the last restrictions were lifted. But by 1787 at least part of the pressure on the island was relieved.

Other symbols were changed as well. The ancient bishoprics at Skálholt and Hólar were united and transferred to Reykjavík by a royal decision. This was a serious breach of tradition, but even more serious from a 'national' point of view was the abolition of the Althing in 1800. The Althing had been the political and conceptual centre of Iceland ever since the beginning of history, and although it had gradually lost its legislative functions under the Danish reign, it had continued to execute judicial functions. No less important, the meeting had served as an integrative mechanism, in the sense that the recurrent event brought people together once a year, and made 'society' visible to the Icelanders living in highly scattered communities. At the meeting, news and commodities were exchanged, and entertainment organized—quite apart from the news and entertainment value of the court verdicts and their execution. In 1800 a royal decree abolished all this; the Althing was suspended and the court functions bureaucratized and transferred to Reykjavík, by then a town of 446 inhabitants, including twenty-seven convicts.

Thus all the institutions symbolizing ancient Icelandic culture and tradition were eclipsed at the close of the poorest and saddest century in Icelandic history. Meanwhile, Denmark collapsed financially due to the Napoleonic wars, resulting in reduced imports into Iceland. Thanks to the Enlightenment reformers in Iceland, the soil had been prepared for an improvement of local gardening and fishing techniques, and new vegetables like cabbage and potato gradually compensated for part of the external losses. This process was very slow, however, much to the exasperation of the reformers who complained about the idle and conservative peasants who did not want to learn.

The Romanticist movement was introduced into this slightly optimistic setting (cf. Hastrup 1990*b*: 103ff.). Like many Enlightenment ideas it was imported mainly by Icelanders who had been or were in Copenhagen for university education. A journal, *Fjölnir*, was started in Copenhagen, in which poets and literati praised the Icelandic heritage. The first issue appeared in 1835; in the opening article the editors clearly state their ambition to pursue three themes, utility, beauty, and truth in search for national values. The natural beauty of the country is praised, and it is claimed that this beauty forever attached the Icelanders to their native land. 'But if you, Icelander, truly want to love your country, then read its life-history, and get to know everything which has ever been written about your ancestors' culture and achievements. If you take away what they have written, not only will the Nordic countries appear empty, but in the history of humanity you will find an emptiness of the kind an astronomer would experience if on the sky he looks in vain for the Polar star.' Great words under the North Pole.

The invocation of the past and of ancient literature was a call for a restoration of Icelandic pride, which had hardly survived the disasters of the preceding centuries. In the line of Romanticism in general, the Icelanders were now to see their precarious natural surroundings as beautiful and conceive of the subarctic and arid island in terms of a warm and loving mother. The process of restoring national pride was supported by the launching of a systematic purification of the language, the written form of which was (re-)constructed on the basis of medieval saga literature. In that way, too, past virtues were proposed as goals for the future.

This first nationalist movement was essentially literary; it was a matter of words and writings in more than one sense. However, it prepared the ground for a more explicitly political movement which under the leadership of Jón Sigurðsson struggled for autonomy. The first victory was the re-establishment of the Althing in 1843 as a local advisory body to the Danish government. The first proper meeting was held in 1845, but it was the meeting of 1851 which was decisive in proposing a separate constitution for Iceland. On hearing this claim the Danish representatives proceeded to close the meeting in the name of the king, but Jón Sigurðsson immediately protested—also in the name of the king. He spoke about the unlawfulness of the act and when he ended his speech, the Icelanders rose and cried: '*Vér mótmælum allir*' ('we all protest') (Sigurðsson 1951: 150–2). This was a turning point in Danish–Icelandic relations as far as almost any Icelandic view of history is concerned. It was the first antagonistic experience that was expressed in an explicitly political idiom. The consequences were far-reaching.

The victories of the nationalists slowly but surely brought Iceland closer to self-government. Among the important events of the decades following the collective protest of the Icelanders were a law that finally liberated Icelandic trade with all nations (1854), and a liberalization of the election law (1857). But still in 1871 the Danish Parliament unilaterally passed a bill which declared Iceland part of the Danish kingdom, although it had its own government in domestic affairs. The Danish supreme court was to remain supreme in Iceland as well. These and other more or less arbitrary measures only served to strengthen the struggle of the Icelanders.

As the millennium of the alleged first settlement in Iceland approached (1874), the nationalists urged the king to grant the Icelanders a new constitution which gave legislative power to the Althing. Jón Sigurðsson was the prime mover, and he succeeded. In 1874 a constitution was adopted which gave the Icelanders self-government in all internal matters. From then onwards Iceland moved inevitably towards full independence. In 1918 it became a sovereign State in personal union with Denmark. On 17 June (Jón Sigurðsson's birthday) 1944, Iceland was declared a sovereign Republic. Thus ended 680 years of foreign rule, through which a remarkable continuity of a national consciousness had survived—at one level probably the most significant precondition of the reclaimed autonomy.

This brief sketch of the nationalist movement in Iceland shows at least one remarkable feature. There was no violence and no weapons used except for those of words. There was never any military in Iceland—until the Allied forces came during the Second World War—neither Icelandic, Norwegian, nor Danish. Since the beginnings of history, the execution of laws and verdicts were left to the Icelanders on behalf of the community and by the directives given at the Althing. Local power was not backed by organized physical force, but by collectively supported self-help.

The rulers were always sparsely represented in Iceland. A handful of governors mediated between the people and their distant king, but generally the Icelanders were left alone—for better or for worse. The laws imposed upon them were only slowly put into practice, but also innovations were only slowly implanted. The isolation of the Icelanders in the North Atlantic contributed to their poverty for centuries, but when it came to the nationalist movement it also helped them avoid the fate of peoples elsewhere where physical force was used to keep down rightful quests for sovereignty. The only weapons used in the Icelandic struggle for independence were words, and extensive reference to the earliest times.

Self-definitions and Contemporary Conditions

In the preceding sketch of the long and well-documented history of the Icelanders the present era has been foreshadowed in many ways, if for nothing but the

remarkable continuity in the image of 'Icelandicness'. The Norse mythology provided the Icelanders with a concentric model of the world, which has influenced
Icelandic cosmology ever since. Although the opposition between the inside and
the outside no longer masks an explicit distinction between humans and non-
humans, there is still an outspoken difference between 'we, the Icelanders' and the
rest of the world.

One possible reason for the tenacity of the ancient cosmological model is the fit
between Iceland as a geographical space and Iceland as a social space. In myth,
Miðgarðr was separated from Útgarðr by an ocean in which the evil serpent lived;
in geography, Iceland is separated from the outer world by the North Atlantic, by
which the external rulers, tax collectors, and merchants came to exploit the island.
Similarly, at the local level, the atomistic social structure made of every single
farmstead a microcosmos, where the fence always provided symbolic protection
against the threats of the uncontrolled forces of the wild. The household epitomized society, and farm life itself was a constant reminder of the basic opposition
between inside and outside.

In their collective representations, the Icelanders continually entertained an idea
of living in the cultivated centre of the world. This was contrary to the actual
experience of many Icelanders, who had been marginalized for centuries, as vagrants, casual labourers, fishermen, or urbanites. To these categories, the inside
provided no actual shelter against the hazards of nature, but 'the Icelanders' were
nevertheless embraced by the sweeping category of insiders who had the power to
define others out of the social space. Due to the conceptual equation between the
centre of the world and a stable farming society, a paradox of identity was created
and maintained which actually alienated large parts of the poorer population from
the social stereotype of 'the Icelanders'.

The paradox was a consequence also of the structural dominance of the farmers
who had the power to objectify their vision of the world. Since the landtakings,
'Icelandicness' had been anchored in sedentary farming—even if it was so named
only a century and a half later. Even today, when only a small proportion of
Icelanders (about 10–11 per cent) are actually farmers, there is still a noticeable
semantic density around the farming population, whenever 'the Icelanders' are
mentioned. Most Icelanders now live in more or less urban surroundings, and by
far the greatest proportion of the gross national income is owing to the fishing
industries, but visitors are still told that in order to get to know Iceland properly,
they must go to the countryside, where people also speak real Icelandic. Somehow
the life and language of the townships are regarded as more or less corrupt.

This is gradually changing, however, and there is now a growing pride in the
fishing enterprise. The concept of Icelandicness is probably in a process of
reorientation. But the image of the ancestors as free and proud settlers is continually invoked in the national rhetoric. The boundaries of Icelandic culture are
continually stressed, and firmly anchored in history. After the declaration of the
Republic of Iceland (1944) one of the major issues was to get back the old manu-

scripts from Denmark; the transfer has now been completed, and there is a distinct feeling that history has finally been reclaimed.

The fear of losing cultural autonomy is apparently still present, however. Immigrants and refugees are not really welcome, and Icelanders who have been educated abroad more often than not hurry home from their chosen exile. This is probably both a sign of a firm sense of belonging, which may have little to do with boundaries, and a reflection of a long tradition of firmly distinguishing between Icelanders and others, as an expression of a claim to uniqueness. For centuries, foreigners were not allowed to winter in Iceland, but had to leave by September at the latest. Dispensation was given only a few times on condition that the foreigner (often a popular healer from elsewhere, who had come with a merchant ship) learned Icelandic. While this restriction was lifted in the nineteenth century, the reservation towards foreigners, such as tourists, has not completely lapsed, while there is also some pleasure taken in being hosts.

There are historical reasons for this; foreigners often were exploiters, whether bishops, kings, merchants, or pirates. The economy was extremely vulnerable for centuries and nobody wanted to be stuck with more circulating paupers than absolutely necessary. In spite of rapid industrial growth after the Second World War and a high level of income and social welfare, the modern Icelandic economy is still vulnerable because it depends on the unstable natural resources of the sea. This vulnerability marks the self-definition of the Icelanders who actually and conceptually protect their remote island in the North Atlantic by insisting on its uniqueness.

In the modern conditions, Iceland has become fully integrated in the world economy and in global streams of consciousness. Modernity and related universalizing modes came late to Iceland, however, and as elsewhere in the world they must coexist with counter-claims to particularity, such as a notion of history consisting in qualitatively defined time spaces, of which 'today' is only the last. The general point is that wherever we are in the world, modernity is transformed locally so as to fit previous experience (Sahlins 1993).

Modernity, whatever it may be, is always incorporated into local history, and into a particular practice of memory. Whether reference is to times past or times present, the meanings of 'pastness' and 'presentness' are mutually implicated. In Iceland, where memory is practised to an extraordinary degree, as we shall see later, history is shaped and reshaped in a collective recollection of age-old themes, partly premissed by the times just described and the knowledge about them stored in words and practices. The 'said', as story and history, is constantly recirculated, and in the process it both surrounds and constitutes the contexture of the Icelandic world.

2

Ethnographic Fieldsites

Ethnographers are travellers; for them travel is not a metaphor and their theoretical landscapes are real. They may be more or less pedestrian, but ethnographers must ground their work in places that are real and practised by people—including their own temporary practice. In this chapter I shall present the principal sites of my own fieldwork, those corners of the Icelandic world that I came to know well through my interlocutions with people who were already there, and who remained and continued to transform their world when I left.

In everyday life, people are afforded the luxury of assuming that they understand what they see or hear; by contrast, anthropologists have to start their work on the assumption of misunderstanding. This is a consequence of the nature of the ethnographic enquiry itself. First, there are no results which are not interpretations, and there is nothing, therefore, which can be understood just like that. Next, the practical nature of anthropological theorizing in a space inhabited by people who are themselves theorizing their society, means that the object changes as the interpretation takes shape. 'The enquiry brings with it answers that change the next question which can be asked' (Paine 1995: 58). Again, we sense the profoundly interpersonal character of the ethnographic enterprise. The nature of the ethnographic enquiry takes shape in a process of experience and conversation. This requires some reflections on the space in which the ethnographic encounter takes place, as well as on the position held by the ethnographer.

In ethnography a mode of social experience is transformed into a kind of text that one way or the other is at one remove from the world but which may, nevertheless, have a certain social efficacy (cf. Bourdieu 1990: ch. 1). By being told, the narrative assumes its own reality and becomes part of lived experience. There is reason to repeat that writing about life in Iceland cannot mirror or reflect local practical knowledge of being an Icelander. The mode of representation implied in the bygone genre of (metaphysical) realism has been dismantled. With Realism went the confidence in our notion of the object, and of interpretation as a kind of correlation with the object in itself. This notion of interpretation is not the only notion available to us, however; we can still seek to correlate discourse with discourse, or to construct a meaningful commentary on one discourse in another (Putnam 1990: 121–2). The latter is my ambition.

As commentary, its meaning is relative to the anthropological scheme of reference before anything else. This does not imply that the views and critiques voiced within the Icelandic scheme of reference are immaterial. The anthropological practice of interpretation must be context-sensitive, and seek to 'get it right', that is aim at a general acceptability of the results (cf. Putnam 1990: 122). Yet, as a scholarly discipline, anthropology *disciplines* the material in particular ways, abiding by certain transcultural notions of justification. In this view, objectivity or scientific ambition has nothing to do with monism or absoluteness, let alone relativism.

My comprehension of the Icelandic world is situated and as much a result of reflection and writing as a consistent quality of my Icelandic experience (cf. Clifford 1988: 110). The point is, however, that reflection and experience cannot be absolutely separated in the practice of anthropology (Hastrup and Hervik 1994). This insight is not new; twenty years ago, Bob Scholte drew our attention to the fact that

Fieldwork and subsequent analysis constitute a unified praxis . . . the ethnographic situation is defined not only by the native society in question, but also the ethnographical tradition 'in the head' of the ethnographer. Once he is actually in the field, the native's presuppositions also become operative, and the entire situation turns into complex intercultural mediation and a dynamic interpersonal experience. (Scholte 1974: 438)

At the time there was little guidance as to how the 'interpersonal experience' might be presented and exploited in writing. During the decades that followed this lack has been amended, some would say to excess. The importance of autobiography and positioning in the ethnographic encounter has been widely acknowledged (Okely and Callaway 1992). It has become generally accepted that the ethnographic experience takes place in a world which in many ways is a world of 'betweenness' (Hastrup 1992c); there is no privileged position from where we can eliminate our own consciousness from our object (Rabinow 1977: 151). Neither is subjectivity a fixed point from which one interacts with the world; experience is the effect of the interaction between the subject and the world (Callaway 1992: 37). If we take it to be axiomatic, that 'the autobiographical is theoretical' in this sense (Okely 1992: 9), it is apposite to give my own position some explicit recognition in the following. This is done only, I should like to stress, in order to get beyond it.

Even if ethnographic authority is not *only* based on the fact that 'I was there', as the textual criticism in anthropology has made us see, there must still be some solid basis for the ethnographic claims—solidity being at least in part defined by having been there and shared the local experience for some time. I have felt the need on this occasion to be rather explicit about my fieldwork, because it has been alleged publicly that my work is based on 'only a few weeks' of fieldwork (Pálsson 1995: 68). If this were the case, I would remain silent. The total of eighteen months that I have spent in Iceland may not be much, but then, when does one ever have 'enough' material? It depends on analytical scope, of course, and mine was one of exploring a world with a general purpose of theoretical understanding.

Autobiography

Fieldwork is situated between autobiography and anthropology. Geertz suggests (1995: 11) that fieldwork is a parenthesis in local history, important because the anthropologists' 'parenthetic experience' shapes their stories. Daniel also takes the parenthesis as axiomatic and suggests 'interclusion' as a metaphor for the relationship between the ethnographer's experience and the ethnography, defining the nature of the by-now almost pre-empted reflexivity in anthropology, which has less to do with narcissism than with epistemology. By itself, reflexivity in anthropology may be more of a hyphen than a parenthesis:

> I am thinking of the ultimate in intercluding marks, the hyphen. Reflexivity in ethnography can be brief, small, a particle in flight or a fleeting particular, a crepuscular detail, hyphen-like: holding together and holding apart, maintaining continuity and creating a breach, uniting and separating, estranging and binding, and most importantly, dividing but also compounding. (Daniel 1985: 247)

When discussing the position of the ethnographer, it is this interclusion that matters rather than biographic details, because it contributes to the shape of ethnography.

Upon reflection, my choice of Iceland as a field has a number of historical precursors. First among them was my childhood wish to become a polar explorer; my hero was Knud Rasmussen, who was the leader of the famous Thule expeditions in the early 1920s and whose work on the (then so-called) Eskimos is widely renowned (e.g. Rasmussen 1929). Among his publications were also more popular ones in my native Danish, and my dream was to follow the trace of his dog sledge. The dream was further stimulated by extensive reading on Greenland and the Eskimos in general. As Judith Okely (1978) has pointed out, in the 1950s (and 1960s, I would add) young girls had very few women heroes with whom to identify, and if they aspired beyond domesticity, the imagery was heavily male biased. So was mine.

Growing up and realizing that at university there was such a subject as anthropology which might provide an outlet for even women's thirst for explorative adventure was a relief. I enrolled as a potential polar anthropologist, but soon I became sidetracked by the East. A planned and initiated fieldwork in India had to be given up, however, partly due to the unhappy circumstances of the war between India and Pakistan, leading to the creation of Bangladesh, and partly due to the precarious state of health of my two young children. The decision to abandon India was made easier by the fact that already before leaving I had an almost prophetic vision of my new field: Iceland.

It was astonishing even to myself. I knew nothing of Iceland, except that it was a rather large but thinly populated island in the North Atlantic. Anthropologically, I only knew it from two papers I had read during my postgraduate years, viz. Victor Turner's paper on the Icelandic sagas (Turner 1971), and Einar Haugen's paper on the semantics of Icelandic orientation (Haugen 1957). In spite of the paucity of my knowledge, I knew instinctively that my choice was right. On my return, I immediately embarked on Icelandic studies, starting with the country's history. The richness of medieval Icelandic literature was impressive, and soon with four children, the incentive to stick to history for a while was relatively strong. Fieldwork had to be postponed. My doctoral thesis at Oxford in 1979 (revised and published in 1985*a*) therefore became a piece of 'historical anthropology'. Unknowingly, I was part of a trend.

Although certainly an anthropological work in its own right, I still considered this historical analysis a prelude to fieldwork. Such were the canons of the discipline that 'writing' meant the writing up of *field* material. A one-month pilot study was undertaken in 1981, and in January 1982 I embarked upon proper fieldwork for one year with my four children, then aged 3 to 10. The five of us arrived in winter and darkness, and installed ourselves in a flat in the capital Reykjavík, which was to be our base for the first seven months. I recall an immense joy looking out at the white winter night. Somewhat accidentally, I had almost become a polar explorer—even if the practicalities of being a single woman with four young children was slightly at odds with this image.

I stayed in Iceland for the year, during eight months of which my children were with me, until they went home with my visiting sister. Due to practical matters such a schooling and housing, I remained in Reykjavík with the children, undertaking the occasional trip to other areas, looking for possible fieldsites in the countryside and/or in a small fishing village. I pursued my historical and archival studies, while also 'exploring the city' (Hannerz 1980), which by some standards is but an outgrown village—although a remarkably cosmopolitan one. As had happened before, I became fascinated by history itself, and I was drawn towards a closer investigation of the period from 1400 to 1800, which was far less well known than the Middle Ages. The 'prelude' to fieldwork again became a separate project, which was eventually published (Hastrup 1990*a*).

For practical as well as academic reasons, then, a great deal of time has lapsed between fieldwork and writing this book. Recurrent revisits during the 1980s kept me in touch with the people I knew, but whenever I sat down to produce the monograph, I shied away from it. A few articles based on fieldwork observations have been published, but the well-known lack of confidence in one's own notes (cf. Sanjek 1990), which is also a vestige of an obsolete paradigm in anthropology within which the ambition is one of providing the whole truth about a particular society, made me uncertain. However, by the end of the first century of professional anthropology we agree that there is no finite knowledge about any society because history is a flux of unprecedented events, and because there is no knowledge independent of a knower.

What has become evident to me during the years of churning my knowledge about Iceland is that it may be less important to write the classical monograph about 'We, the Icelanders' than to investigate the historical and social premisses of the 'we'. The result is a more comprehensive analysis of some recurrent themes in Icelandic history up to this day. My fieldwork experience is not the sole source of my reflections, although it is still of immense importance as *experience*. As such it informs the whole book, including its more or less implicit epistemological concerns, for which there still seems to be enough food for thought in the ethnographic material that I have. What is more, I have to write it 'out' if not 'up'. Even if there is no sense of unused objective data, which I owe the world to publish, there is still a pressure to externalize my experience and the theoretical reflections it implies. 'No tension is more acute than the intrapersonal experience of unfinished work, all the more so because, on this personal level, we experience the *presence* of the Other' (Fabian 1996: 221). This experience of presence may grow with time and, at any rate, needs time to grow, as Fabian says, in a manner which aptly summarizes my own struggles with writing on contemporary Iceland.

One more note on autobiography remains to be told. In 1988 my life history, including the story of my failed fieldwork in India and my later intensive experience of the Icelandic world, was turned into a theatre play by the famous Danish group theatre, Odin Teatret. Upon reading some of my fieldwork based reflections and later meetings and talks, the director commissioned my autobiography. Parts of it were then, literally, put into the play and as such it toured the world for two years. For me, and my anthropological consciousness, it had two major consequences. First, it was in the writing of my autobiography, in the shape of about fifty 'key-scenes' from my life, that I became aware of (or created) a pattern: indeed, I had become a lonely polar explorer. Second, my own sense of devastation upon seeing the final play about me, in which the main character bore my proper name and spoke my words, gave me an idea of how 'fieldworking' upon other people, and staging their lives in a different (academic) context, may deprive them of their sense of self to an unbearable degree. This experience, which I have analysed elsewhere (Hastrup 1992*d*), was to be followed by a commentary, which was also revealing. While elated by the performance itself, an Icelandic critic of the play nevertheless bemoaned the fact that my impression of the Icelanders had been of such a brutal and almost hostile kind: '*það sem hinsvegar kemur manni á óvart er að Kirsten Hastrup skuli hafa upplifað Ísland sem framandi, villt, frumstætt og fjandsamlegt þjóðfélag*' ('what on the other hand is unexpected is that Kirsten Hastrup should have experienced Iceland as an alien, wild, primitive, and hostile society') (Hólmarsson 1989: 56). First, there is a conflation here between Kirsten of the play and Kirsten the anthropologist, which is interesting; next, there is a gliding from the actual sensation of estrangement to an alleged feeling of hostility, which was never part of my experience, let alone of my writings. This was my first lesson in the self-evident fact that 'the natives' speak back, but more than that it was a lesson in the difficulty of balancing between the literal and the literary, and ultimately in the vast emotional problem in having to publish your friendships. However sensitive one is to ethical matters and to the integrity of the subjects of study, the fact that they have to be written about implies a dramatization of their lives, and possibly symbolic violence. Writing, therefore, feels like treason, and it may block your writing for years. The lack of anonymity in Iceland, as in any small-scale society, makes everyone aware of whom and where in the ethnographic account. This realization has made it difficult for me to go back to Iceland for the past few years, as writing became more pressing. I had to distance myself emotionally to be able to write at all, while naturally also keeping in touch with those sensational experiences that the Icelanders gave me. It also made me choose not to blur my sites in the usual manner. My experiences were localized, if my afterthoughts transcend the local.

The Field

Modern Iceland is a society which for better or for worse is integrated into world economics, and suffering the same problems of industrial pollution, inflation, and rapid social change as the rest of the Western world. It is an island society, reflecting global issues. I have introduced the place already; in this section I shall turn to a more detailed presentation of the space of my fieldwork, understood as a practised place (de Certeau 1984: 117). The practice of fieldwork itself implies a creation of a particular space. In the process of 'taking' place, my fieldwork in Iceland spurred the creation of a space through the ethnographer's movements and courses of action. These movements took me between three fieldsites.

FIG. 2. The field 1: studying a manuscript at Árnastofnun.

My first fieldsite was in Reykjavík, where the centre of my historical research activities was the Stofnun Árna Magnússonar (in daily speech just called Árnastofnun), the Manuscript Institute of the University of Iceland, named after the first systematic manuscript collector in Iceland, Árni Magnússon (1663–1730). Strong antiquarian interests took root at the time under the patronage of King Frederik the Third, and the young Icelander who was sent to study in Copenhagen in 1683 was soon caught up in the general pursuit of historical learning and was eventually appointed the first professor of Danish Antiquities, and the first professor at all of Icelandic origin (Bekker-Nielsen and Widding 1972). In that capacity he travelled extensively in Iceland, collecting any bits and pieces of manuscripts from the Middle Ages onwards. Among them were whole sagas and well-known books, which today form the core of the manuscript collection. Part of his original archive was burnt in a devastaing fire in Copenhagen 1728, after which the remains were bequeathed to the University of Copenhagen, where ever since there has been an Arnamagnæan Collection and, later, an Institute. During the 1960s negotiations were made between the now independent Republic of Iceland and Denmark about the return of the manuscripts to Iceland, and in 1971 the first of them were officially handed back with great national interest. By now the exchange has been completed, and the Manuscript Institute in Iceland is a rich, learned younger brother to the Institute in Copenhagen.

At Árnastofnun a dozen or more permanent scholars and many visitors work on the literary heritage of Iceland, as transmitted on parchment or, later, on paper through the centuries. Texts are deciphered, 'hands' identified, stories connected, and histories traced. The publications from this Institute are pre-eminent in Icelandic studies, and I soon came to venerate this unique centre of learning and tradition. Apart from access to its library and manuscripts, and being provided with a desk and a key to the back door, possibly my chief benefit was admission into a field of embodied cultural tradition. Each morning, the safe is unlocked and the scholars get their manuscripts, and each evening they are put back. During weekends, the scholars take turns in showing the small amount of manuscripts on display to visitors, and the ambience is one of a national treasury, which indeed it is.

Árnastofnun is a secluded area, locked off from the rest of the university, permanently under guard; the protection of the manuscripts is a major concern. Within it, a small world unfolds that seems to transcend both time and space. In the *kaffistofa*, coffee room, where the permanent staff and visiting scholars join for coffee every morning and every afternoon, the air was loaded with Icelandicness. The brief philological exchanges, interpretative queries, and anecdotes were packed with meaning for the visiting anthropologist. My being accepted as a 'resident' of the *kaffistofa* for seven months taught me more than I shall ever be able to acknowledge. My (at first) naïve questions on various matters on Icelandic history were always met with wise answers and a degree of patience that allowed for sidetracks into other areas of knowledge. Of course, my area of scholarship was unusual in this context, and my friends would make occasional hints at the anthropologist studying them, and on later revisits some would ask when my book of the *kaffistofa* was due to come out. While not solely a book on the *kaffistofa*, the present work is deeply informed by its unique athmosphere. Indeed, the *kaffistofa* is a place of shared knowledge and intellectual generosity, of wisdom and history—of *fræði* and *saga*.

Exploring the city from the vantage point of Árnastofnun made me acutely aware of the recent and rapid transition of Icelandic society. Although by the end of the twentieth century there are of course families that have been living in Reykjavík for generations, and hence many people who are native to the city, among most there still seems to be a strong connection to a particular tract of countryside Iceland, a *sveit*. Through various kinship bonds, many city-dwellers retained a sense of belonging to a particular place; their social space comprised a locality elsewhere, to which their urbanite children would often go and spend the long summer vacation.

This ethnographic observation was one reason why I wanted to spend some time in the countryside. Another inducement was provided by my university colleagues' recurrent insistence that if one were to learn proper Icelandic, one had to go to the countryside. In the town, and most notably in the fishing villages, language was corrupt. While it can be unmasked as an ideological more than a linguistic observation (Pálsson 1989, and see Chapter 4), the repeated stress on 'proper' Icelandic

Fig. 3. The field 2: the farm of Hali.

being spoken only in *sveit*, was a piece of ethnographic information that deserved attention. I was grateful, therefore, to be allowed to stay at a farm, where I was to spend a couple of months in the first round, to be followed by repeated revisits for the next five years. I was very cordially received and felt accepted almost as if I were a member of the family, as will be recalled from the story of the cows in the Prelude. The friendly atmosphere at this farm, inhabited by three generations of the same family, its learnedness, and their collective pride of being farmers and Icelanders engulfed me and nourished my sense of local significance.

In Iceland, most farms lie widely scattered and far between in the unlimited and rough landscape, and fieldwork presupposes affiliation with a particular farmstead. There are no villages and no village squares with out-of-doors cafés from where life can be observed. In the subarctic, one is either part of indoor life or completely shut off from it. It was my good fortune to become part of one family's life, and to be assigned various tasks, thus enabling me to truly experience farming life in Suðursveit of eastern Iceland. Even though Þórbergur Þórðarson writes about life there two or three generations back, before roads and cars, his observation on the farm's 'singularity' is still in some sense true: *Allir, sem ekki áttu heima á Hala, voru útlendingar . . . allir bæir voru útlönd nema Halabærinn. Svona byrjaði ættjarðarástin* (1981: 35) ('All who were not at home at Hali were outlanders . . . all farms except Hali were foreign country. Thus the love for family land began'). While life has changed a lot since then, it was still my general feeling that farm life in Iceland is remarkably centred. This probably is a feature of farm life everywhere, but it is a feature which is emphasized in Iceland due to the thinly scattered population. The point here is that I could only study farm life by being accepted as an 'honorary' member of the family, much as in earlier generations there had always been the odd, distant relative by blood, marriage, or fostering who found shelter and work at the farm. My being accepted was also, I believe, a feature of the age-old tradition of welcoming travellers, passers-by, and distant acquaintances who had *fréttir* (news) to tell, or *sögur* (stories) to impart. In a learned family like 'mine' this openness was legendary, and while there it was my own privilege often to meet and listen to people from all over the place making a point of stopping and sharing news as they went by.

As I have already indicated, Hali is situated on a narrow strip of land on the south-eastern coast of Iceland between the sea and the mountains, and towering in the background on clear days is a huge glacier. One feels rather small and insignificant in this landscape, unless one learns to meet it on local terms, as it were. Between the farm and the 'world-ocean', as Þórbergur has it, there is a longish lagoon (*lón*), and behind it are the inaccessible rocks. As he reminisces from his childhood perception:

Allar hæðir voru ákaflega háar og allar brekkur brattar og næstum ómögulegt að komast þær upp. Allir staðir voru langt í burtu og ókunnuglegir, álíka og manni fundust síðar önnur lönd. Það var enginn vegur að komast þangað, nema einhver vildi lofa manni með sér. Og öll ferðalög voru löng og nýstárleg. (Þórbergur Þórðarson 1981: 36)

FIG. 4. The field 3: the village of Hellisandur.

(All heights were exceedingly high and all slopes steep and almost impossible to negotiate. All places were faraway and unknown, almost as one would later find other countries. There were no ways of getting there, unless one could get someone to go along. And all travel was long and rare.)

Orientation in such landscape inevitably is centred on the home. The world is measured *from* there. It is a fixed place from where one goes out into the rest of the world.

By contrast, the fishing villages are places that seem to be mentally constructed by the reverse movement. They are places *to* where one moves. Historically, this has been true to an extraordinary degree, because permanent settlements on the coasts were prohibited as we have seen, effectively making fishing life a seasonal enterprise, as implied by the notion of (*ver-*)*búðir*, (fishing-abodes) in contrast to the farmstead or *bú*. My third fieldsite was such a place: Hellisandur on the western part of the headland Snæfellsnes, epitomizing life *undir jökli* (under the glacier), the tough life in the shadow of cone-shaped beautiful Snæfellsjökull. In his work on legends from Snæfellsnes, Oscar Clausen notes how by the first census in the eighteenth century *þurrabúðarmennirnir í sjóplássunum undir Jökli voru komnir úr öllum áttum* (the cottage-dwellers at the fishing places under the Glacier had come from all corners of the world) (Clausen 1968: 58). Although today it is possible to find families with several generations having lived in the same village, there is still

RARITAN VALLEY COMMUNITY COLLEGE
EVELYN S. FIELD LIBRARY

a remarkable feeling of the place being somewhere one lands, but not where one starts. Movement is part of life in the fishing villages, and it is epitomized by the presence of a *verbúð*, a fishing barrack, in all villages, designed for migrant labour.

Generally, I had been warned in Reykjavík that fishing villages were rough places where no one would want to live, and where people were violent and language corrupt. Part of the reputation for violence was sustained in local legend having it that *á fyrri öldum, þegar sjóplássin á Snæfellsnesi voru svo að segja einu þorpin hér á landi, fluttust þangað ýmiss kunar vandræðamenn og uppflosingar úr öðrum héruðum landsins* (Clausen 1967: 167), ('in previous centuries, when the fishing places on Snæfellsnes were so to speak the only village in the country, all sorts of troublesome people and bankrupt peasants from other counties moved there'). It seems that the dual nature of the population as troubled and alien has stuck to the mental image of the fishing places for ages. I naturally wanted to see such a place for myself, and from Hali I moved to Hellisandur, and took up residence in the *verbúð*. Some 600 people are living there and making their living either as fishermen or in the fish factories.

Hellisandur is one of the oldest-known fishing 'villages' in Iceland, and the history of the place made my choice rather easy. Often, the place is referred to simply as Sandur (sand), and it is situated in what is called Neshreppur utan Ennis, the commune of the headland that is outside the mountain Enni, guarded by a fierce troll woman and (until the late 1980s, when a new road was opened on an artificial 'shore' by the sea) not always easily accessible. I recall a drive on the old road with rocks and stones flying around from above and the roaring sea appearing to be claiming passers-by from below. Beyond Enni, there was never any farming of significance, the land being mainly lava and old ash fields, and the weather rough and stormy. In *Landnámabók* we hear of a certain Ingjaldur claiming land out there, and close to Hellisandur the name of Ingjaldshóll survives at the site of the church, now rather isolated in the landscape. The farm itself, as lesser farms out there, fell into disuse years ago. One may still encounter flocks of semi-wild horses and some sheep, but grazing is nowhere sufficient for modern large-scale animal farming, and it always was extremely scarce.

Nevertheless, since the Middle Ages, the place has attracted people from all over Iceland, who until this century went there to earn a living from fishing on a seasonal basis. *Líf þess fólks, sem ól aldur sinn í þessum verstöðvum, mótaðist mjög af baráttu við óblíð náttúruöfl, þegar það var að sækja lífsbjörgina handa sér og sínum í djúp hafsins* ('The life of people who spent their lives in these fishing places, was profoundly shaped by the fight with unkind forces of nature, when they sought a living for themselves and their families in the deep sea') (Haukur Kristjánsson 1982: 124). My own experience of the place was also one of tough natural conditions. It was snowy, stormy, and dark during the almost two months I initially spent there; few people went out of doors except when hurrying to work and back. My own wanderings to 'map out' the place were considered mysterious not to say hazardous and silly. Later visits at other seasons have softened the image, but on the fringe of the Arctic and the North Atlantic, activities are generally ruled by cold and wind.

I set myself up in the *verbúð* and forced myself to play the hero ethnographer, while being actually initially rather terrified by the darkness, the storm, and the shatterings and sounds of this house on the margins of the world. Recalling Evans-Pritchard's remark, that one can never get enough tables during fieldwork (Evans-Pritchard 1973), and finding myself without one, my first self-assigned task was to construct a table from whatever was at hand in the ragged house. Having done this, I bought a lamp so that I could write my fieldnotes even though it was pitch dark twenty hours a day. I then hung up a piece of cloth in front of the window, through which the wind blew incessantly and noisily, and made my bed on a mattress on the floor with a sleeping-bag and an extra blanket. The polar explorer was ready.

As it happened, the *verbúð* soon proved to be inhabited also by a handful of fishermen who had been away at sea during the first days after my arrival. I had a room of my own, and learned to lock my door. The scenery was totally different from the courtesy and calm of the farm. The *verbúð* was a centre of youthful partying, drinking, occasional outbursts of violence, and more or less anti-social behaviour. Inadvertently, the stereotypes I had been presented with in Reykjavík were confirmed.

I shall return to the ethnography of these fieldsites at various points. Here it suffices to stress that my living in these three places, to which I have returned again and again, remains the basis of my experiential knowledge of the Icelandic world. This knowledge is partial and positioned, and the experience upon which it is based is personal and unrepeatable. This does not prevent it from being generalizable, however, as I hope to be able to demonstrate. Although three separate places, my experience of them makes up a single 'Icelandic' space, in which the ethnographer's voice once was only one among others, but which she now 'writes' and dramatizes in the mode of her own scholarly world. 'The responsibility for ethnography, or the credit, can be placed at no other door than that of the romancers who have dreamt it up' (Geertz 1988: 140).

However much fieldwork is betweenness, we should be careful not to equate it with some transcendental experience. It is certainly also *work*. It is a systematic attempt to aquire detailed factual knowledge about a different world, and of pursuing the bits and pieces of information almost to the point of exhaustion. The point is that 'systematics' cannot be learnt exclusively from classical anthropological handbooks like *Notes and Queries* or other (more recent) 'guides to ethnographic conduct' (e.g. Ellen 1984). The systematics of fieldwork are defined and redefined in the course of the ethnographer's shifting involvement in the local social dramas, for which one can only partly prepare oneself.

In my own case, the systematics of fieldwork implied work in a very well-defined sense as well. Given the nature of my sites, and the practical context of my particular fieldwork, I had to take on special kinds of local work to get access to the places I studied. At Árnastofnun I worked as a historian while also making ethnographic observations on the definition of tradition and the self-definitions of its caretakers. At the farm I was given the role of milkmaid, helping in the milking of some thirty cows, taking them out to pasture in the morning, and collecting them in the evening. I also gave a hand with the children and with general domestic chores. While I was initially embarrassed by my own limited competence in tending cows and rounding up sheep, I soon learned the basic skills and enjoyed embodying farm life. It also greatly facilitated my transition from stranger to friend. In the fishing village I started working in one of the fish factories after having realized that there was no other way of access to the community. Assuming a well-defined role in the community, which also fitted with my place of living, was the only way to penetrate local darkness. In all of my three fieldsites, fieldwork thus implied participation in local, well-defined work as well.

At the farm and in the fishing village, my role assignments were clearly those of a woman. At the farm I was half-laughingly referred to as *fjósakona* (cowshed woman). Both 'my' family and the wider social environment knew perfectly well that I was an anthropologist, and acknowledged my aim of studying Icelandic culture and language. My position as milkmaid somehow gave me a more clearly defined position to speak and to observe from, and it also gave my friends a proper person to relate to. I was neither simply a stranger, nor a guest staying too long, but someone with a well-defined role in the life of the farm. At least my hosts were generous enough to let me believe that.

In the fishing village my gender role was even more marked. To escape the total silence and break my way into the community, the only means was to take women's work at the factory. During the first weeks, I would work up to fourteen hours a day, cutting and packing endless amounts of icy cod, haddock, and halibut. While getting close to the reality of most women at this place, I felt somewhat removed from my image of the hero-anthropologist exploring the subarctic. The cold itself did not quite qualify for heroism. The woman labourers were at the bottom of the local status hierarchy, and my work score at the bottom of the bottom, but at least I had a position to operate from. It was as a fishwoman that I first became visible in the darkness. After a few weeks I could leave this role behind, having acquired an identity with which I could move around in pursuit of my general aims. I had become known and named, not only noted and classified.

The old notion in anthropology of female ethnographers becoming honorary males in the culture under study has been unmasked as a particular Western idea of maleness being somehow superior to femaleness (Okely 1975: 176). While it may be true that in some places the female ethnographers may lack some of the critical specification markers of women (S. Ardener 1984: 126), it is absurd to assume that the sex of the fieldworker passes unnoticed. Certainly, in my own case my gender was read locally in a completely unambiguous way, and any idea of being an honorary male had no correspondance to reality. Many of the 'revelatory events'

(Fernandez 1986: p. xi) in the field were actually related to my being so distinctly female by local ascription.

If the ethnographer were a distinctly gendered sign in the field, her sites were no less marked. The locations or places of fieldwork were not semantically or emotionally neutral. My association with Árnastofnun, for instance, spurred some almost standardized reactions wherever I went. After all, it was the national treasury chamber. Given the nature and the history of Iceland, there are no old castles, no medieval cathedrals, or no crown jewels that of themselves are tokens of the past. There are virtually only textual relics from before the nineteenth century, apart from place names of extraordinary semantic density. In consequence the Manuscript Institute was very highly regarded.

The farm where I lived, too, was a place of some renown. It was the birthplace of Þórbergur Þórðarson, one of Iceland's most cherished twentieth-century authors, whom we have met already; the present senior man of the three-generations household was the author's brother's son. The senior's father had himself been a renowned storyteller, whose oral narratives had been collected by folklorists. My association with this farm thus both meant taking part in its life, and sharing for a while its distinction. Conversely, my dwelling in the more negatively marked *verbúð* in the fishing village associated me with the perceived back stage of Icelandic society.

The point I want to make is that the 'ethnographer's magic' in the format of common-sense rules and scientific principles (Malinowski 1922: 6) could not be applied from a neutral position, let alone at a safe distance. In general, no ethnography is uncontaminated evidence, as Edmund Leach has formulated it. Culture as such is simply not available for inspection; the observer is always a key part of the changing scene that is observed (Leach 1989: 39). This provides the theoretical impetus for some degree of autobiographical reflection in ethnographical writing.

Language

The problem of writing is complicated by the fact that fieldwork and anthropology as a whole is a heteroglot encounter. To some extent the experience of fieldwork is beyond language, but still highly dependent upon it. There are many languages involved before the ethnographic dialogue, whether actually spoken or silent, is 'written up'. Even when one does fieldwork in one's own society, one has to learn another language in one's mother tongue (Okely 1984, 1996). The meaning of words cannot be taken for granted; the context of fieldwork makes it shift.

Fieldwork in other societies than your own makes the problem of heteroglossia even more obvious. Again, with James Clifford we may refer to Malinowski as a model case, and a case, furthermore, from which it is obvious that the heteroglot situation is much more than linguistic (Clifford 1988: 102). Malinowski's mother tongue was Polish, his fieldwork was conducted in Kiriwinian, and he addressed his anthropological audience in English. For him, the linguistic complexities mirrored autobiographical and emotional ones; Polish was the language of the past and of intimacy; Kiriwinian was a temporary language of ethnographic dialogue and desire; meanwhile, English had become the language of career, marriage, and restraint.

Although, as James Clifford is aware, this picture is probably too neat, it may still serve as a parable of the linguistic reality of many ethnographies, including my own. Danish is my language of intimacy; it is largely the language of my diaries and of all my letters from the field, and it was the language I spoke with my children—being transported to an unknown linguistic world with a single parent. In my notebooks the occasional passage in English would slip in; this is my main language of anthropological interpretation, and of my audience. It is, therefore, also a language of restraint and of a certain muteness, when it comes to finer nuances of description. Between the two, a third one intervenes, directly associated with the ethnographic experience itself. Icelandic was the language of my ethnographic dialogues, and to some extent of my desire as well—the general desire to become at one with the others.

At first, I had not quite realized the complexity of the linguistic situation. I tended to perceive of it as a personal problem of learning actually to speak a new language. I found myself an incredibly slow learner in spite of the fact that I read both old and modern Icelandic. This was largely self-taught book-learning, however, and there seemed to be a huge gap between the reading and speaking faculties. It took many months of listening before I felt sure of my understanding; it was not until I became directly involved in the tending of cows, and the cutting up of fish that practical mastery was achieved. As recently argued by Tamara Kohn (1994), what the ethnographer learns before a reasonable linguistic competence is achieved is in no way 'wasted', but leaves a lasting imprint upon the perception of the goings-on in the field.

I have since then realized that my difficulties of learning to speak Icelandic were very much a function of the particular ethnography of this isolated North Atlantic community. The language is archaic by comparison with the Scandinavian languages, with which Icelandic shares the roots in Old Norse (Haugen 1976). For the Icelanders, so much goes without saying; the words have many hidden referents to a tradition that is shared and accessible to all Icelanders. This is why I could not 'know' Icelandic before I knew how it was actually lived, and not only spoken. Even if to most anthropologists embarking on fieldwork the learning of the language spoken in the field is most often presented as a purely instrumental, preparatory device—like having the necessary inoculations—this is not so. While language learning in this sense is of course a good way to begin, it never gives one more than encyclopedic knowledge. That is, precisely, book knowledge. And life does not go by the book any more than cultural knowledge belongs to the domain of words. The difficulty of learning a foreign language, even one that belongs to the same family of languages as one's own, thus is not so much a matter of the language itself being difficult, as it is matter of a series of interrelated socio-linguistic complexities that are intractable at the level of words. The *experience* of the foreign language, including its silent parts, is a vital part of ethnographic fieldwork, and—incidentally— this is one of the marks that distinguishes anthropology from history or other disciplines working on texts out of context. In anthropology we have to shift the focus from reference meaning to speaker's meaning, that is from a semantic to a pragmatic view of language.

In my experience, Icelandic is a language of silences; a few words, a raised eyebrow, and five minutes' silence, followed by another person's sighing that 'that is how it is', seem to equal ten minutes of uninterrupted dramatic speech-performance elsewhere (the relative silence is necessarily a matter of comparative experience, not absolute truth). Silences, of course, are not semantically empty. They mean something in the context. My desire was to be allowed into the silence and share the sensation of density; this was beyond the learning of lexicon and grammar. My initial feeling of linguistic incapacity was only partly a problem of language; it was primarily a problem of my lack of knowledge about the experiential space within which the hidden referents of silence would reveal themselves.

This point was brought clearly home to me on the occasion of one of my returns to the farm, where I had for the first time brought a friend with me. My friend was not exactly heir to the throne of patience, and he wanted to know what we were talking about all the time, and wanted to pose questions of his own. I translated and told, only to find that my answers never satisfied him; in the process of translation the rich and significant conversation was reduced to few and relatively simple words. To my attuned ear, the smallest hint about the grandfather, the sheep, the neighbours, or the upcoming feasts carried extensive meaning which could not be captured by the 'literalization' of the conversation through translation. My friend felt excluded and even hurt when I occasionally would refuse to translate; sometimes I felt that my breaking up my conversation would take me too far away from what was going on, and for professional reasons I wanted to pursue certain matters. Conversely, I sometimes found my friend's probing questions too insensitive to the context, and would also refuse to pass them on. My friend was excluded, of course, but the problem could not have been solved with words. Our shared Danish could not capture the Icelandic reality of which I had once been part. At a more general level, this experience—and hosts of others—made it abundantly clear to me that language is not only a systematic potential, but also a practical feasibility, and thus it involves timing and other features of historicity.

The three languages involved in my fieldwork correspond to three 'selves': the (Danish) private self, of past and future family life; the (English) academic self, of anthropological reflection; and the (Icelandic) ethnographic self, of experience and of being objectified by the others. There were, and remain, discrepancies between these selves, but it is important to stress that in the ethnographic experience, the person, the time, and the unresolved linguistic contradictions are fused. It is

precisely this fusion of disparate selves, languages, and ultimately worlds which
provides anthropology with its most creative instance because it brings into contact
worlds and views that were previously apart. The 'third-person' experience in the
field (Hastrup 1987*a*) teaches the ethnographer that a shared vocabulary is not the
sole prerequisite of understanding, neither within or between cultures.

One reason why it is important to spell out the linguistic situation is that
languages have a built-in tendency to make the speaker notice some things about
the world, and let others pass unnoticed (Geertz 1995: 46–7). The spoken language
introduces its own evaluations upon the world; it fuses or falls silent about certain
issues. What is spoken is not everything worth noticing, and to conceive of
fieldwork as primarily a linguistic event (e.g. Clifford 1988: 41) is to reduce
the complexity of the contact to a technical matter of mastering the dialogical
conventions.

In many ways, the linguistic condition of one's fieldwork is paradigmatic of the
subsequent construction of the world in narrative. It highlights the nature of the
contact zone, within which the work takes place, and it contributes vastly to an
understanding of the meanings that emerge beyond the words. As in music, the
sounds of language are events, breaking the original silence to which one must
return. Melodies and sentences are arabesques upon a silence within which the
possibilities for other sound events are stored. The conversations in the field are
realizations of some of these possible events, and while we cannot realize them all,
the keys and the themes that manifest themselves in the process of becoming allow
us to generalize—if not about culture, then about a particular mode of attending to
the world. After which one cannot but return to the silence which is never empty,
just suspended form, the silence of the contexture of the local world surrounding
and constituting it.

First Impressions

As has been demonstrated in a number of cases, the 'first' impressions in the field
that often predate a proper linguistic competence remain valid clues to the cultural
goings-on—themselves largely beyond language (e.g. Kohn 1994; Rudie 1994). In
the words of Geertz 'such first impressions, because they are first, and perhaps as
well because they are impressions rather than worked-up theories or pinned-down
facts, set a frame of perception and understanding . . . that could not afterwards be
wholly discarded, only critiqued, developed, filled out, moralized upon, and
brought to bear on more exact experiences' (Geertz 1995: 13).

The present work is informed by my own first impressions in a rather complex
way. My first knowledge of Iceland was a knowledge about history; my earliest
research on Iceland concentrated on the Middle Ages, and later the subsequent
centuries up to and including the nationalist movement in the nineteenth century.
Thus, when I eventually made my way to the field, I saw the Icelanders through the

categories that they themselves had laid out for me during previous centuries. Next, approaching the farming and the fishing communities, I saw these with the eyes of the tradition-keepers in Reykjavík where I had spent my first precious field time. This is no apology, but a statement to the effect that whatever else the field-sites are, they are always zones or points of contact, in which the implicitly comparative statements about people living different parts within the local scenario blend with the contrasting experiences of the moving ethnographer. It is this contrasting quality of the contact zone that brings unexpected matters into view.

At this point in time, my fieldwork is as much memory as it is experience, and no doubt I have fallen prey to a risk of embellishing the relics (cf. Boon 1986: 244). Nevertheless, the circumstances of the actual field experience are still important; they provide fuel for the 'headnotes' that by now seem as important as the actual fieldnotes (Ottenberg 1990). The ethnographic writing is informed by both autobiography and refracted memories of the field.

Yet there remains a chasm between 'the brute material of information . . . and the final authoritative presentation of the results' (Malinowski 1922: 3–4). As echoed by James Boon: 'It is a venerable custom among anthropologists to present the *humble* facts of ethnography in *sublime* style' (Boon 1986: 225). While it is easy to laugh at recognition of this particular kind of embellishing the remains of fieldwork in others' writing, it is less evident in one's own. Seen from within the horizon of one's own ethnographic experience, there are no truly humble facts, nor neccesarily a sublime style of writing of course. There are sensational recollections from within the walls of another time space. One comes back transformed, as if by a Moebius loop.

If fieldwork takes place in the contact zone, the ethnographer herself is like a double agent. She has to act convincingly in two spaces, and to perform competently—as if by nature. Her powers of double agency derive from her training; the rewards are not in shining silver but in ambiguous identity: who is she to herself? So, the duality pervades the entire practice of anthropology, and it hits hard on some occasions. Maybe it is a general problem of ethnographers, being both inside and outside, but it is also a specifically Icelandic phenomenon, because Iceland at one and the same time is so like and so different from home. In India I only noticed the difference.

The experience of double agency provides part of the context of my writing about the Icelandic world where familiar meanings are always twisted and brought to bear on one's own lack of competence. Studying Iceland is not just studying any old space on the earth. It is studying a very particular space, created through a practice that lends its own materiality to the world. The invisible and the silent are always uninvited guests in Iceland; so much is hidden from view to the uninitiated, and the world seems manageable. Once inside, however, the space extends vastly beyond the words; the silence is incarnate history. I had to live this silence to sense its density, and to get a feel of the contexture of the Icelandic world which embraces so many fieldsites and makes them one.

3

The Contact Zone

Social life unfolds in a community of potential conversational partners. The audience is implied in any reasoning, any social action, however unrecognized. This also applies to the social action of scholarship. When studying a world anthropologically we are doubly caught in the contact zone, the space wherein we meet and where our histories become mutually implicated. The life world of people is established in *practice*, and for the anthropologist to get near to it, she has to enter the contact zone. In some sense localized, but certainly not a place or a simple locality that can be organized visually; most of its defining parameters are invisible and exist only in action.

One evening during my stay in the fishing village I was invited to coffee by a young workmate of mine. She and her baby daughter lived with her parents and her two brothers. The family apparently had not been blessed by life and they lived under rather poor conditions. They were very welcoming, and revealed that they felt rather bad about my living in the *verbúð*, and had wanted to show me a proper home. I was not only offered coffee that evening but also a look at their photos. The pictures of family ceremonies were among their dearest treasures and—like other people I visited—they wanted to share their pride with me. I looked at these icons of memory and tried to figure out the true meaning of the pictures here on the back of welfare society. It seemed obvious that they functioned as archives of personal histories, but a couple of pictures questioned the nature of the 'archive'.

The pictures in question were from the baptisms of the two boys in the house, then 11 and 14 years of age. First I saw the picture of the youngest boy in a fine christening robe. I thought he looked rather big for a christening, which in the Nordic countries usually takes place when the child is about three months old. When I asked about his age, I was told that he was about 1 year at the time when the photo was taken. Possibly there had been economic reasons for his delayed christening, I thought, and did not probe further into the matter. When the next christening picture appeared, the question arose most forcefully again, however. The photo showed an enormous 4-year-old child, who had been squeezed into a christening robe and posed in an armchair from where he looked sullenly at the camera. I asked if it was not unusual that children were baptized so late. The mother replied that they had not been late; truly, the youngest boy had been just over six months old, but the oldest had been christened at the usual age of three months. Further questioning revealed that when the boys had actually been christened the family had no camera; but when they were 1 and 4 years old, respectively, the parents had the opportunity to borrow one. Then they had dressed the huge babies in their old christening robe and taken photographs of them 'so that we had their christening pictures', the mother explained.

Christening pictures they were, but on which scale were they authentic, and in which sense were they archives to the family's past. They certainly were representation of 'pastness' but they were not history (cf. Tonkin 1990: 27). This incident taught me, first, that we have to question the relationship between visibility and veracity. Next, I learnt by direct experience that history is not fixed, it consists in a series of representations that may or may not coincide with one's own conventions of representation. When working close to one's own world, it may be more difficult than for 'exotic' anthropology to spot the differences in such conventions and take local notions of history, legend, or myth at face value—the face being what they immediately look like to us.

The forms of representations on the other hand are not absolutely 'local' once they are invoked by an other, be she anthropologist or simply a guest to the scene. They are deeply implicated by the contact. In the case just related, the whole situation bears the mark of the visitor; the mother's pride in her sons and their christening pictures was directed at an audience. In contrast to other kinds of archives, photos have to be made public to be effective. They have to be talked about; they do not tell their own story. Like Judith Okely in her study of elderly people in rural France (Okely 1994), I could use family pictures as an entry into a conversational space, which bore its own marks of history and interpretation. This is the point: ethnography never speaks for itself. However much dialogue and information and conversation take place in the field, once it is constructed as 'field', speech is premissed by the contact zone.

As Geertz has recently argued, anthropology these days exists in an altered medium: 'To convey this, what it is to be an anthropologist not off somewhere beyond the reach of headlines but on some fault line between the large and the little, photographs are quite inadequate. There is nothing to picture. So too are prefaces and appendices. They marginalize what is central. What is needed, or anyway must serve, is tableaus, anecdotes, parables, tales: mini-narratives with the narrator in them' (Geertz 1995: 65). Photographs and prefaces are not archives to anything but what someone wants to say about them. Realism occurs between the lines.

Intertextuality

In this little preamble I am not simply talking about intersubjectivity or anthropological reflexivity; I also want to point to the feature of intertextuality which is an ever-present feature of ethnographic and historical writing. Whether the Icelanders that I came to know had actually read the sagas or the modern literature, they were part of a literate society which entertained images of past and present that derived from this literature (which again draw on real experiences, of course). Very little springs from a vacuum. Medieval sagas, humanist treatises, Enlightenment reports, and modern literature blend and inform contemporary images of Icelandicness. Sometimes they are referred to explicitly, but most often they are implicit frames of understanding. As such they often form unacknowledged bases for the feeling of a collectivity. The integrity of the Icelanders is not a feature of literal insularity, it is a feature of sharing certain images. As Nigel Rapport has observed, texts may be sites for the proliferation of meaning within the individual consciousness; what is striking is how individuals make use of relatively stable collective forms for making and expressing diverse and often quite idiosyncratic meanings (Rapport 1994: 24). Thus, far from reducing individual Icelanders' perceptions to a common denominator, my emphasis on shared images points to a dual phenomenology of sharing on the one hand, and individual attribution of meaning on the other.

Among the images I encountered was the image of a past dominated by Danish merchants. This past was not precisely defined in historical terms, but many of my interlocutors would mention the author Halldór Laxness as someone who had written about it. At some point when I probed further into this matter, my friends admitted that they found Laxness 'heavy' reading, and that his style 'was too special for ordinary Icelanders to read'. People would buy his books but they were meant for the bookshelf, not for reading, a male farmer argued, while his wife maintained that people at least 'knew' *Sjálfstætt fólk* (1934–5; English translation, *Independent People*, 1946) and *Íslandsklukkan* (*Iceland's Bell*, 1943). The former features the poor farmers as true heroes, while the latter deals with the time around 1700 when Iceland was deeply implicated in Danish legislation. Clearly these (and other) works refurbish local notions of right and wrong, and give a common verbal shape to individual experiences. I myself read a lot of Laxness while in Iceland, and whatever the truth value of his observations, his texts filtered into mine in intractable ways.

The feature of intertextuality was prominent at the farmstead where I worked. As mentioned before, it was the native home of one of the greatest authors of Iceland in this century, Þórbergur Þórðarson, and my friends would constantly quote him or direct my attention to his work when they were short of an answer to my questions, or just deferred to the expert on life in *sveit*. The textual presence was prominent in all our conversations about local history. This history could not be separated from the local *awareness* of history as verbally framed by shared images. Intertextuality also worked the other way round, of course. People translated me into their own categories of researchers and answered me accordingly. My questions about history would be answered within a particular frame of reference, incorporating their image of me both as a member of the one-time oppressive nation, and as a person interested in the documented, the written, the truth.

I was particularly interested in the use of history in the construction of modern Icelandic identity, and from my extensive historical research I was familiar with 'the old days' to which people referred whenever we talked about history. I was also familiar with the supernatual inhabitants of earlier landscapes, such as trolls (*tröll*), hidden people (*huldufólk*), and ghosts (*draugar*). Inevitably, we talked about them and about the folktales (*þjóðsögur*) that we all knew, and which had been widely told and read in Iceland until these days. Allegedly, the present children of the farm where I worked represented the first generation not to have been brought up with extensive reading and singing as an evening pastime, and their parents would often regret that television had now replaced it. With the two adult generations I was really treading common ground and sharing an interest in these stories, however, and I marvelled at the vitality of tradition.

Only gradually would I come to realize that tradition was still with us in a much more direct sense as well. Although talked about as a discourse on the past, the characters that inhabited this discursive space were still present in the Icelandic landscape. I had been caught in the trap of taking statements that were made in the past tense for statements about past conditions, of which I knew 'too much'. The three kinds of beings mentioned above were not equal with respect to their position in time, however. Upon probing (carefully, of course), I learnt that trolls had effectively become extinct. Their one-time reality was not explicitly questioned; some petrified ones were rather laughingly pointed out in the landscape. My question of when they had disappeared was answered with 'about two hundred years ago'. I suppose this was a rather arbitrary choice of time indication, prompted by the wish to be precise in a sense that was believed to be acceptable to the 'writer' of Icelandic history. Whether or not the trolls had ever really existed was a more or less irrelevant question; they were dead and gone anyway.

Curiously, when later I became acquainted with the collection of stories and prehistoric remnants made by Icelandic vicars in the early nineteenth century on the demand of the Danish king, the entry for the parish of Ingjaldshóll on Snæfelsnes (from 1817), which was another of my fieldsites, has it: 'About trolls here by the Glacier, there are . . . some, who have not been dead for long, and some who are still alive. Elves are all over in slopes and holes, and they have the same behaviour as men' (Rafnsson 1983: 333). This actually suggests that trolls were actually dying out some two hundred years ago, while elves were still all over the place.

As regards elves or the 'hidden people', it was also an entirely different matter at the farm. The *huldufólk* represented a category of metaphorical humans, closely associated with particular features of the landscape. Around the farmstead there were two or three places where *huldufólk* had been known to dwell, and these were rocky hills or ravines breaking through the even surface of the infields. Þórbergur Þórðarson writes about these places and about the doings of the hidden people when he was young (e.g. 1981: 173). Today the people with whom I talked about it stated that they did not know whether the *huldufólk* were still living there, because they had not been seen for a long time. My question of 'how long' was met with hesitant reflections and some internal debate. Clearly, we were moving within personal memories, and discussion centred upon the situating of particular events to which the last appearance of the *huldufólk* was tied. Eventually, an internal chronology was agreed upon, and the first answer produced: 'about twenty years'. Further collective memorizing brought forth a more recent event. About ten years ago a whole group of hidden people had been seen at the corner of the farmhouse; I was given details about the particular encounter and the event to which it was connected, namely the arrival of a person whom they had not seen for a long time, and which was clearly remembered. What I, much later and long since back behind my desk, came to think of as a major correlate if not the cause of the disappearance of the *huldufólk* was the introduction of electricity. It had been a significant event at the farm, and one which had also taken place about ten years previously. It felt reasonable to suggest that the light cast by the enormous outdoor lamps would chase off a people who wanted to retain their most distinctive feature: their being 'hidden'. As suggested to me by David Koester (pers. comm. 1996), another thing about electric lights is that they make the outside so much blacker when you go out; part of what made the Icelandic landscape so full of half-shadows probably were the long periods of semi-darkness that have been transformed into blackness by bright electric lights.

If not actually seen, the *huldufólk* were still somehow in evidence, in that they would more or less jokingly be accused of borrowing or hiding tools that were temporarily missing. The elderly wise woman of the farm told me that whatever was missing it would be no good searching for it. It would be a waste of time, since inevitably the items would reappear, once the hidden people had finished with it. There is no question of 'belief' involved in this. There is a shared image, to which present-day experience can connect. The image of the hidden people is real, and it serves as a point of convergence of individual interpretations of past and present. That this is not simply a feature of a remote farmstead can be inferred from the fact that recently a map of Reykjavík was produced that showed the dwelling places of the hidden people (and other related beings), and which should be respected by the city planners.

The third category, *draugar* (or ghosts), were also still in evidence, if talked about in the past tense as well. *Draugar* were revenants, most often associated with drowned fishermen, but also—at the farm—simply experienced as unpleasant, if actually harmless, encounters in the night. Characteristically, these beings were more often referred to in the fishing village. They were portrayed as wandering all over the place in the dark. In the village I myself would often wander about in darkness; after all, in winter it is dark most of the time. In connection with evening visits to the houses of my workmates from the factory and to other friends, I was recurrently asked whether I had no fear of *draugar*. The women I knew would only unwillingly walk alone in the dark and some appeared genuinely petrified on my behalf. With my knowledge of *draugar*, and with my recent farm experience, I felt relatively safe, however.

Once again I had to realize that my knowledge was like a veil over reality. The fear of the local women was partly due to the fact that in the village context, the category of *draugar* was inhabited by real, living people—if the word was still used metaphorically. One night I stumbled upon at least one of them, a middle-aged, somewhat deviant man, whom I took no particular delight in meeting. He, and others, could roam about in the dark under cover of an age-old category of non-humans. Because of my book knowledge I had failed to understand that the category could materialize right in front of me, and I had been unable to perceive the warnings I had been given by the persistent reference to *draugar* as a real threat, not a belief. Incidentally, this also contributed to my own ambiguous classification in the eyes of local men; researcher, perhaps, but also a woman who could be approached under the cover of darkness.

There is more than one lesson to be learnt from this, I believe. First of all, it seems that the sheer amount of my (textual) knowledge of Icelandic history and folklore made me hear statements made in the past tense as statements about the past. This could be a general feature of doing fieldwork in societies with a long historical record. Secondly, because the people I dealt with were brought up and educated in a cultural context that was in many ways similar to mine, I could readily be identified as an academic with particular knowledge interests. In order to converse with this person, they organized their stories in the past tense whenever they were talking about matters of folklore—known to be only popular images for the urbanized élites. Third, having eventually realized that some of the beings talked about were still present, I still failed to discover the real content of some of these categories. I read the ghost as a sign of the past, without realizing that the signified had changed. Because I did not take it for real, I ran the risk of colluding with a living signifier.

The problem of shifting from the coevalness in the field to the allochronism in writing, as identified by Fabian (1983), is vastly complicated by features of intertextuality once we work in literate societies with a long written tradition. When 'the ethnographic present' is formulated in the past tense by the people themselves, they are the ones who deny coevalness. They answer the ethnographer's questions, posed in her own autobiographic present, in an ethnographic past. They know who *you* are, and are left with no choice of grammatical tense. The verbalizing process itself *generates reality as folktale*, to be heard and interpreted as 'tradition', even 'genre'—when it is actually life itself. The real nature of the shared images to which individuals connect their singular experiences is blurred by their endless intertextual reference. The temporal distancing that occurs in language is a consequence of the encounter; the nature of the discursive space in which the interlocutors meet is premissed by the contact itself.

This applies to my encounters with the Icelanders, but it also applies to the relationship between Icelanders. Ultimately, any sentence that breaks the silence between people is predicated by the self and the other; there is an 'I' speaking, but the way of speech is determined as much by 'you' who listen to this. The 'we' is created on the assumption that we share some words and images to which we may attach our individual understanding.

Icelandic Studies

From this brief discussion of intertextuality, I shall now equally briefly deal with its particular expression in the field of Icelandic studies, where the meeting of different textual versions of the Icelandic reality seems to have led to rather remarkable viewpoints.

One of the reasons for my choice of the musical allegory as an organizing principle of this work is my wish to stress the aspect of non-linearity and non-representation in the study of societies, eternally moving out of the frame within which we have understood them. There are no structures to which we can defer our explanations, no givens to which we can appeal for meaning. There are endless possibilities for elaboration and improvisation. The practice of anthropology by itself contributes to the moving frame.

But there is another reason which has less to do with the object than with the writing about it. We take it for granted that music appeals to emotion as well as intellect, and that it affects its listeners in diverse ways by encapsulating them in sound. By contrast, we have tended to believe that books and other textual material appeal only to the intellect and that their reception is a matter of pure understanding and of the verdict of reason; the gaze is carefully directed towards the words, which appear on print. There is no understanding which is also not an evaluation, and an emotional reaction, however. The distance is fictional; there is always a degree of imagination in our appreciation of a particular work, but we have rarely made a point of the emotional component in any reading.

We have to distinguish, of course, between discourses on emotion and emotional discourses (Lutz and Abu-Lughod 1992). The former distances itself from the emotions it portrays; it objectifies them, so to speak, such as may be embedded in literary expressions, be they books written by established authors and read in print or be they the individual's expression of passion, whether sorrow or love. It is common for Icelanders writing obituaries of kinsmen or friends to compose a poem in their honour, which is emotionally loaded in easily recognizable terms; also it is not at all uncommon for women to receive lyrical notes from men who fancy them, notes that in my experience contain much more passion than will ever pass in ordinary speech—or in action for that matter. Thus, in the field of social relations there is an ever-accompanying discourse on emotion, residing in its own discursive space.

Apart from the passionate poetic discourse on emotion, it seems that any discourse on Iceland is inherently emotional. The values and feelings of the Icelanders are intrinsic to any narrative about matters Icelandic; I suppose this holds good for other societies as well, but my case here is the Icelandic one. The field of Icelandic studies is a prime example, as known from the debate on the origin of the sagas, either in an oral tradition or as literary compositions. It certainly was more than a technical debate on the nature of the sagas; it was also a highly emotional debate on Icelandic culture and its uniqueness and singular achievements in the

Middle Ages. Let me refer to just one example from a recent history of Iceland's medieval literature, published by the then director of the Manuscript Institute, who in his preface to the English translation says:

[T]here is little change from the Icelandic version. As a consequence the book occasionally presupposes an Icelander's knowledge of the subject or gives a different emphasis than would have been the case if it had been originally intended for foreign readers. But if there is a slight disadvantage in the fact that the book was written *for Icelanders*, there ought to be a decided advantage in the fact that it was written *by an Icelander*, for none but Icelanders can fully participate in this unique national literature. Only we speak this ancient language and only we have the setting of the sagas in our daily view. Thus it ought to be of benefit for foreigners to be led through this landscape by an Icelandic guide. (Jónas Kristjánsson 1988: 7)

This is actually a very peculiar declaration from a scholar addressing the international community; 'participation' in national literature in the sense suggested by Jónas Kristjánsson may not be what literary scholarship is all about. Yet it is an implicit element in much of the discussion within the field of Icelandic studies.

Anthropology, and other disciplines dealing with people, involves a theorizing which is a kind of practice, in the sense that it affects its object in a way which makes it different from any natural science. In society, there is always a pre-theoretical understanding of what is going on, and those practices which make up the society require certain self-descriptions on the part of the participants; the object is also always a subject with its own view of the world. Self-understanding is constitutive of our world. This is a theoretical statement, of course. And this is where the nature of theorizing becomes apparent. Theories, including anthropological theories of the world 'do not just make our constitutive self-understandings explicit, but extend, or criticize or even challenge them' (Taylor 1985a: 94). This is where a declared 'nationalist' literary criticism seems out of tune with the scholarly practice.

As far as I am concerned, there simply is no single truth where the interpretation of human life is concerned, and any idea of a privileged path to understanding therefore is based on false assumptions of objectivism. This applies to all scholars as historical and positioned subjects. To assume, therefore, that only Icelanders can fully participate in the world of the sagas is to assume both objectivism and essentialism. In my own view, what is most fascinating about the sagas—and by extension of the Icelandic world as a whole—is that they make sense to all and sundry, across time and space.

Maybe new and interesting interpretations will even emerge between the different perspectives suggested by different scholars. In many cases, the distinct viewpoints are more a matter of different vocabularies than of incompatibility. All anthropology is the product of the contact zone, that is the space in which the anthropologist meets her people. It is a product, however, which distances itself somewhat from the meeting itself, because of the essentially theoretical nature of the anthropological endeavour. Whatever shape we give to the product, it is part of a knowledge project in which one can approach the world in the attempt to reach a more general understanding—more general, that is, than the individual talk about the world that we may hear in the field, whether close or far away. In this way, all anthropologists go 'beyond' whatever it is that they are studying, while also encompassing it.

In the contact zone, several selves meet and must negotiate their perception of reality. As recently discussed by Anthony Cohen (1994), anthropology has become self-conscious. This implies not only the by-now evident importance of reflexivity, but also that we are aware of the selves of those 'others' that we study. This tallies with my proposition that it is for anthropology to assume the position of 'other' *vis-à-vis* the world under study (be it within one's home society or not). 'For the anthropologist to give others back their selfhood is to contribute modestly to the decolonisation of the human subject' (Cohen 1994: 192). However, the meaning of 'selfhood' has to be established empirically, and in no way posits a barrier to theoretical generalization about the context within which selfhood is premissed. The purpose of anthropology, as I see it, is not to speculate about individual selves as closed circuits or minds but to study their motivation by culture and their contribution to society.

At one level of analysis, people inhabit disparate, even mutually inaccessible subjective universes (Linger 1994: 289), and we can never reach 'the native point of view', as launched by Malinowski (1922) in this subjective sense. Nor can we study people as if they were 'objects'—or somehow make up a unified cultural agent. What we can do is to enter into the communicative space, where meaning is established in the course of interaction. Meaning is not something which social facts 'have'; it is something which is attributed to them by people in their negotiations of reality. Whether the interlocutors are born in the same country or in different ones, meaning is emergent, not given or prefabricated. Understanding is a social event. It is not simply a clarification of intrinsic properties. Therefore, while the Icelandic literary critic may have the landscape of the sagas within view, this does not give him the key to the final meaning of literature and life in Iceland. There is no such absolute meaning in the world of human contact.

The view of a privileged participation based in a national or cultural essentialism actually seems curiously out of tune with the 'saga-world' itself, where stories are passed on for everyone to hear and understand. *Sagt er*, or 'it is said' that this, that, or the other happened at a particular place, normally, but the whole point of telling is precisely to make the story able to travel beyond that place, and to share with people who were not already witnesses to the event. From the saga world itself, we thus get a glimpse of a radically different notion of participation, and one which tallies with the notion implied by ethnographic fieldwork, which is a participation in a particular communicative space. In this sense, participation is a practice in which everyone can engage, and scholarship, accordingly, is not simply a matter of reporting on local absolutes but of analysing and refashioning them. There are places where we feel at home, temporarily or permanently, but 'homeliness' cannot be a diacritical feature of scholarship, which must always question its own assumptions. Maybe anthropologists explicitly working in a contact zone, where there is the possibility of refashioning one's own viewpoint as a consequence of meeting another, are more aware of the pitfalls inherent in the implicit essentialism; anthropologist Gísli Pálsson thus has elegantly unmasked much of the discourse within Icelandic studies and Icelandic linguistics as based on nationalist ideology (Pálsson 1989).

By way of ending this brief debate on the pitfalls of essentialism in Icelandic studies (and surely in other 'national studies', by definition), I would like to remind us about the distinction made by Said between the (professional) expert and the (amateur) philosopher (1994: 49ff.). The former provides answers to any question put by authority or economic power; the latter poses further questions and stirs the conscience of people. The true intellectual must act as philosopher in this sense. There are no final answers, but a lot of further questions to be posed—also to the anthropology of Iceland—if we have the courage to enter the contact zone between academics of different backgrounds, genders, nationalities, inclinations, and writing styles. The contact zone is a zone of historical dynamism, unless it is mined to maim and silence different people. It is also the place from where our theoretical language grows.

The Theoretical Language

Anthropology has to theorize the contact zone. Because theories are but sentences, the theoretical language becomes an issue. In many ways the discussion of the theoretical language of anthropology reflects the discussion of language in general. The theories represent the voiced events of understanding, taking place on the backdrop of silence and possible misunderstanding. It is in the nature of anthropological theory, being 'expressive' rather than 'designative' (cf. Hastrup 1995*a*: 181–2), that it expresses what otherwise remains untold. It spans across difference without neutralizing it and in the process the possible is made manifest by way of radical interpretation. Much debate on native anthropology, and to some extent a side effect of the recent interest in self-consciousness, has been misguided by the assumption that radical interpretation by definition is ethnocentric and that the language of our cross-cultural theories has to be either 'theirs' or 'ours'.

If this were so, then any attempt at understanding across cultures would be faced with an impossible dilemma: either accept incorrigibility, or be arrogantly ethnocentric. But as a matter of fact, while challenging their language of self-understanding, we may also be challenging ours. (Taylor 1985*b*: 125)

The theoretical language of anthropology is a language of perspicuous contrast, which is neither theirs nor ours, but a separate language in which we can formulate both their and our ways of life as alternative possibilities—and as such it is contingent to the ethnographer's double agency in the field. To the extent that anthropology can be conceived of as 'giving voice' to different viewpoints, it must be remembered that giving voice is an art, 'the art of discovering the language of the Other' (Daniel 1996*a*: 7)—and making it accessible to somebody else. This kind of 'cultural translation' is not about the levelling of difference or making the other sound like oneself. Anthropological understanding is about 'disequation rather than equation' (E. Ardener 1989*a*: 183).

Taking this to its practical conclusion means that theorizing in anthropology is not about simple understanding of the others, because the language of contrast presupposes that we understand ourselves as well—from the same critical perspective. The theoretical language of anthropology thus brings the manifest reality of the contact zone to discursive effect. Articulating the anthropological insight in a language of contrast means understanding human practices in relation to each other. This is the only passable route between the Objectivist refutation of real differences on the one hand, and the Relativist view of absolute incommensurability on the other. Understanding is an event of juxtaposition. Radical interpretation thus brings about the opposite of ethnocentrism.

The theoretical project of anthropology is reducible neither to behaviourism nor to ventriloquism. We cannot just map behavioural units in linear sequences, nor should we simply give voice to other people by way of our own lips. By involving ourselves in the field our task is to identify connections that are not linear, and which may not be spoken at all. Such connections are real, yet they are also theoretical in that they are constructed in theories that are but sentences, internally linked by logic, proposing particular interpretations of the world. Theories are ways of making the constitutive self-understandings explicit, of articulating motivations, of recontextualizing the world of experience; articulation is different from clarification in that it is also always definition. In that sense, anthropological theory may influence, confirm, or alter the constitutive self-description of particular people. In that sense, theories do not only make the constitutive self-descriptions explicit, they also extend, criticize, and even challenge them.

Because of the nature of the anthropological object—people—the anthropologist is always in some important sense part of the class of phenomena she is studying. More importantly, perhaps, is the fact that *the object itself is a subject*. There is always a pre-theoretical understanding of society, always a set of constitutive self-descriptions which cannot be bypassed by the anthropologist; but because of the constitutive self-descriptions, anthropology stands in a particular relationship to its object. Theorizing the social potentially affects local understanding; whereas theorizing the atom does not by itself alter the object, theorizing people changes the object immediately because it infiltrates self-understanding (especially, of course, if it is presented in a not too alienating way). This is where intertextuality in the field becomes inevitable: the presence of the ethnographer alters self-perceptions, even if one should not overestimate the change affected. By and large, at a general level the other reality persists and changes independent of how it is reconstituted in the anthropological text (Daniel 1996*a*: 3).

Where natural theories can to some extent be exhaustively described as means to clarify or explicate the innate properties of nature, social theory never just articulates what is already part of the object. 'The stronger motive for making and adopting theories is the sense that our implicit understanding is in some way crucially inadequate or even wrong' (Taylor 1985*a*: 94). Theories may alter ways of seeing the world, and must therefore be taken seriously as theory, and not simply 'representation'. This is important in the following argument about the world of the Icelanders.

Again, Charles Taylor may be of help clarifying the issue, in his spelling out of two common misapprehensions in the social sciences:

The first is that what it demands of us is empathy with our subjects. But this is to miss the point. Empathy may certainly be useful in coming to have the understanding we seek; but it is not what understanding consists in. Science is a form of discourse, and what we want is an account which sets out the significance of action and situation. (Taylor 1985*b*: 117)

In fact this amounts to another way of saying that in terms of the *theoretical understanding*, no one has a more immediate access than others.

The second misapprehension is related to this, and consists in the idea 'that understanding the agent involves adopting his point of view; or, to speak in terms of language, describing and accounting for what he does in his own terms, or those of his society and time' (Taylor 1985*b*: 117). Normally, a theoretical proposition would have to be a different and possibly clearer statement of what somebody is doing than what he or she is able to account for him- or herself. Understanding cannot, therefore, be adopting the agent's point of view, because in that case a theory would never be able to form the basis for an altered practice. So, while an interpretive social science cannot bypass the agent's self-understanding (and selfhood), there is no point of view which is incorrigible. 'The incorrigibility thesis'—in requiring that we explain or understand each society and culture in its own terms—'rules out an account which shows them up as wrong, confused or deluded. Each culture on this view is incorrigible' (Taylor 1985*b*: 123).

Accepting this extremely relativist view means that any social or cultural theorizing is disempowered from the outset. My own position is a different one, one which sees anthropological theory as a practice, potentially changing the world and hopefully for the better. Without being unduly romantic and naïve about it, I still think that there is an element of creativity in anthropological theorizing: its ability to speak in a language, in which one can maintain the unique and the shared at the same time—and thereby make room for alternative ways of seeing the world.

Interclusion

In this last statement there is a recognition of the power of anthropology to impart newness in the world. By conversing with pre-existing understandings, social theory is essentially inventive. As Robert Paine has suggested, there are two ways of introducing newness in the world: newness by *discovery* and newness by *invention* (Paine 1995: 52ff.). To discover a new planet may be an accomplishment, but it is predicated on previous conceptualizations of planets; this conceptualization is the original invention. 'Whereas discovery *implies* that the nature of the thing found was previously known, with invention we do find the ontologically new' (Paine 1995: 53). I agree with Paine when he states that this difference is immensely significant with regard to the possiblities for the advancement of knowledge. It certainly has an acute bearing on the anthropological project.

Before, in the era of representationist assumptions in anthropology, the newness one could hope for from anthropology was of the first kind: new tribes, new kinship systems, or modes of production were discovered. Today, and with the acknowledgement of expressive theory, the newness we may expect from anthropology is the newness of invention. If we have the courage to now move beyond the designative ethnographic mode, while still adhering to notions of realism, we may be on the verge of the ontologically new. The invention is not that of the 'Other' but that of the same: the shared human condition of involvement in social process, historical circumstance, and cultural canonicity.

This grand scope can, in fact, be quite modestly described, as does Geertz: 'Understanding a form of life, or anyway some aspects of it to some degree, and convincing others that you have indeed done so, involves more than the assembly of telling particulars or the imposition of general narratives. It involves bringing figure and ground, the passing occasion and the long story, into coincident view' (Geertz 1995: 51). In conveying this coincident view, we may hope for insight into the ontologically new. Theorizing the contact zone means giving expression to the space between people, the world of recognition through disequation.

In this space, people tune in to one another and establish social relationships that allow them to generalize about the workings of their shared world. Theories represent victories over the silence inherent in that space. Like music, theory must be incarnate in ordinary time, but should not be confused with it. 'The musical work, which has a certain duration, is not compelled to occupy a given moment in time. And, transcending that actual time from which it takes its flight, in time music escapes from time; for the nature of music is to be forever contemporaneous with those very moments during which performance makes it actual' (Brelet 1961: 104). The nature of anthropology is to transcend the instance of fieldwork, if always incarnating the duration of the contact, and temporarily conquering the zone of silent implications between people.

By her interclusion in the world of other people, the ethnographer aims not at discovering what they themselves know better, but at articulating the non-verbalized contexture of the world in which their selfhood is anchored, and their actions motivated.

PART II
Orchestration

4

Tradition and Ideology

Tradition connects people to their history and thus informs their sense of self or their identity. Tradition gives shape to the collective remembrance of the past; it is memory rephrased in words and action. In this view, tradition is not only what is handed down, it is also the way it is shaped and by its shape influences the present. In other words traditions are those myths we live by (Samuel and Thompson 1990). By being *lived* by, they are of course part of contemporary reality. If contexture is what surrounds and constitutes the world, as I have argued, tradition provides contexture with a depth of time. This is pre-eminently true in Iceland, where historical self-consciousness is constantly reaffirmed by reference to shared stories from and about the past.

The conflation of story and history in the Icelandic word *saga* (cf. Chapter 2) immediately questions a dominant theme in the discussion of tradition, viz. its relationship to history, often conceived of in terms of an opposition, tradition being invented and history being true. This is far from my own view, as informed by my Icelandic experience. Tradition and history are mutually implicated; with the Icelandic case in mind one could go even further and suggest that they are mutually immanent categories, much like reflexivity and representation (cf. Daniel 1996a: 10). Tradition makes history because it largely consists in a search for the truth about the past, and as time goes by this truth will change. In his chronicle of Suðursveit, Þórbergur Þórðarson (1981: 405) relates how during the evening reading aloud, the family and others around would often make a break in the reading and speak about particular points in the sagas. In the process the story took on a new meaning and the deeds of heroes like Njáll and Skarpheðinn would be measured against common sense. In this way, the Icelandic tradition can be seen as a chain of interpretations that modern historians cannot bypass, even though they have often desperately wanted to, in order to get to the true meaning of the past somewhere outside the transmitted interpretations. Accordingly, historians have rejected narrative sources, such as the Icelandic sagas for instance, on the grounds that they are not reliable. Recently, they have been recirculated by anthropologists and others as patently truthful, irrespective of their being first a text and only second a 'source'. Reliability, of course, is a relational matter, and it very much depends on the scope of the investigation which sources are relevant, if not 'reliable'. There are differences in focus and in bearing which must be taken into account. As far as the Icelandic sagas are concerned, and we shall deal with one shortly, there is the inherent complication that they usually do not present us with reliable chronologies, which means 'that our social history is by default relegated to a kind of ethnographic present' (Andersson and Miller 1989: 5). Anthropologists are used to living with that, not because they are uninterested in 'real' history, but because they are concerned with general themes as well as with singular events. The rejection of narrative and other sources can only lead to a loss of history, and hence to a loss of knowledge. There are different conventions of representation but these do not necessarily reflect different degrees of truth. In the case of the Icelandic sagas, their source value is underscored also by their own reference to 'tradition' as a source of authority; *svá er sagt* and *svá segja menn* ('so it is said', 'so people tell') are characteristic phrases in the sagas, by which the authors defer to general knowledge and living memory for authenticity (Sørensen 1977, 1993). From the point of view of the literature itself, tradition is what marks truth from invention. This is still the case today in the popular rendition of history, which is also prefaced by reference to what is said (*sagt er*), or to *munnmæli*, 'oral tradition', which at one and the same time gives authority to the story and dispenses with demands of verification.

Tradition is both a product and a process as Jan Vansina has said about oral tradition (1985: 3). The product is the message that is passed on, while the process refers to the transmission. Both of these dimensions are important parameters in what follows about Icelandic tradition, of which I can only deal with a small part. I have chosen to focus on 'oral' tradition in a very broad sense, by discussing matters of language, of narrative, and of food. Together these fields point to a particular ideology of Icelandicness. Often, ideology is understood as 'something other than what it appears to be' (Blau 1992: 37), and without falling into the trap of 'false consciousness' I believe that this way of seeing it points to a paradox inherent in ideology: its being what it is not, but which thereby becomes so. Ideology thus becomes an active force in shaping both history and tradition.

Ideology reflects what Robert Paine (1995) would call cultural canonicity, in contrast to mere referentiality. If, generally, anthropology has given up the vision of culture as an entitity governed by systematics, it is still bound to question the thematicities inherent in the life worlds of people. The shift from the inherent logic of culture to the coherence in people's lives extends to action as well as models and categories. Tradition and ideology work together in defining such themes of directive force within the 'contextural' field of the Icelanders, and others.

Studying a world in time means acknowledging both facts of succession and facts of repetition (Burguière 1982: 425). In studying tradition this is an important point; while tradition may point to a certain way of organizing one's collective representations, this is not outside history. In this chapter I shall start by a discussion of the most important means whereby tradition is transmitted, namely the language. If nothing else, this seems pertinent because of the stress on speaking and telling as the most significant means of trajecting history and of collective remembrance. It also appears that the ethnolinguistics of the Icelanders by itself points to an inherent ideological feature in the traditional view of proper Icelandic.

Next, we shall turn to the narrative tradition of the sagas and trace the particular character of Grettir the Outlaw, or Grettir the Strong, in order to substantiate tradition. It appears that Grettir is a figure of thought which we can identify as of continuous import in Iceland (see Hastrup 1986 for a more detailed account). Grettir originally is the main character of *Grettis saga Ásmundarsonar*, one of the younger family sagas of Iceland, dating back to the early fourteenth century, and transmitted in manuscripts from the fifteenth to seventeenth centuries. One of its editors claimed that *Grettis saga* is 'the most popular of all stories' (Jónsson 1936: p. lviii). We shall attempt to elucidate the basis of this popularity, which is manifest also in the tenacity of the image of the outlaw-hero in the Icelandic oral tradition until today. By exposing the basic imagery of this particular saga, I hope to identify a cultural theme of directive force in the Icelandic world through time.

The oral tradition of the Icelanders is not only sustained by ways of talking and telling, it is also made manifest in eating; as a complement to tracing the tradition of Grettir I shall, therefore, investigate a particular food ritual of similar time-depth. The ritual meal, *þorrablót*, which is a popular, festive occasion in February is constructed upon an age-old ritual notion, which has been transposed into modern times (see also Hastrup 1991). With Grettir as well as with the *þorrablót*, we will be able to discern patterns of succession as well as patterns of repetition. Tradition is closely linked with history, as well as with ideology. These linkages will be discussed in the last part of this chapter, where I shall also connect the argument to present-day Icelandic experience and lift it into the theoretical concerns of anthropology. But first we must know the language.

Language: Speaking the Icelandic Way

Icelandic philologists have been heavily preoccupied with the purification of Icelandic. As elsewhere, the legitimacy of particular ways of speaking has been centrally established, thereby masking social difference in linguistic terms (cf. Bourdieu 1991). As demonstrated in detail by Gísli Pálsson, linguists have been busy making a claim for a standard Icelandic, neglecting variation and subverting everyday language (Pálsson 1979, 1989). The idealized version of Icelandic, which is supposedly based on classical literary Icelandic, must be preserved at all costs. Speech that fails to live up to this standard is diseased, as the recurrent reference to the *þágufallssýki* (the dative disease) bears witness. This and other 'diseases' were often mentioned to me during my fieldwork when I—with good reason—made linguistic inquiries. On the radio were daily broadcasts on linguistic matters, stressing the importance of speaking properly and not corrupting the inflections, as for instance the tendency to use the dative form where it had rightly to be the accusative or nominative (whence the dative disease). One recurrent example is the use of *mér* (dat.) *vantar* (I need) instead of the syntactically correct *mig* (acc.) *vantar*, or *mér hlakkar til* (I look forward to) instead of *ég* (nom.) *hlakka til*. Analysis seems to show rather unambiguously that the dative plague is particularly contagious among lower-status groups, even if class differentiation is rarely acknowledged. There is evidence also that in modern Icelandic literature, the (incorrect) use of the dative among the characters almost invariably signals a low social standing (Ásta Svavarsdóttir 1982, quoted by Pálsson 1989: 128–9). The broadcasts that I heard often concerned such syntactic matters, and I recall listening for days to warnings against overlooking the fact that in case of the genitive all words must be equally inflected, and no short cuts made. These broadcasts (called *Daglegt mál*, Everyday Language) were given by untiring university linguists in the interest of the Icelandic language committee, founded in 1965.

On the whole, the message from this committee is that language must be cultivated, literally: 'Language cultivation is similar to the conservation of nature, the protection of plants and the soil. It is an equally noble act of purifying . . . Frankly speaking the Icelanders are somewhat sloppy in their pronunciation' (Baldur Jónsson 1978, quoted by Pálsson 1989: 123). As Pálsson has shown, in spite of their insistence on the homogeneity of Icelandic, the purists spend most of the time complaining about symptoms of emerging heterogeneity, largely labelled as evil. 'Bad' language is inherently stigmatizing. It seems that we have a clear-cut example of what Mary Douglas noted as the 'danger' emerging from matter out of place, threatening the conceptual order (Douglas 1966). In between the clear-cut categories of dative and accusative, disorder threatens pure speech.

One of the first Icelanders to note the specificity of Icelandic was the so-called First Grammarian whose grammatical treatise from the mid-twelfth century proposes a particular alphabet for 'us, the Icelanders' (*First Grammatical Treatise*, p. 21). At the time, the common name for the Nordic language(s) was *dönsk tunga* (Danish tongue), but two and a half centuries after their emigration from Norway and elsewhere in Scandinavia, the Norse settlers apparently had a new sense of speaking their own way. In turn, this linguistic specificity could be used to mark a separate nation (cf. Hastrup 1982). In the twelfth and thirteenth centuries an extensive literature was created in this language, which was to have repercussions in the identity-making of later centuries. But at this stage there was no language problem, no diseases. The first to make some comment to that effect was Arngrímur Jónsson, a humanist writing in Latin about the history of Iceland, *Crymogæa*, in 1609. He suggests that the Icelanders consciously cultivate the ancient pure language, as found in the manuscripts, and do not let foreigners, notably Danes, destroy it (Benediktsson 1985: 104–5), but it was not until some two hundred years later that a deliberate effort was made towards a (re-)construction of a pure and noble Icelandic. In the nineteenth and twentieth centuries the process of purification was closely tied up with Icelandic nationalism, which emphasized the historical stability of Icelandic on the one hand, and glossed over internal linguistic differentiation on the other (Pálsson 1989).

The archaic character has been praised as a virtue which links the Icelanders directly with the past. Let us have an example:

Finally it should be observed that the fate of our language and our literature have always been closely coupled. Now Icelandic is our mother tongue, the marker of our nation, and it is unnecessary to explain its value to our people. But it should be recalled that the special value of the Icelandic language, compared with other modern languages, is to a great extent comprised in the fact that it has not changed more than it has in a thousand years . . . it is not without significance that the language is so transparent that it is a school of memory for the people, while many of the words in modern languages are more like worn coins, which people know the value of, but never think to compare with other words. French writers find it necessary to learn Latin in order to understand their words from the roots so they can make better use of them. We do not need anything like that. And no one can doubt that for this reason (other things being equal) there is more opportunity for a writer's talent in Icelandic than in other languages. (Nordal 1931: p. xxviii; trans. by Haugen 1976: 435)

Archaism in language is here linked with literary achievement, and we hear a distant echo of the 'native literary critic', quoted above (in Chapter 3). A more important feature of the passage is the understanding of language as the marker of the peculiar national identity (*þjóðareinkunn vor*) and as a 'school of thought' (or school of memory, as Haugen has it) for the people (*hún er skóli í hugsun fyrir þjóðina*). The link between people, history, and country is found in the language. This idea is closely linked with the vision of Icelandic integrity as established in the Romantic period. In this vision, present-day *götumál*, street language, carries little weight and is seen more as a kind of temporary and youthful predilection among urbanites who have not yet come to cherish the classical literature.

Nordal was an influential philologist between the wars whose work earned him international fame. His work was based on a strong conviction of the immense value of the literary heritage of the Icelanders, otherwise so ill-fated and overlooked. His studies gradually widened from philology in the strict sense of the term to embracing Icelandic culture in general. His *Íslenzk menning* (*Icelandic Culture*) from 1942 reflects this as well as his conviction that not only had the ancient literature an obvious literary value, which made it worth reporting to the rest of the world, it was also the main reason why the Icelanders had survived at all. As Stefán Einarsson has it:

He soon came to the conclusion that not only the Eddas and the sagas had intrinsic value, but also the way this old literature had become, so to speak, the very bread on which the people as a whole had survived during long centuries of famine and depressions, up to the rebirth in the nineteenth century. (Einarsson 1957: 299)

This 'rebirth' was, to a remarkable degree, linguistic, and it is difficult to overlook the fact that by the early nineteenth century there were strong voices of fear that Icelandic would die out altogether. Thus in 1813 the Danish linguist Rasmus Rask wrote to an Icelandic friend:

Annars . . . held ég ad íslendskan brádum mun útaf deyia, reikna eg ad vallu mun nockur skilia hana í Reikiavík ad 100 árum lidnun, enn valla nockur í landinu ad ödrum 200 þaruppfrá, ef alt fer eins og híngad tíl og ecki verda rammar skordur vidreistar, jafnvel hiá bestu mönnum er annadhvört ord á dönsku, hiá almuganum mun hún haldast vid leingst. (Hjelmslev 1941: 164)

(Otherwise I believe that Icelandic will die out shortly, I reckon that hardly anyone will understand it in Reykjavík in a hundred years' time, and hardly anybody else in the country in another two hundred years from then, if everything goes as until now and if strong support is not raised, since with the best of men every second word is Danish, with the peasants she [Icelandic] may stay the longest.)

There is reason to render the letter in its original Icelandic because it immediately demonstrates how written Icelandic had not yet become standardized, and how it was heavily influenced by Danish, for some 400 years the language of the kingdom to which Iceland formally belonged. Icelandic certainly had changed since the Middle Ages; it was one of the achievements of Romanticism and of the literary establishment of Iceland (largely living in Copenhagen) to reconstruct a 'pure' Icelandic on the basis of the medieval texts (in collaboration with Rasmus Rask)—after which they could proclaim absolute continuity. This continuity is a strong ideological feature even today, at least in the popular image of the language, even if some Icelandic scholars do not subscribe to Nordal's thesis anymore. Among the latter are Jakob Benediktsson who has confirmed that at least the phonological system has undergone radical change in the course of time. However, even he emphasizes the close connection between Icelandic language and culture, and answers critics of 'romantic' conservatism that Icelandic must still be the link between modern people and the past, including its literature (Benediktsson 1964: 109).

By the end of the nineteenth century the notability of Icelandic as a key to history was axiomatic. In 1898 the poet Matthías Jochumsson wrote a poem called *Íslenzk tunga* ('Icelandic Language') for the Icelandic emigrants in America, characteristically named 'western Icelanders'. The idea of writing a poem on language was not peculiar to Matthías Jochumsson—it was almost part of a trend in Scandinavia at the time—yet the content of the statement was distinct (cf. Haugen 1976). Two stanzas from the Icelandic poem run like this:

> What is our language?—Let no one think
> that empty words are the fullness of life,—
> it is *art*, that flashes with power,
> living soul in steel engraved,
> *form* of the spirit in gentle images,
> *memory's saga* of bygone days,
> *floods of life*, in the riverbed
> of a flowing wave that never ends.
>
> Our language bears in the stream of time
> the faith and hopes of our country's sons,

their groans of death and deepest travail,
the web of the Norns from ancient times;
the smell of hate and the breakers of love,
the echo of fates and judgements,
land and time in living images,
hallowed in verse—it bears in its bosom.

(Trans. by Haugen 1976: 434)

While representing a fairly widespread romantic view of the mother tongue, Matthías Jochumsson also foreshadows the present-day concern with the purity of Icelandic. The 'purity' is not only a matter of having few loan words and inventing Icelandic terms for imported objects and ideas, it is also a matter of ideologically glossing over the class difference. As Halldór Halldórsson has it, it is one of the characteristics of Icelandic that it is hardly class-bound; he is worried, though, that a mob language (*skrílmál*) is emerging in Reykjavík, and he urges people who are concerned about this to stand guard around language so that *þeir, sem meira mega sín andlega, láti ekki óvitana móta málfar sitt og þar með hugsun* (Halldórsson 1964: 157) ('those who are spiritually gifted, don't let the unenlightened spoil their language and thereby their thought'). Because bad language gives bad thoughts it is necessary to cure *flámæli* (slack-jawed speech) and *hljóðvilla* (sound mistake), notions that were often heard even in the 1980s when my field research took place.

If not a 'class-language' in any simple way, there are remarkable internal differences. As an acclaimed vehicle of Icelandic memory—and since this memory relates to the landscape in particular (as we shall see in Chapter 5)—it is little to be wondered that true Icelandic has been constructed as 'rooted' in the life of the farming population. Already in Rasmus Rask's comments on the state of Icelandic we note the explicit view of the peasants' language being less corrupt than the language of the towns. This notion is still entertained, as I noted in Chapter 2. In the farm where I worked, and where the author Þórbergur Þórðarson was born, it was generally acknowledged that his language was a remarkably fine Icelandic; the implication was that such was generally the language spoken there, and a lot of effort went into teaching the children the correct grammar. No 'street language' there—no streets at all for that matter.

By contrast, in the fishing village the women with whom I worked readily admitted that they had difficulties in speaking good Icelandic; there were 'too many inflections'. We often talked about it, since my own lack of fluency was a good way to enter into a conversation, initially on language matters but eventually on anything emerging from this. What struck me in the fishing village, and notably among the labourers of the fish factory, was the extent to which they had internalized the view of themselves as poor Icelandic speakers; they had come to suffer from what has generally become known as *málótti* (fear of speaking). The paradoxical effect of the insistence on a pure everyday language has been an image of only specialists being able to speak correctly. This points to another distinction made by Icelandic linguists, the distinction between clever and stupid.

It cannot be denied that the level of intelligence varies within the population and that the structure of Icelandic is complicated. I doubt if all Icelanders are or have ever been able to master the structure of Icelandic. (Halldór Halldórsson 1971, quoted and trans. by Gísli Pálsson 1989: 131)

This attitude on behalf of the language guards and the repeated appeal to an archaic and allegedly pure mode of speech has had the effect of alienating a number of people from their own mode of expression. As Gísli Pálsson has shown, the sonorous claim to represent a *standard* Icelandic, as against various sources of pollution, masks an emergent class-differentiation. This was certainly confirmed by my own experience in the field.

Asking questions of lexicon is generally acknowledged as a way of entry into 'a culture'. Yet, as we know, encyclopedic knowledge is a poor key to action. In the field of linguistics itself there has been a recent shift in focus from structure and grammar to practise and actual events (Lakoff 1987). It is stressed that there is no language without speakers; whenever we talk about the world in which humans live 'we are talking about the perceived world and not a metaphysical world without a knower' (Rosch 1978: 29). With an actor-centred approach to the world, the 'semantic space' yields to the strategies of motivated action as the main issue of research. Such strategies are partly formed by tradition, including the tradition of a pure and unchanging language. They are not formed by this language itself. Language is just one yardstick among others, seeking to 'measure' experience.

When fieldwork is construed as 'significantly composed of language events' (Clifford 1988: 41), and when the interlocution in the field is seen as dialogue (Tedlock 1983), the 'thickness' of the encounter—and the world—is obscured. 'Information' is but a fraction of what constitutes the material which is built up from experience rather than dialogue. Silences are a very important part of this experience, as I foreshadowed in Chapter 2. My own fieldwork certainly taught me that most cultural knowledge is transmitted by way of the body (rather than words). It is the body-in-life, the living person, that is the locus of experience. In order to really *know* culture, one has to suffer it, as it were.

Let me give you an example. In Iceland, half the population lives from fishing. This is thoroughly documented both in statistics and in local images. There would be no point in my simply collecting more information on this, or in conveying local images to the rest of the world, as if they were a fixed system of meanings. As an anthropologist, my aim was to get to the experiential core of these images in order that I might understand their motivational force in the daily life of the Icelanders. After all, this is what gradually becomes history.

So I went living the fishing. The natural place to start was the filleting factory, since that was where women worked. I filleted and packed endless amounts of iced cod and haddock, rather unskilfully I may add, and I could still feel the cold in my fingers after twelve hours of work. I also wanted to go fishing for myself, as it were, that is being with the men. It was difficult to find a vessel that would take me on board, however; clearly I would be a nuisance—and as a woman I had no natural place in the fishermen's world. Women had been known to fish, but there seemed to be an image of female bad luck at sea that could be invoked against my participation. Insistent as anthropologists are, I finally succeeded, and one early morning at 3 o'clock, I was on my way. The weather was extremely rough—as it very often is on the North Atlantic—and once beyond the harbour, I was certain that I would never return. The image of the hero-anthropologist (exploring the precarious life of the northern seas), vanished—or rather it melted into that of a forlorn woman, facing her imminent drowning with some dread.

After some time, this woman nevertheless remembered that she was an anthropologist and started asking the skipper all sorts of questions. Skipper was a man of few words, however, and only occasionally would he answer me by way of a grunt or a silent nod. The crew was also a silent lot, and after a while I, too, stopped talking. Words seemed out of order.

As day and night passed, I realized that if I wanted coffee, food, or sleep, I had to organize myself. No one was going to offer me anything, or tell me what to do. And certainly nobody was going to comfort me, or to reassure me about my survival. If, at first, I was slightly hurt by the fishermen's negligence, afterwards I realized that they had in fact taken me very seriously. They had let me *experience* the uncertainty of fishing, and the actual powerlessness of words in this violent nature. What is more, by reducing me to invisibility, they had truly treated me as a woman. I *had* no place in their world.

Through this experience I learnt that the 'maleness' of fishing was not simply a statistical feature, it was a cultural model, which contained its own motivational force, also in the relation between men and women ashore. Once I had realized this, everything fell into a distinctive pattern. And from my nowhere-position in the men's world I looked towards land with a new comprehension. The silence at sea was packed with meaning. But I could not hear it, until I let myself become part of it. I had to tune in to the music of the social before I could sense the density of silence.

The general point is that *living* a culture, as we attempt to do also in fieldwork, implies a *merging of action and awareness*. This merging is the basis for the self-evidence of incorporated cultural knowledge—in everyday life in Iceland and elsewhere. As Ardener has it, in this life it can sometimes be difficult to tease out 'whether we are dealing with a "social" or a "linguistic" phenomenon. Language is to the social as the measuring rod is to the measured, where, however, the inches or centimetres stretch or contract at the same time as the object itself deforms in related or independent directions' (Ardener 1989*a*: 180). With language we are definitely outside the metrical—if within the canonical.

If this holds on the theoretical level, it is forgotten by the the linguistic purists in Iceland who have identified Icelandic as the metering device for more or less prototypical Icelandicness: 'language cultivation . . . [represents] the morality of language. This morality is applied to . . . many other issues. . . . It is expressed, for example, in civilized appearance, and good manners in general' (Baldur Jónsson 1978, quoted by Pálsson 1989: 132).

By stressing the unity of people, history, and language an ideology of Icelandicness is created, which makes speaking a moral issue, rooted in a tradition that spans a thousand years of telling.

Telling the Past: The Story of Grettir

In the final chapter of *Grettis saga*, Sturla *lögmaðr* Þórðarson is quoted as saying about Grettir that he was a quite exceptional man for three reasons. First, he was the one who had lived the longest as an outlaw; second, he was the strongest man in the country at his time and the most efficient in fighting ghosts; and, third, his death had been revenged in Miklagarðr, the Norse name for Constantinople, which had happened to no Icelander before him (Jónsson 1936: 289–90). Sturla died in 1284, so if one way or the other he is the originator of the passage, we are faced with a thirteenth-century evaluation of a tenth- to eleventh-century person.

In 1982, when engaged in the autumn collection of sheep in the mountains with a group of local Icelandic farmers, I heard part of this judgement repeated. When passing a cave (*hellir*) bearing a man's name, I was told by one of the farmers that this man had been an *útilegumaður* (outlying man). Sensing that perhaps this statement needed further qualification, he volunteered the information that *útilegumenn* were a relatively common feature of the past, and that they were generally gigantic, strong, sometimes mischievous but very often brave men, who for some reasons had been expelled from society. 'The most famous are Grettir Ásmundarson and Fjalla-Eyvindur, who lived as *útilegumenn* longer than anyone else.'

Seven hundred years separate the two statements which may, nevertheless, be seen as outer points of a continuous tradition of Grettir the Strong. The continuity is so conspicuous that the twentieth-century statement might have been heard as merely a reproduction of the saga's evaluation. This is so only indirectly, however. The continuity is no simple matter of sameness; the seven hundred years separating the two verbal events have not passed without leaving a trace. Significant changes in both content and context stand out even from the few lines quoted above. There is a switch from Grettir as 'outlaw' to 'outlier', from his being a singular character 'at his time' to his being classified with others in a non-distinct past. Obviously, there is also a shift from a literary to a popular image belonging to a largely oral tradition.

Tradition is deeply embedded in history, even if it has very often been separated from it and presented as if consisting only in stable forms and motifs. Tracing the tradition of Grettir, therefore, is not simply an exercise in tracing a motif through the centuries, but also a study of the visions held by the Icelanders who in different historical circumstances measured themselves in relation to particular 'others'.

'Others' are no more unchanging than 'selves', and in spite of Grettir's immense tenacity in the Icelandic tradition, he has not stayed the same.

The framework of *Grettis saga* consists of Grettir's life history, and the episodes of the story are chronologically organized in relation to this biographical skeleton. Starting with the Norwegian ancestry and other genealogical information (chs. 1–13), the story runs through Grettir's childhood and adolescence in Iceland (chs. 14–16), his exile in Norway for three years (chs. 17–24), through a couple of interims in his adult life (chs. 25–46), and on to the main body of the narrative concerning Grettir's life as an outlaw in Iceland and terminating with his death (chs. 47–84). After this follows a narration of the excursion of vengeance by Grettir's half-brother Þorsteinn, and his love story with Lady Spes in Miklagarðr (chs. 85–92). Finally, an epilogue containing Sturla's evaluation of Grettir closes the saga.

Among the ancestors we notice an Önundr *tréfótr*, (wooden foot) and an Ófeigr *burlufótr* (clumsy foot). With this ancestry Grettir's *ætt* (kin group) is marked by an element of human imperfection. In the course of the narrative this element is enlarged to a general theme concerning the boundary between the human and the non-human worlds. This boundary is realized at several layers of discourse. It occurs, first, as an opposition between the 'noble Icelanders' and the less noble Norwegian kingship, who claimed the land and thus made the would-be-Icelanders flee. Next, it is expressed as a boundary between proper *ætt*-membership on the one hand, and a blurred or denigrated *ætt*-affiliation on the other. At yet another level, the boundary between the human and the non-human world is associated with the definition of society as coterminous with the law, beyond which a wild and uncontrolled space encloses the outlaws and related anti-social elements. Cosmologically and mythologically the boundary between society and non-society is reflected in the opposition between humans and non-humans, such as trolls, giants, and ghosts.

Boundaries are a means of creating discrete categories, and they are, therefore, a primary tool in all sorts of social and symbolic classification. It is Grettir's fate to be constantly moving across one or another otherwise insurmountable boundary in the Icelandic systems of classification. He is noble and ignoble at the same time. He belongs to a particular *ætt*, yet his father refuses him love and paternal support. He protects society against evil, yet he is an outlaw. He cleanses the wild, uncontrolled space of trolls and ghosts, yet he is also a human, craving for manly honour and fame in this world. It is from this transgression of boundaries that Grettir derives both his strength and his weakness; it takes a man like him to fight the evil forces threatening society, one who is able to meet them on common ground as it were. Yet at the same time he is disqualified as a consort of decent people.

In the fight with the ghost-monster Glámr (ch. 35), so often noted as the turning point of the saga (and connected to the tradition of Beowulf), the humanity of Grettir is seriously at stake, as he himself is henceforward to be haunted by Glámr's eye. Thus in spite of Grettir's victory he is also defeated. The fight with Glámr changes Grettir's relationship to society (cf. Hume 1974: 473); he has reached the point of no return in his moving across the boundary between the human and the non-human world. In his deeds, Grettir has put the opposition between 'inside' and 'outside' (the kin group, the community, the law, the human world) into focus. Normally, the outside would be the negative counterpart of the positively marked inside, yet as *Grettis saga* progresses with Grettir's increasingly firm association with the outside or non-human world, the relative marking of the two spaces seems less certain. It has certainly been inverted towards the end of Grettir's life story, when it is a representative from society who is playing the villain in his killing the now glorified outlaw. In the epilogue Grettir is fully reintegrated into society, even if his personal fate was to be expelled from it, when the lawman Sturla recalls his glory.

As other main characters in the Icelandic sagas, the image of Grettir has been subject to many a literary analysis and interpretation. A recurrent theme is his dual nature as outlaw-hero. By comparison with other Icelandic sagas, this one has been claimed to be of particular unity, owing to the fact that the thematic design takes precedence over the antiquarian desire to recount the history of the early Icelanders (Hume 1974: 477). The literary debates on the true nature of the sagas is extensive and beyond our scope here, however. It suffices to note that Grettir is invariably associated with the 'outside'—as giant-killer (Ciklamini 1966), as connected with ghosts (Chadwick 1946), and with sorcery (Ellis Davidson 1973). In this position, however, Grettir has also aspired to a status of hero, operating between two worlds in order to negotiate the opposition between the profane order and the demonic disorder (Greenway 1973: 8). In this capacity of hero, Grettir even amounts to a particular type within the Icelandic saga literature (Lönnroth 1976: 62). At a still more general level, Grettir is claimed to transcend the limits of Icelandic culture and relate to ancient and universal matters of myth and ritual, which is why he has been able to hold our interest and emotion through the ages (Motz 1973: 92).

This multidimensionality of the literary character of Grettir may be seen as a parallel to many mythical characters from all over the world. Like tricksters, for instance, Grettir takes on different roles during the narrative; he mediates between the human and the non-human world, but never achieves a balance between his own simultaneous sub- and super-humanity. He is always more or less human than anybody else, culture-hero or fool, exorcist or outlaw.

As culture-hero Grettir truly achieves mythical proportions. His superhuman strength and his quality of defender of the Earth links him to the Norse god Thorr in a very direct way; his fight against demonic powers, like those of Glámr, haunting the country is the ultimate heroism. Also, his going through all sorts of perils to bring fire to his freezing company at vital points in their joint history, links him to traditional notions of culture-heroes in the anthropological literature. He even finds an unknown valley of plenty and thereby gives life to an old myth of a different world of unlimited resources. This valley, Þórisdalur, becomes a topological representation of the 'other world'.

As a fool Grettir is of less than human nature. Human imperfection was always in the *ætt*, and potentially Grettir was a *mannskræfa* (miserable coward) as much as a man. This was pointed out to him already in his childhood by his father (Jónsson 1936: 38), and not surprisingly Grettir has a hard time proving to the world that he is fit for anything but *löðrmannlegt verk* (unmanly work) (ibid. 37). In some episodes of the saga, the fool turns into a virtual buffoon such as in the fight in curds with a man he had happened to offend. This side of Grettir's character further relates him to the role played by the jesters at medieval European courts. They, too, were subhuman, i.e. hunchbacks or dwarfs, and they were licensed to tell the ruler what nobody else could say. Grettir's brief sojourn at the Norwegian court did not position him as jester in this direct sense, but his actions were potentially subversive and ambiguously evaluated. Up to a certain point the king greatly appreciated his extraordinary powers, but he finally exiled him because he could have no such an *ógæfumaðr* (ill-fated man) among his housecarls (Jónsson 1936: 133–4).

Grettir's role as an exorcist shows him of superhuman strength and potency, as implied also by his gifts as *skáld* (poet). In this capacity Grettir acts on behalf of society, of which he is still very much part. Through his acts of *landhreinsan* (land-cleansing), among which the fight of Glámr is the epitome though not the only one, Grettir wins fame and manly honour in the social space. An example is provided by the episode at Sandhaugar (chs. 64–5), where Grettir arrives as Gestr (guest or stranger) in search of human company, exorcizes some haunting ghosts, and wins a woman by whom he has a son. His fighting of the dark forces of Iceland is an expression of his superhuman qualities, yet it is decidedly a social act for which the rewards are those of a man.

As an outlaw, by contrast, Grettir is by definition asocial. He belongs to a space which in many ways provides the negative mirror image of society. Even this space has its own code of honour, which gives Grettir a much better position than most of his outlaw companions. In some episodes, Grettir behaves like 'a noble bandit' (Hobsbawm 1969), helping the weak and thus personifying peasant revolt against usurping rulers. This theme is not fully exploited in the saga; in many ways the image is anachronistic, given the fact that the scene of Grettir's life is set in the early eleventh century. Yet, written as it is in the early fourteenth century, the author of the saga does not fail to allude to the possible illegitimacy of power—through the very construction of Grettir as an outlaw-hero, or a noble bandit. Significantly, Grettir's main abode as an outlaw, Drangey, is an island cut off from Iceland proper. The metaphorical 'social' space of the outlaw is geographically fixed in topography as something distant, separate, and dangerous.

Clearly, Grettir is a strong image and he has had a remarkable grip upon the imagination of the Icelanders through the centuries. A multitude of manuscripts have been handed down, and there is reason to believe that Grettir was a frequent 'guest' at the popular *sagnaskemmtun* (saga entertainment), consisting of a reading aloud of sagas for purposes of common entertainment and a recasting of old tales (Pálsson 1962). By way of this institution the literary images became known to (potentially) everyone and became part of a shared 'vocabulary' in which the Icelanders could speak of themselves and their history. In other words the literary motif became a popular image belonging to a more comprehensive conceptual order (cf. Lönnroth 1976: 56).

The popular image of Grettir was nourished from other sources than the saga itself. A popular mode of expression since the fifteenth century was the *ríma*. *Rímur* (rhymes) generally borrowed their motifs from the literature but gave them a new form, and certainly made their selections. Several cycles of *Grettisrímur* are known today, in which Grettir is presented as of mythical proportion while the historical backdrop of farm life and kinship has faded. If the evidence is given full weight, there is little doubt that Grettir was among the images most often recycled in the popular genres of entertainment in Iceland from the fourteenth-century saga onwards.

When, during the nineteenth century, the *rímur* gave way to modern poetry, Grettir continued to inspire the poets. In a late nineteenth-century poem, Matthías Jochumsson, whom we met above as a poet also of the Icelandic language, compares Grettir's life history to the history of the Icelanders. In his *Grettisljóð* Grettir thus comes to personify the Icelandic people (*þjóð*):

> Þú ert Grettir, þjóðin mín
> þarna sá ég fylgjur þín
> þó að ljós þinn lýsi draum
> losast muntu seint við Glaum.
> (Jochumsson 1936: 573)

> (My people, you are Grettir,
> there I saw your *fylgjur*,
> although a light illuminates your dream
> only late will you be freed from Glaum.)

A *fylgja* (lit., follower) in more than one way is a shadow of oneself; its behaviour is often an augury of one's own fate. This is how in the eyes of Matthías Jochumsson *Grettis saga* contains for the Icelanders *örlög vor og hjartablóð* ('our fate and heart's blood'). That this was more than a passing sentiment is testified to by Sigurður Nordal who confidently asserts that *þjóðin hefur þekkt sín eigin örlög í örlögum Grettis* ('the people have recognized their own fate in the fate of Grettir') (Nordal 1938: 4).

Outside 'official' evaluation, where many echoes of Nordal are heard, Grettir also appears in amusement lore of diverse kinds, relating to his sexual and other appetites, and in treatises on Icelandic nature, alluding to the hidden valleys of plenty first discovered by Grettir. The latter are mainly seventeenth-century works (to which we shall return in the next chapter) composed at a time when famine was prevalent in Iceland. It goes on and on, across times, genres, and spaces; Grettir stayed alive through periods that were otherwise completely different. Thus, the image of Grettir is by all standards a stable element in Icelandic tradition. As such it was, of course, interpreted differently. The outlaw-hero gradually was transformed into only a hero in which the Icelanders could see their own image. They, too, had been in some sense 'outlawed' by the Danes, but they had known how to answer back from their retreat.

Because Grettir was a born joker, he could remain of significance through shifting historical contexts. If the saga is a particular kind of signifier, the knowledge or *fræði* is the signified in the Icelandic universe of meaning (Sørensen 1977: 24). *Fræði* sums up a body of historical knowledge which is shared by society and transmitted from one generation to the next. In the course of time, historical knowledge will of necessity undergo some changes, and the relationship between saga and society is transformed into a relationship between tradition and history; at any point we have to identify the meaning of tradition. While the text, motif, or image persists, its *valeur* may change dramatically. Far from being a stable and essentially ahistorical category, 'tradition' is deeply embedded in history.

The nature of its embeddedness is twofold. The content of tradition is continuously reinterpreted in the light of new historical experience; in turn, the reinterpretation of old texts may lead to a redefinition of the context with which it is so intimately linked. This is how the relationship between tradition and history becomes one of mutual implication. While tradition articulates a collective historical experience, it also feeds back into history by giving later action a particular sense of direction. In that sense, history is as much an interpretation of tradition as the reverse.

As with language, so also for narrative; there are proper ways of emphasizing the theme of Icelandicness. There are correct and incorrect inflections, proper and improper cases to be made. In spite of the ideological insistence on continuity, the ways of telling shift through the ages. Indeed, one way of telling 'ages' from one another is their distinctive thematicities, their different socialities. In the case of Grettir, the outlaw of the autonomous medieval society transformed into an outlaw-hero under colonial impact—starting when the saga was first written down, in fact. Today, in the Republic of Iceland, Grettir has become the token of the hard times of the past, when people had to fight the forces of the outside, be they evil powers or foreign merchants.

In other words, the image of Grettir may contain both times of famine and times of feast. Thus is the last lesson of Grettir the Strong, whose appetite for life was legendary:

> *Grettir át í málið eitt*
> *uxalæri og fleski feitt*
> *flotfjórðung og fiska tólf*
> *fjóra sauði og endakólf.*
> (Árnason 1860, IV: 114)

> (Grettir ate in one meal
> a ham of beef and fat pork

ten pounds of grease and twelve fish
four sheep and a sausage.)

This, I believe, is an appropriate *entrée* to our next course in this three-course meal
of oral traditions in Iceland.

Eating the Past: the Meal of Þorrablót

In the history of things, food has often been neglected due to its transitory character. Once something has been eaten, it is quickly forgotten. The evanescence of
meals as compared to other material objects should not delude us, however. Their
actual history may be short but their tradition may span a considerable period of
time. The brief period of consumption can be seen as an event which transcends the
instant and points to the *longue durée* of any history. From an anthropological
perspective, the substance of food is not only protein or fibre, but the world in
which it is consumed.

There is a certain piquancy about the anthropological subject matter of food, as
Gellner has observed (Gellner 1985: 159). To the outsider, 'at any rate if of genteel
background', the interest in food may seem a bit gross or even vulgar (ibid.). For
the anthropologists, however, such vulgarities are part and parcel of the complex
realities that we savour in the field. 'One reason why the anthropologists are so
interested in food is that it is such an apt medium for purely social symbolism, from
private hospitality to great ceremonial dramas' (Douglas 1977: 2). Although eating
is a biological necessity, it is also a social fact in the Durkheimian sense, a 'thing' to
be studied sociologically (Durkheim 1938). Food is an object of exchange, too; as
objects of thought and possibly pride, giving away food implies giving part of
yourself to somebody else; the gift entails its own obligations (Mauss 1950). Meals
have to be shared; cuisine creates social groups (cf. Goody 1982). Anthropologists
sharing meals with 'their' peoples gradually learn the local table manners, which in
turn may provide them with clues to a larger social order. Also, modes of cooking
and consumption involve a 'placing' of oneself in relation to others: the smaller the
group the greater the boundary problems and the less one can ignore the distinct-
ness of local as opposed to foreign cuisine, according to Goody (1982: 2). Food,
therefore, may provide a gourmet clue to the self-understanding of a particular
people. So much for my general point of departure into the culinary tangle of
Icelandic eating.

The route passes by an attempt to situate the meaning of a modern Icelandic
ritual, which is little more than a festival of traditional foods. During my fieldwork
in Iceland I was struck by the fact that sometime in early February, supermarkets
would abound in peculiarly Icelandic dishes and lure consumers into buying certain
kinds of food at high prices through the invocation of *þorrablót*, being the name of
a pre-Christian rite of sacrifice. The food in question was 'traditional' peasant food

of the most lavish kind, which I myself had once helped prepare during the slaughtering season at the farmstead where I had one of my stations in the field (Hastrup 1985*b*).

The spur of this section is thus the common curiosity of the ethnographer. It is more than that, however, because it is also a wish to show how food can serve as an entry into inedible social facts. The correlation between eating and sexual intercourse is widespread and often noted in the anthropological literature (e.g. Goody 1982: 192). It is well known also that cultural contempt or misapprehension is often expressed in culinary ridicule; the French 'frogs' are a case in point. Beyond analogies of this kind we may even find clues to a social space which otherwise seems to defy our categories. Savouring the Icelandic food ritual thus leads us far into the cultural condition of a remote island. In order to arrive there we must start with a presentation of the long tradition of *þorrablót* in Iceland. The tradition stretches back into the earliest history of the island community, as founded in the late Viking Age in the ninth century.

The tradition of *þorrablót* goes back to pre-Christian times. As the name indicates, it was originally a feast of sacrifice (*blót*). The sacrifice involved blood—possibly once human blood—but in historic times the sacrifice was one of oxen or goats. When the first settlers came to Iceland such sacrifices were a recurrent feature of social life and stand out as celebrations of the successful colonization of new land. In *Landnámabók* ('The Book of Settlements') from the mid-twelfth century, we learn for instance of a certain settler Þórólfr Mostrarskegg that *hann var blótmaðr mikill ok trúði á Þór*—meaning that he was a great '*blót*-man' and believed in Thorr (*Landnámabók* 1968: 124). Judging from the sources, including place names, Thorr was by far the most 'popular' of the pagan gods in Iceland, and it was to his name that most sacrifices were connected. It is therefore of little surprise that the folk etymology of *þorrablót* relates it to a feast celebrating Thorr. Certainly, when *þorrablót* was revitalized in the last part of the nineteenth century, this was the popular explanation of its origin (Björnsson 1986: 14, 59–78).

Folk etymologies are significant in the reconstruction of implicit relations of meaning even if 'wrong' from a strictly philological point of view (cf. Ardener 1971: 224–5). The correct etymology of *þorrablót* is contested, but in the popular imagination the connection between the sacrificial feast and Thorr is readily made. Grammatically, it is barely possible for the name to be a derivative of Thorr, however. It is more likely to be derived from *þorri*, which is the name of a 'month' in the old Icelandic calendar, running roughly from the middle of January to the middle of February (Hastrup 1985*a*: 29ff.). It is a month name of considerable age, and one which certainly goes far back into the prehistory of the Nordic peoples.

It is also the name of a legendary king in the stories of the first settlements in Norway; his ancestors and kinsmen bore winter names ('Snow', 'Frost', 'Glacier', etc.), and one of his sons was Nórr, 'North', who gave the name to Norvegr, 'the Way North'—Norway. Of the king it is said that *Þorri var blótmaðr mikill; hann hafði blót á hverju ári á miðjum vetri; þad kölluðu þeir þorrablót; af því tók manaðurin heiti* (*Orkneyinga saga* 1965: 3)—'Þorri was a great *blót*-man, he made a sacrifice every year at midwinter, which they called *þorrablót*; from this the month got its name.' In his *Crymogæa* (1609), the learned Arngrímur Jónsson seems to be in no doubt that the name of the month is the name of this king (Benediktsson 1985: 107).

The calendrical position of *þorrablót* invariably is tied to the harshest month of winter; in *Hænsa-Þóris saga* we learn *er þorri kemur, þá ekur hart að mönnum, og eru margir þá upp tefldir* (1938: 12)—'when *þorri* comes, times are hard for men, and many are thus at stake.' The origin of both the sacrifice and the word seems harder to ascertain. In addition to the complexities introduced above, it has also been suggested that *þorri* was the name of a land spirit for whom sacrifices were made (Lid 1934: 163–9). Philologists have discussed the original meaning of the word *þorri* as a derivative from either *þverra*, 'diminish', probably related to the ebbing out of winter at this time of the year, or *þurr*, 'dry', because this part of winter is dry and cold (*Kulturhistorisk Leksikon* XX: 395ff.). These speculations need not detain us further. All we need to know in the present connection is that *þorrablót* is a rite of considerable age, that it originally implied a kind of live sacrifice, and was held in midwinter.

Sacrifices were prohibited by the advent of Christianity, which was accepted as the 'national' faith in the year 1000. In the first place the prohibition was modified by the clause that men could still make sacrifices in secrecy (*skyldu menn blóta á laun, ef vildu*); it was criminal offence only if witnesses came by (*Íslendingabók* 1968: 17). Even secret sacrifices soon came to a halt, however, and all that was left of *þorrablót* was the name which appears over and again in the sources from the Middle Ages onwards (cf. Björnsson 1986). In the seventeenth and eighteenth centuries, a character by the name of Þorri appears in popular verse of many kinds. He appears as an old man with a huge beard full of frost and clad in a wide cloak; in some ways he is like a poor wanderer, to whom the Icelanders owe part of their surplus, in others he is a more divine figure, who augurs the fate of the local people (cf. Björnsson 1986: 23–9). At this time, the literary élite links the image of Þorri to the simple-minded peasantry, still prone to superstition.

Þorrablót, however, was part of a tenacious structure. In the Icelandic oral tradition, it has left a trace as a recurrent winter feast, taking place on the first day of the month of *þorri*. '*Sumstaðar á Norðurlandi er fyrsti þorradagur enn í dag kallaður "bóndadagur"; á þá húsfreyjan að halda vel til bónda sins og heita þau hátíðabrigði enn þorrablót*' (Árnason 1860, II: 551)—'somewhere in the Northlands the first day of *þorri* is still called "farmer's day"; on that day, the housewife must cater well for her husband and the feast is still called *þorrablót*.' The ritual welcoming of *þorri* was widespread, and invariably implied a lavish meal; folklorists have established evidence of this and have recorded how in the nineteenth century the first day of *þorri* was a day of pleasure and abundance of food: *hangið kjöt, súr svið og brauð, svo og gefið kaffi og brauð með* (Björnsson 1986: 50). This was the more conspicuous because at that time of winter the stores were beginning to get meagre, and there was still some time to spring. In the Icelandic tradition, the midwinter feast thus seems to be a more or less permanent feature. Under the name of *þorrablót* the feast changed from a live sacrifice to the pre-Christian deities to the eating of a ritual meal consisting mainly of meat produce—traditionally a scarce treat among the Icelandic peasantry living mainly on fish and whey. The apparent discontinuity between the two kinds of ritual that are separated by centuries reflects a deep-rooted continuity at another level, however. Before discussing this, we must briefly present the latest manifestations of the tradition.

In the last half of the nineteenth century, Iceland witnessed a revitalization of *þorrablót*. Generally, this period was one of strong national feelings, and increasingly forceful claims to Icelandic sovereignty directed against Danish rule. This context was probably important in reshaping the feast of *þorrablót*. Until then the ritual had been a private feast taking place within the social space of a single farmstead and celebrating the winter stores, as it were. But for the first time it now appeared as a 'public' ritual. According to the minutes of a small 'Evening Society' in Reykjavík it was suggested on 7 February 1867 that the society should meet for a *þorrablót* the next time and have some drinks together. One of the participants (again) was the poet Matthías Jochumsson, and for the actual *blót* he made a song of three verses (with the tune of the Danish national anthem!). The Icelandic past is invoked in a eulogy of local strength, and the song ends, on *þvi framfor Íslands, frelsi, trú—i fornum anda signum nu,—vort 'blót'* (quoted by Björnsson 1986: 56)—'thus to Iceland, freedom, faith, let us now in the ancient spirit, bless our "sacrifice".' A tradition had been reinvented. The idea of making a feast spread rapidly—also to the Icelandic student community in Copenhagen (ibid. 59ff.). The common theme is one of invoking the past and praising the virtues of Iceland. The communal eating and drinking became inextricably linked to nationalism, and with the celebrations of the millennium of the first settlements in Iceland (in 1874) the idea of *þorrablót* became part and parcel of the romanticizing of the past.

The countryside also took up the renewed tradition of communal feasting (ibid. 78ff.). From the last decade of the nineteenth century and onwards to the Second World War announcements of such gatherings were made every year in the local media. People were invited to 'Icelandic food, speeches, singing and dancing'. Among the peasants the emphasis seems to have been more on the local community than the 'nation' of the urbanites. Apparently the *þorrablót* became a focus of nostalgia; tradition—oral, poetic, musical—was the implicit scale for measuring the values of local peasant life.

In the countryside the feast became conceptually linked with the ancient ritual of welcoming the month of *þorri*, and eating the right (Icelandic) food was as important as singing nationalistic hymns. Meanwhile, the number of the feasts declined in the townships, which were under heavy foreign influence from the beginning of this century. However, after 1950 and increasingly in the 1970s and 1980s, the

Icelanders have experienced yet another revitalization of the feast in the towns, where the descendants of the farming population now express their deliberate wish to have traditional Icelandic food. *Þorrablót* has become a commercial success. Once a year in midwinter, people now make a point of celebrating *þorrablót* with their friends—and possibly with a visiting anthropologist. The experience is one of a ritualized eating of traditional peasant food of the richest kind. In the newspapers, the tradition is rehearsed and recipes given.

The food consists mainly in *svið* (singed and halved sheep heads, eaten with eyes, brain, and everything), and *slátur* (liver and blood sausages, sewn into small bags (*keppir*) made of lambs' stomachs). This basic foodstuff may be supplemented with rams' testicles (*hrútspungar*) also sewn into *keppir* and preserved in *sýra* (sour whey), at least in the countryside where the food is still entirely home-made. It is often completed with various fish produce, notably *hákarl* (half-rotten) shark, of which W. H. Auden said, it 'is white inside with a prickly horn rind outside, as tough as an old boot. Owing to the smell it has to be eaten out of doors. It is shaved off with a knife and eaten with brandy. It tastes more like boot polish than anything else I can think of' (Auden and MacNeice 1985: 42). I would agree that the taste is somewhat special.

Today, there will also be less special festive foods like smoked salmon in some families, but at the core of the meal is the appeal to age-old dishes. There are local variations in the eating tradition, but the general theme of *þorrablót* is one of eating rich traditional food, which more or less explicitly is linked to life in the celebrated *sveit* (countryside or local tract). For people in town, there are shops offering *þorramatarbakkar* (*þorri*-food packages), making up for the lack of one's own produce. Thus in my local supermarket in Reykjavík, the package advertised contained *hrútspungar* (rams' testicles), *lundabaggi* (sausage in sheep's intestines), *hvalur* (whale), *smjör* (butter), *sviðasulta* (brawn made of *svið*), *bringukollar* (briskets), *hangikjöt* (hung and smoked mutton), *blóðmör* (blood pudding), *lifrarpylsa* (liver sausage), *harðfiskur* (dried fish), *hákarl* (shark), and *rúgbrauð* (rye bread). This much would suffice for a taste of tradition. Much of it is considered rather exotic these days, but, generally, 'the more exotic the more Icelandic' (Pálsson 1995: 16).

The above sketch of the tradition of *þorrablót* in Iceland provides an interesting point of departure into the construction of Icelandicness, however modest it may seem. The individual piece of *svið* may have but a short life, but the feast itself is part of a long tradition. In spite of the variations at the level of actual events there is a noticeable general theme underlying the actual ritual events, which links them with the structures of the *longue durée*. At the same time the discontinuity from an actual (human) sacrifice to the celebratory consumption of particular food items points to a general change in the context of *þorrablót*. In order to assess both the continuity and the discontinuity we shall move on to some observations on the modern food festival.

Let us start with the meal itself and rehearse the question put by Mary Douglas:

'If food is a code, where is the precoded message?' (Douglas 1975: 249). Somehow for the meal to be anthropologically interesting it must have a social or cultural component alongside the obvious nutritional or biological one. In *Mythologiques*, a masterpiece in culinary anthropology, Lévi-Strauss has set out to prove the universal patterns of meaning in any food habit, thus attempting to establish what we might call a panhuman culinary message:

La nourriture s'offre en effet à l'homme dans trois états principaux: elle peut etre crue, cuite ou pourrie. Par rapport à la cuisine, l'état cru constitue le pole non marqué, tandis que les deux autres le sont fortement, mais dans les directions opposées: le cuit comme transformation culturelle du cru, et le pourri comme sa transformation naturelle. Sous-jacente au triangle principal, on discerne donc une double opposition entre: élaboré/non-élaboré d'une part, et: culture/nature d'autre part. (Lévi-Strauss 1968: 396)

All culinary systems are variations on this scheme which I suppose would qualify as the 'precoded message' asked for by Mary Douglas—even if of a more universal kind than to her taste.

In the Icelandic case this kind of analysis has something to offer. The food eaten at the *þorrablót* draws upon all the poles of this scheme. The things eaten cover all the aspects of the triangular scheme. Dried fish, buried eggs, rotten shark, singed heads, smoked meat, whey-preserved uncooked rams' testicles, cooked blood-pudding, and liver sausages are eternally trapped in the dual oppositions between nature and culture, elaborated and non-elaborated. This not only obtains for the results—that is the actual things eaten—but also for the processes involved in the cooking. Nature and culture alternate as agents in this process. Obviously, then, the Icelandic meal is eligible for structural analysis by exposing simultaneously the entire culinary triangle.

This analysis leaves us not completely satisfied, however. The binary contrasts of the isolated meal must be placed in its syntagmatic relations to other meals and other features of the social in order for us to perceive the local contextual meaning of *þorrablót*. Doing so makes us realize that meals are ordered according to a scale of relative importance both during the day and during the year. As Mary Douglas puts it: 'The smallest, meanest meal metonymically figures the structure of the grandest, and each unit of the grand meal figures again the whole meal—or the meanest meal' (Douglas 1975: 257). It is this perspective of repeated analogies which invests the individual meal with additional meaning. For centuries the normal Icelandic meal was rather poor, and certainly repetitive. According to the *Búalög*, the Icelandic 'household law' governing the relationships between farmers, farm hands, and servants, the workers were to receive daily meals consisting of fish, butter, and milk produce; only rarely was there any meat (*Búalög* 1915–22: *passim*). According to one eighteenth-century observer, the daily rations for men were one dried fish of two pounds, half a pound of butter, and some whey; women received half the amount (Jochumsson 1977: 51). The point here is not so much the quantity, however, as it is the quality of the meal.

For it to be a proper meal it had to contain butter and whey in addition to the fish. Fish was a kind of staple 'crop'—and in its dried state it was almost 'nature'—but for it to be a socially recognized meal and not just a snack to kill hunger, enculturated butter and whey had to be supplied. Both of these were products of farming which 'marked' Icelandic social life by culture, while fishing just sustained it by protein.

In every single meal we rediscover this pattern, combining fish and farm produce, 'nature' and 'culture'. Poverty may sometimes have made butter supplies very short, but whey (*sýra*) was always part of the diet. Apart from providing a drink, it also served the purpose of preservation in this country so short of salt. Meat, sausages, and blood-puddings were preserved in *sýra*. Thus the sour taste of the daily drink invoked times of feast and plenty, even when they were farthest away. It is tempting to quote a rather long passage, describing an Icelandic supper in 1809, which certainly is plentiful, if savoured only by a small group of guests. It is worth noting that the banquet takes place only a few years after the 'great famine' (*móðuharðindin*) in Iceland, killing thousands of people, and certainly still within the collective memory—not least because it was just one final catastrophe after some four hundred years of recurrent famines. There is nothing wanting here, however, so let us approach the table.

On the cloth was nothing but a plate, a knife and fork, a wine glass, and a bottle of claret, for each guest, except that in the middle stood a large and handsome glass-castor of sugar, with a magnificent silver top. The dishes are brought in singly; our first was a large tureen of soup, which is a favourite addition to the dinners of the richer people, and made of sago, claret, and raisins, boiled so as to become almost a mucilage. We were helped to two soup plates full of this, which we ate without knowing if anything was to come. No sooner, however, was the soup removed, than two large salmon, boiled and cut in slices, were brought on and, with them, melted butter looking like oil, mixed with vinegar and pepper; this likewise, was very good and when we had with some difficulty cleared our plates, we hoped we had finished our dinners. Not so, for there was then introduced a tureen full of eggs of the Cree, a great tern, boiled hard, of which a dozen were put upon each of our plates; and for sauce, we had a large basin of cream, mixed with sugar, in which were four spoons, so that we all ate out of the same bowl, placed in the middle of the table. We devoured with difficulty our eggs and cream, but had no sooner dismissed our plates, than half a sheep, well roasted, came on with a mess of sorrel called by the Danes, scurvy-grass, boiled, mashed and sweetened with sugar. However, even this was not all; for a large dish of waffels as they are here called, that is to say a sort of pancake made out of wheat flour, flat, and roasted in a mould, which forms a number of squares on top, succeeded the mutton. This was not more than half an inch thick and about the size of an octavo book. Then bread, Norway biscuit and loaves made of rye were served up: for our drink we had nothing but claret, of which we were all compelled to empty the bottle that stood by us, and this too out of tumblers rather than wine-glasses. The coffee was extremely good and we trusted it would terminate the feast; but all was not yet over; for a large bowl of rum punch was brought in and handed round in glasses pretty freely, and to every glass a toast was given. Another bowl actually came which we were with difficulty allowed to refuse to empty entirely; nor could this be done but by the ordering our people to get the boat ready for our departure, when, having concluded this extraordinary feast by three cups of tea each, we took our leave and reached Reykjavík about ten o'clock, but did not for some time recover from the effects of this most involuntary intemperance. (Hooker 1811; quoted by Auden and MacNeice 1985: 80–1)

There are shades of *Babette's Feast* in this meal, but more importantly, there are not only shades but manifestos of an Icelandic meal here. The dishes reflect the local resources (save for the wine), and they have had a high degree of continuity through the ages. If not as lavishly displayed as in Hooker's supper, its elements are still present in feasts. The meal repeats itself and presents us with a relatively stable element in the taste of Icelandicness.

If it is true that part of the meaning of a meal is found in a system of repeated analogies of different scales, then 'each meal is a structured social event which structures others in its own image' (Douglas 1975: 260). This could also be said about the Icelandic *þorrablót*. In the culinary medium it amplifies the meaning of any meal, which is to uphold a social system (rather than a biological regime). In this case, the social system is marked by 'farming' and the diacritical feature of the meal is farm produce.

In many ways this view of the Icelandic social system is anachronistic; today fishing is the main enterprise and provides by far the major part of the gross national product. The anachronism is not only economic, however, since the collective feast on pre-modern foods also marks a step back from the 'literate' use of international recipes to an 'oral' tradition of local cuisine; the modern and internally differentiated society momentarily cedes to the old concept of the Icelandic world as unified against the outside (cf. Goody 1982). Thus, by 'eating the past' the Icelanders continue to celebrate themselves—in the past tense.

Having deciphered the meal and seen how the eating of the past is in fact a feast by which a particular Icelandic identity is celebrated, we may move on to a more comprehensive understanding of *þorrablót* in the Icelandic context by discussing its ritual nature. In the anthropological study of ritual we are immediately faced with a simultaneity of meaning, action, and object. In even more general terms a ritual is obviously both irrational and symbolic, as well as material and highly empirical. In the thought and practice of the Icelanders these features of the ritual are not separated from each other. It is only analysis that allows us to separate them, but to little avail because the point of the ritual is not to be found in either the symbolic or the material dimension but in their simultaneity. It is neither the past nor the eating that of themselves are of interest. It is the eating of the past that gives us the taste of Icelandicness.

As with other rituals, Icelandic *þorrablót* is remarkably empty once we have penetrated it. From the secret sacrifice of life in the early Middle Ages to today's almost cannibalistic feast on past peasant life, the ritual seems to contain little more than the obvious. 'We all know examples of "secret" rites that, from the outside, seem pregnant with the promise of structure and meaning. When they are penetrated, however, there is nothing there. Or rather, the secrecy is the

meaning, and there is no need of other structures than those of concealment'
(Ardener 1993: 6).

The symbolic and the material do not interact, as it were. They are enacted
together in performance and understanding—being their own message rather than
carrying another meaning. When analysed, the 'content' of any ritual may dissolve;
its meaning is content-free, as Ardener puts it. This paradox is the clue: the ritual
is not something that has a total meaning, but something else is not meaningful
without it. The ritual is not an entity to be dissected and understood by itself, it is
rather a marker of a particular social space, or a context-definer.

Approaching the Icelandic *þorrablót* from this perspective of ritual frees us from
the burden of finding its own meaning. It need not be immediately meaningful in
itself; to sacrifice a goat or to indulge in marinated rams' testicles and rotten shark's
meat does not necessarily carry a heavy load of inner meaning. However, it may
mark a social space which may seem meaningless without this (and other)
ritual(s). In this case the space is 'Iceland'. And *þorrablót* is one of its commemorative practices, that is, one of the practices that continually recreate the Icelandic
social space. The eating of the past is a social action that ties the individual
Icelander not only to a place but also to a particular history and a peculiar culture.

Analysing modern Icelandic *þorrablót* in terms of the anthropological study of
ritual allows us to penetrate its content-free meaning. It is not unlike the case of the
wedding-cake in Scottish marriage celebrations (Charlsley 1987). The elaborate
ecclesiastical procedures and symbols may be legally sufficient for the marriage to
be formally binding, but informally and popularly for a marriage to have taken
place there must be a wedding cake. It is the cake that activates the meaning of the
wedding. Similarly for the Icelandic meal. We can easily see how the Icelanders
may survive without it, but given the fact that the food ritual is being revitalized we
are forced to look for its contribution to the marking of the wider context of
'Iceland'. The paradox of the content-free meaning in ritual thus leads directly to
the context of the ritual. If we take into account the fact that people are not only
defined by their social space but are also the defining consciousness of that space we
can see how the remoteness of Iceland implies a continuous effort on the part of the
Icelanders to redefine their space as unique and peculiarly 'Icelandic'. Following
Goody, who claims that the smaller a particular society the greater the importance
of local cuisine in boundary-marking (Goody 1982: 2), I claim that the ritual eating
of peculiarly local dishes can be understood in these terms. With the increasing
internationalization of Icelandic society and the influx of more and more un-
Icelandic elements the sense of vulnerability grows, while at the same time the
uniquely 'Icelandic' events seem to be fewer. I suggest that is one reason why
traditions are (re)invented—and *þorrablót* recreated (cf. Hobsbawm and Ranger
1983).

We have seen how the food ritual reflects traditional peasant values and through
them emphasizes the singularities of Icelandic culture. As a context marker the
ritual of eating the past is a metaphor for a social space that always required

sacrifice—in the widest sense of this term. If, generally, 'the idea of food underlies the idea of sacrifice' (Douglas 1977: 1), this relationship between food and sacrifice seems almost overdetermined in the specific case of the ritual meal in Iceland.

In order fully to understand the actual implications of this relationship we shall briefly consider the nature of sacrifice in general terms. Any act of sacrifice contains two radically opposed aspects: at certain points in time the sacrifice is a sacred obligation to be neglected only at great peril, while at other points a similiar act would count as a major criminal offence. To account for this duality inherent in particular ritual practices Hubert and Mauss invoked the sacred character of the victim (Hubert and Mauss 1964). In a circular line of reasoning they argued that because the victim is sacred it is criminal to kill him, but the victim is sacred only because he is to be killed. As pointed out by Girard, the implicit notion of ambivalence is no real explanation, only a displacement of the problem. Instead, Girard sets out to understand the violence that is expressed in the sacrifice (Girard 1972).

Essentially, the violence is directed against a surrogate victim. In pastoral societies that are characterized by an extraordinary degree of closeness between people and cattle, the substitute is easily found (Girard 1972: 3). Generally, the animal victim is the one that is most human in nature. In Viking Age Nordic society, oxen or goats were sacrificed in the place of people as the *blót* required; fox or bear would be inconceivable. *Þorrablót* telescopes the act of substitution right from the beginning of the tradition.

Sacrificial substitution implies a degree of misunderstanding. Its vitality as an institution depends on its ability to conceal the displacement upon which the rite is based. It must never lose sight entirely, however, of the original object, or cease to be aware of the act of transference from that object to the surrogate victim; without that awareness no substitution can take place and the sacrifice loses all efficacy. (Girard 1972: 5)

The displacement from human to animal victim is actually superimposed upon another substitution, namely that of one member of the community for all (Girard 1972: 102). Any ritual sacrifice is founded upon this double substitution. In the case of *Þorrablót* the goats that were originally sacrificed to Thorr can immediately be attributed with the mimetic quality so characteristic of ritual sacrifice, according to Girard. I suggest that the modern food festival be read along the same lines. The ritual eating of the past is a mimetic act which invokes the original sacrifice of a surrogate victim, which allowed the community to unite. Today the scapegoat is eaten straightaway and the nature of the unification has changed, but there is still a trace of real violence and original mimetic desire.

Over the centuries, however, another displacement has taken place: the world against which the Icelanders unite is no longer the 'other' world of gods and demons. The great (implicational) divide between the 'inside' and the 'outside' is no longer coterminous with the distinction between the human and the non-human world, but between 'Iceland' and elsewhere, as we saw also when we traced the tradition of Grettir. In order to specify the uniqueness of Icelandic culture, the ritual sacrifice has been transformed into a feast which—given the double substitution and the mimetic desire—has a conspicuous cannibalistic flavour.

The question naturally arises whether modern *þorrablót* is just another feast giving 'pigs for the ancestors'—and thus essentially serving the purpose of ecosystemic regulation (cf. Rappaport 1968). In a country so consistently marked by poverty as Iceland it is hard to maintain that the ritual meal ever served the purpose of eliminating surplus animals; quite the contrary, as feasting in February was a real sacrifice of scarce resources. In that case, one could perhaps argue that the feast is just an empty tradition, reflecting a past when people were short of protein, and therefore had to 'ritualize' the eating of animals that were otherwise both too few and too close to be eaten. Even 'real' cannibalism has often been explained in these terms (e.g. Harris 1977). This is no more than a rationalization of a disturbing phenomenon, however (cf. Liep 1987: 35).

If we claim that there is at least some analogy with cannibalism in *þorrablót*, we must give it one more thought. It has been suggested that 'to eat and to be eaten is one and the same thing; cannibalism is a metaphor for the ultimate consequence of Narcissism—the engulfing of the Self by the Other and the Other by the Self' (Sjørslev 1987: 21). In other words, cannibalism is an ultimate form of self-objectification. At the end of this merry tour through the doors of analytical imagination, we may finally glimpse a major feature of the Icelandic world, the subjective objectifying of 'ourselves' (in past and present tense), enabling Icelanders to declare their unique identity over and over again by invoking a subject called 'we, the Icelanders' (cf. Chapter 8). I suggest that this feature of self-objectification is part of the context of the culinary ritual which it marks.

Time has come to draw this discussion to a conclusion. In Iceland material objects were always few, and the history of things consequently sparse. This feature has sustained an image of the Icelanders as a highly 'spiritual' people concerned more with honour and literature than with material goods—at least in earlier generations. Against this background the modern pattern of consumption in Iceland seems to represent a break with Icelandic history. The break can be located more or less precisely in the Second World War, when the traditional value of work (preferably hard work) as an end in itself became replaced by much too easy wage-work for the British, and entailed the 'end of an epoch' (Magnússon 1990: 129ff.). This discontinuity, however, is largely a *trompe l'œil* owing to the culture-specific distinction between the spiritual and the material. The Icelandic experience transcends the dichotomy. Whether 'said' or 'eaten', the savouring of history in Iceland creates a relationship of internalization between the people and their world. Just as people are never just defined by their social space but are also the defining consciousness of that space, as I said above, consumers are never just objects of external interest but also actors (Löfgren 1990: 35). In the case of *þorrablót*, the Icelanders are both acting according to age-old tradition, and redefining it through their actions. Through the reproduction of an essentially material act of consumption the Icelanders fill the gap between the cultural order as constituted in society and as lived by the people (cf. Sahlins 1985: p. ix). By eating the past, a synthesis is created which confirms the uniqueness of the remote island within the 'global village'.

Canonicity: The 'As If' Model

What we have done here is to run through three modes of 'oral tradition', or conventional articulations of Icelandicness, all of which stress archaism and purity though history, and put a high value on farming virtues. Icelandic history is peculiar in one sense: it has left virtually no trace in the landscape. There are no castles or medieval churches, no ancient towns or ports, no houses of great age. The modest turf-and-stone house construction that was used also for churches, always transformed back into nature when abandoned. Only an occasional overgrown heap of stones may indicate a relatively recent dwelling to the untrained eye, even if one should not underestimate the archeological record in general. Things have changed since the Second World War, when concrete and stone have made their impact on the landscape, also outside the recent towns.

Because of the relative poverty in objects, history has been transmitted mainly in words. Speaking Icelandic has been and is still a major signposting of Icelandicness. The ideology of purity in speech is a forceful example of what Daniel has noted as a quality of words: 'Words are symbols, which, even at the edges, pull one toward culture's center' (Daniel 1996*b*: 362). If this is a general feature of language, the idelogical emphasis of pure Icelandic makes the pull towards the centre of Icelandicness even stronger. As we saw with the example of the silence at sea, the deed of non-speaking separated the stranger from the world of fishing, the woman anthropologist from the men.

Words in Iceland take on a monumental import, in place names and in narratives. We have already noted a peculiar quality of the Icelandic historical narrative, namely the conflation of the concepts of story and history in the word *saga*; it means 'said', and what is said is historical truth. The Icelandic sagas are well known to the international audience as an important literary contribution. Less widely known is the scholarly debate about the veracity of the sagas: are they history or just story? (see e.g. Andersson and Miller 1989). I contend that the question is wrong. The absolute distinction makes no sense in an Icelandic perspective. Obviously, this is not to say that the Icelanders cannot distinguish between fact and fiction, but to stress that in the particular tradition of Iceland the story aspect of history has always been acknowledged.

The point I wish to make here is simply this: the tradition, that is the transmission of history, of Iceland is principally oral. It is 'said'. During a certain period of time the endless repetition of stories about past deeds, the reading aloud of the sagas as popular entertainment, seems to have been counter-productive to the continuation of society (Hastrup 1990*a*). In an almost liturgical form, the sagas set a fixed frame for historical conception, which made current events register in an 'anachronistic' way. The oral nature of history and its recurrent incantation generally produced a degree of intimacy between the Icelanders and their history which made it difficult to maintain the distinction between now and then, and ultimately between 'us' (the present people) and 'them' (the ancestors). The particular Icelandic consumption of history may, therefore, be interpreted metaphorically as an instance of cannibalism. Between the communal reading of the past and eating it there is but a small step.

Images of tradition are resting places for thought. They do not compel Icelanders to think or act alike, but they scaffold the space of self-evidence, the 'home'. Traditional images of this kind are never just referential; rather they are or become canonical through repetition and consumption. 'The canonical embrace', in turn, 'turns thought into ideology' (Paine 1995: 52). It is with ideology as with culture— it is not prescriptive, nor does it level individual difference. In this vein, Cohen phrases an important question about the self in society: 'Do his provenance and his culture mean that he must think certain things, and about things in a certain way? Or do they, rather, provide him with the means to think about them, and the terms in which to express approximately what he thinks?' (Cohen 1994: 89). This is the key, to which Cohen himself provided the implicit answer. Approximation is all we can get from tradition; a common vocabulary does not point to shared meanings— only to a shared vocabulary, in fact, to which the individual may attach his or her own assumptions of meaning.

Communities operate on an 'as if' model implying a model of working misunderstandings. As Cohen has it about the people of Wanet, studied by Nigel Rapport, they 'are revealed as habitual users of "as if" models who find in them precisely the self-validating competence that we noted earlier' (Cohen 1994: 117). Rapport's book 'is a microscopic study of interpretive differences, concealed by a shared vocabulary, among a handful of closely related individuals. . . . Rapport shows how each of them spins the common verbal currency into individually distinctive "loops" of meaning which constitute their respective "world views"' (ibid. 116). This is important: by identifying some pertinent images of Icelandic tradition we have not pre-empted the issue of how the individual Icelander thinks. Far less have we exhausted the discussion of how he or she may act; if words pull towards the centre of a world, deeds 'threaten to push against culture's limits' (Daniel 1996*b*: 362).

What we have done is to establish a common verbal currency, which by any standard is the wrong currency for action, even if it is the right one for articulating aspects of Icelandicness. Of the aspects we have so far dealt with, the definition of Icelandicness as an ancient identity is prominent. This was particularly conspicuous with the way language was seen, reproduced—and changed. Another aspect is the delineation of a concentric model, in which the centre is Icelandic proper, the periphery un-Icelandic. Grettir showed us how the boundary between inside and outside was ever shifting, and when his image was reproduced in later times, he often represented Iceland himself. This points to a paradoxical conception of uniqueness within an ever-present contact zone.

If words of a shared language pull towards the centre, the poetical or narrative images of the shared sagas contributes to the same trend. As Paul Friedrich suggests for the great epics of the world, so also for the Icelandic sagas; they 'are not just corpora of texts but also underlying cultural charters, paradigms, precedents, and templates in terms of which to live. Modest guidelines for the small individual who is having trouble on deck in the storms at sea that life contains. They are also poetical charters for political acts and attitudes of national or international import, such as territorial claims and counterclaims.' (Friedrich 1996: 40).

This has been a forceful element in the general conception of the sagas in Iceland; for a long time the key issue between Denmark and Iceland in the post-colonial era was the 'ownership' of the medieval texts, stored in the Royal Library in Copenhagen since the seventeenth century. It was not only a battle over national antiquities, it was also a battle on the definition of the nature of the texts. For the Icelanders it was world literature. Sigurður Nordal wrote in 1931 'no Germanic people, in fact no nation in Northern Europe, has a medieval literature which in originality and brilliance can be compared with the literature of the Icelanders from the first five centuries after the settlement period' (quoted by Byock 1992: 43). World literature, indeed, yet also definitely Icelandic, as testified to by Einar Ólafur Sveinsson (identified by Pálsson (1995: 14) as 'another authoritative indigenous scholar'), when he writes about the saga literature that 'it is still a vital force, it is the root that draws the juices from the soil of ancient times, passing them on to the lively and maturing branches of modern culture' (Sveinsson 1959: 103; cf. Pálsson 1995: 14). Like other peoples, suddenly freed of external definitions, the Icelanders needed a golden past. Given the nature of Icelandic history and its lack of material trace, the role of fulfilling this need fell to the oral traditions. As noted by Gísli Pálsson, 'the sagas and more recent texts, chronicles and folk tales, have provided an important avenue for the fetishization of Icelandic culture and the national heritage' (Pálsson 1995: 15).

From a slightly different angle we may see the sagas reinterpreted so as to fill the gap between the 'little' traditions of the Icelandic peasants and a 'great' tradition of a literary culture, which nevertheless portrays and sustains a quite conservative image of a rural society (Byock 1990–91). Icelandic scholars in the early twentieth century launched a view upon the sagas that detached them from the oral, popular, tradition and made of them a particularly Icelandic contribution to the world literature, as we saw above. They are, of course, but one need not subscribe to the 'book prosaists'' wholesale view of the literature as distinct from the oral tradition to note that.

In the 'Icelandic school' (of book prosaists) we find a similar tendency as that noted for the language purists before. In both cases there is a will to distinction, a comparative self-consciousness, as it were, which contains an assumption of hierarchy *within* the Icelandic world itself. Some ways of speaking, and some ways of writing are better and more properly Icelandic than others. Icelandicness in this way is largely rendered as a matter of 'taste'—of which we know that it marks social classes (Bourdieu 1986) if apparently denied by the shared features of the Icelandic meal. The taste of famine and the taste of feast is the same, and one which unites the Icelanders through the ages.

When, during the twentieth century, the sagas were recast as the basis for the public image of the Icelandic nation, the language naturally became also of renewed interest. With the expansion of the school system, the standardized Icelandic became strictly enforced, sustaining the view of the purists—and the ideology of cultural homogeneity. Inherent in the celebration of both language and literature is a stress upon antiquity and rootedness. This is apparent also in the revitalized ritual meal. Age is a hallmark of value, and actual rooting in the land is a virtue.

The canonic embrace thus has turned antiquity, purity, and the practising of the land (i.e. farming) into ideology; the image of Icelandicness has become what Iceland is not quite. This does not imply that the Icelanders think alike about their country, or that they can all be portrayed as variants upon a particular cultural image; rather the ideological construction of proper Icelandicness gives any individual Icelander a shared vocabulary to think with and to relate to in his or her own way. Also, by the end of the twentieth century, 'the textual imagination of Icelanders will, no doubt, have to face a series of threats and challenges. In particular, notions of Icelandicness, language, tradition, and cultural boundaries are subject to change' (Pálsson 1995: 16–17). But ideology will probably continue to be constructed as tradition in Iceland as elsewhere in the world.

5

Landscape and Memory

During the hay harvest in Suðursveit in 1982 I was told that the yield from one *tún* (infield), always fell short of expectations. The young farmer explained to me that there was an *álög* (spell), upon it. However much the field looked like other fields, and often it would look even more promising, something would invariably go wrong. The farmer had no opinion when or why this *álög* had occurred, it was a retrospective explanation of present-day experience. As such it has affinities all over the world where people have to cope conceptually with haphazard misfortune. At another level, it also points to the fact that the Icelandic landscape is deeply 'marked', even if there are no ruins of ancient palaces. It is marked by a history that goes beyond local memory, but which is part of a collective conscious-ness of space.

It is a common assumption that the relation between landscape and memory results from the capture of memories in architecture, monuments, or other visual landmarks, while the landscape itself is seen as an objective, fixed, and measurable surface which is unaffected by the processes of remembrance (Küchler 1993: 103–4). The baseline taken here is different. I see the Icelandic landscape as deeply historicized itself. It is not simply a surface, or a stage upon which people play their social roles: it is part of the social space. It infiltrates practice and makes history. There is, as it were, agency on both sides; the opposition between nature and culture dissolves. This serves to stress that whatever else we may say about land-scape and memory the relationship is never stable. The spell on the land has shifting relevance and may be forgotten.

The naturalistic view of the landscape as the backdrop of human activities is out of tune with anthropological insights into the culturally constructed environment that will not allow an external perspective of nature (Ingold 1992). 'People and environment are constitutive components of the *same* world' (Tilley 1994: 23). As Gísli Pálsson has convincingly argued with special reference to Iceland, we have to get beyond the language of nature and reconcile the discursive and the ecological if we want properly to understand society's embeddedness in nature (Pálsson 1991).

Discourse or narrative is a means of describing the world in relation to human agency; 'it is a means of linking locales, landscapes, actions, events and experiences together providing a synthesis of heterogenous phenomena' (Tilley 1994: 32). As we have seen, this tendency to synthesizing, or to 'centring' experience by way of words, is of particular power in Iceland. Michel de Certeau (1984) has pointed out that all stories have a temporal as well as a spatial component, organizing a spatial practice; stories relate the movements of people, transforming places to social spaces. In the narrative of Grettir Ásmundarson, recast in the previous chapter, we were not only met with a life history, but also a life space. While the appearance of the landscape may be *mapped* according to certain well-established codes of abstract notation because it is something substantial and measurable, the actual territory of a people is less easy to depict. The map is not the territory, as Bateson said (1972), because for one thing it strips away the paths of human movement, the points of remembrance, the articulations of space, and the bodily itineraries and routines.

Naturally(!), the naming practices of particular topographical features such as mountains, rocks, bays, beaches, and settlements are crucial for the establishment and maintenance of their identity. 'Through an act of naming and through the development of human and mythological assocations such places become invested with meaning and significance' (Tilley 1994: 18). This applies to generic terms as well as place names; the act of naming is the first step towards the establishment of 'commonplaces', that is shared notions of sites and values.

In the 'arts of memory' studied so extensively by Frances Yates (1992), yet by her exclusively attached to human-made structures, the landscape stands out as the most generally applicable *aide-mémoire* of a society's knowledge of itself (Küchler 1993: 85). In that sense, landscape becomes a *topos* of identity. In Vico's terms, identities relate to 'sensory topics', moments or instances where a shared feeling for common circumstances is created and commonplaces established (Hirsch 1995: 17). This is a key to my concern with the Icelandic landscape at this stage: the everyday spatial practice, imbued with feelings deriving from age-old notions and events of bygone centuries and sustained by ideology, clad as tradition.

Remembering

Remembering and forgetting are profoundly social activities, 'embodied and constituted within ordinary social and communicative practices, and the symbolic significances of the natural and made world' (Middleton and Edwards 1990: 10). In other words, society is not just the backdrop of individual memories; memory itself is social in nature. If a sense of collectivity is created by people's movements in a shared space, the social nature of memory adds a temporal component to this. To remember is not simply to be able to recall isolated events but also to relate them to others in narrative form, or to invoke them in other communicative or social practices. In their daily lives, people are constantly reminded by images, objects, and landscapes about what has come before them, and in their movements within the vast mnemonic of their environment they reassess or re-enact the past (cf. Radley 1990). In this chapter we shall substantiate this claim with specific reference to the Icelandic landscape.

It seems useful here to introduce a distinction between recollection and memory, as made by Søren Kierkegaard. Recollections are outside time, eternally present in one's life; their imprint cannot be erased. It is the active if voiceless presence of the whole past, forgotten as history and deposited as self-evidence. Memories, on the other hand, are extracted from history and placed in time; they are remembered, narrated, reinterpreted, sometimes rejected, and often soon forgotten. Recollections are unmediated experiences. Memory makes a critical difference to these: in being remembered, experience 'becomes "a memory"', with all that this entails, not merely of the consistent, the enduring, the reliable, but also of the fragile, the errant, the confabulated' (Casey 1987: p. xii). The process of making memory explicit, of foregrounding it from the archive of implicit recollection and habituated knowledge, has a parallel in the transformation of mere experience into *an* experience, as discussed by Victor Turner (1986: 35). This transformation is made by way of narrative expression; by telling we carve out units of experience and meaning from the continuity of life. An experience, therefore, has an explicit temporal dimension (Bruner 1986: 7). In real life, there are no absolute beginnings or ends to particular events; there are antecedents and successors to every moment. Yet we cannot but punctuate this in narrative, and in memory.

In addition to the memories stored in narrative, societies remember by what Connerton calls the 'social habit-memory' (Connerton 1989: 36). It is the active remembrance and performance of social rules and codes, and it consists primarily in commemorative rituals and bodily practices, such as we have seen with the *þorrablót*. The rhetorics of re-enactment in ritual, and the silent continuity in daily gesture are both of them tokens of a collective identity, transcending time and space. They are means by which people *practise* their communality—if within an imagined community. They are a means of explicating a shared imagery of the social—if not of shared thoughts about it. Explicitness is precisely what makes the awareness of land and history social, rather than individual, since explicating something, if only to oneself, of necessity involves particular cultural schemes and values. There is no 'explication' outside a conversational community, whether this is actually addressed or not in the particular instance. While meaning is certainly always emergent rather than prior to events or phenomena, it must still in some sense be shared. 'Mad' acts cannot, by definition, be understood (Vendler 1984: 209). The semantic features of language are public features: 'What no one can, in the nature of the case, figure out from the totality of the relevant evidence cannot be part of meaning' (Davidson 1984: 235).

All awareness of the past is founded on memory; at one level all memories are profoundly personal in their recalling individual experiences. Through narration, however, they become public, not only in the sense of being told, but also in the sense of taking shape from the context of telling. Events that we have heard told may even become indistinguishable from our own memory, to the point where 'other people's recollections of past events occlude and often masquerade as our own' (Lowenthal 1985: 196). Different kinds of memory afford differing perspectives on the past, but in the process of recalling the perspectives merge. Histories are collectively created from individual memories. History and memory are distinguishable less as types of knowledge, however, than as attitudes towards knowledge (ibid. 213). History seeks to arrange memory in an orderly narrative structure, which by its nature must be collective for it to have meaning. Intertextuality is a prominent feature in the process.

Recollection, like consciousness, is indistinguishable from our continuous being in between time past and time future, while historical awareness cuts us loose from this; just as narrative punctuates experience, historical awareness constantly arrests the flow of consciousness—to make room for action, as it were. Space is a medium for action, not its container, and action therefore is shot through with differentiated spatial experiences. Depending on social position, mode of livelihood, age and gender, and so forth, people will sense the landscape differently; space is intimately linked with biography and social relationships (Tilley 1994: 11). Across perceived difference and relative awareness of the landscape as party to one's own history, a collective consciousness of the world—forming a simultaneity of time, space, and language—constantly informs social agency. Relating the question of consciousness and awareness to agency is to seek a theoretical understanding of motivation, constituting the link between culture and action (D'Andrade 1992: 41). Motivation is the moving force between these (analytical) entities; as such it is timeless in itself, but by inducing movement it spills over into time and informs local action. Action, in turn, makes up the locale.

Motivation is deeply marked by previous experience, individual and collective, as retained in memory. Memory in a peculiar way attaches simultaneously to words and landscape as succintly put by Grettir Ásmundarson, this time speaking though Auden's poetical vision of his ghost in conversation with an English visitor:

> Too many people. My memory will go,
> Lose itself in the hordes of modern people.
> Memory is words; we remember what others
> Say and record of ourselves—stones with the runes,
> Too many people—sandstorm over the words.
> Is your land also an island?
> There is only hope for people who live upon islands
> Where the Lowest Common labels will not stick
> And the unpolluted hills will hold your echo.

> (in Auden and MacNeice 1985: 124)

In this chapter we shall listen to these echos of the unpolluted hills of the Icelandic landscape with a view to understanding how its marks of memory and recollection spill over into history by motivating action. We shall seek out rune stones amidst the sandstorm over the words.

Journeys and Paths

On a number of occasions, the people living on the farm where I worked told me that the farm was situated at *landnámsland* (settlement land). They would refer to *Landnámabók* ('The Book of Settlements') from the mid-twelfth century and point out how a certain Hrollaugr had claimed land at the site around 900, coming from the sea and landing somewhere 'down there' at the nearby coastline. Now the site had three farms on it; closely related by the nature of the place—and by intermarriage. The name of the first settler survives in the name of a group of small rocky islands off the coast, Hrollaugseyjar, that are visible from the farm in clear weather. According to the friend who first told me about it, Hrollaugr was son of Rögnvaldr Jarl the Great of Norway, and a brother of Göngu-Hrólfr, who conquered the land of the Franks.

In *Landnámabók*, the story is slightly more elaborate (Benediktsson 1968: 316ff.). Rögnvaldr Jarl had three legitimate sons, among whom was Göngu-Hrólfr 'who claimed Normandy'. He also had three sons by a thrall woman, one of whom was Hrollaugr; and although there was no immediate legal or moral problem in having illegitimate children who were equal members of the earl's household, they were socially less well placed when it came to inheritance and political influence. The Jarl, therefore, advised his three extramarital sons to seek their fortune elsewhere, and suggested that Hrollaugr go to Iceland (while another one, Einarr, went and claimed the Orkney Islands). After having consulted the king, Harald, Hrollaugr embarked towards Iceland with his wife and son. On the east coast at Horn, he threw his high seat pillars overboard, and like other settlers, he claimed land where they drifted ashore. His land extended far on what was then and still is a rather narrow strip of coastal soil between the huge glaciers and the sea; an estimate of 80–90 kilometres in length has been made. On this land, Hrollaugr became a 'great chief' who remained a close friend of the Norwegian king, but who never left Iceland again.

As a token of his friendship, the king gave Hrollaugr a golden ring, 'worth five *aurar*', and other items including a renowned sword, whose history and later owners are given in some detail. But, as the chronicler of Suðursveit, Þórbergur Þórðarson, has it about the ring: *Hann var týndur, þegar ég mundi eftir, og enginn vissi, hvað hefði orðið af honum. Svona hefur mikið af gulli týnzt á Íslandi* ('it was thin, now I come to think about it, and nobody knows what became of it. Like this, much gold has been thinning in Iceland') (1981: 95). The slight melancholy felt at the thinning of values in Iceland both reflects and sustains the shared feeling of a glorious past, a time when the inhabitants were truly pioneers, and when their lands stretched much farther than today. Among the present inhabitants the past is still noted with some veneration, and the fact that the actual farmstead of Hrollaugr probably was right here, at 'our' place, is a matter of shared interest. There is no sense of regret or nostalgia, rather a sense of interest and of historical depth.

All over Iceland, when engaged in conversations about the land, reference to the *landnám* will be made. It signifies the original domestication of the land, the roots of Icelandicness as something distinct from the shared Nordic past. The settlers were primordial Icelanders; they colonized virgin land and made a lawful society where before only wilderness had been. In *Landnámabók* it is claimed that it was written in order to establish the noble ancestry of the Icelanders, who allegedly had been accused of being all of them descendants of slaves and robbers. In this it certainly succeeded, even if the motive for writing was probably also a wish to keep track of landownership at a time when all available (inhabitable) land had been claimed and the population continued to grow (Rafnsson 1974). Today the reference to the *landnám* has another significance, which in its own way subordinates the other two. It is part of a comprehensive and continual discourse establishing the antiquity of Icelandicness. The Icelandic landscape is spoken of in terms of what happened during the *landnámsöld*, the age of settlements, or the First Times, in a way that is not totally unlike the way the indigenous Australian landscape is referred to as the Dreaming (cf. Layton 1995: 213). Of course, the landscape is also the 'object' of subsistence activities and a discourse on subsistence, in which the Icelanders speak of *tún* (infields), other kinds of fields and meadows, pastures and grazings, as well as fishing and other resources. In this sense, the landscape has a rather plain referential meaning, if far from a stable one, as we shall see later. No less important, however, is the 'song-line' created by the ancestral past and transmitted in words, the meaning of which transcends the present and the economic domain. It is a landscape of shared knowledge of history and the value of gold.

The history alluded to here may be unauthenticated, in the sense discussed before, yet the knowledge itself of course is authentic. How could it be otherwise? In the renditions of the First Times, as marked in the landscape by the indications and names of settlement lands, there is a shared consciousness of the original journey to Iceland, by which Iceland was created and entered into history. It is this knowledge of the original journey which feeds into present-day sentiments about the landscape. In this way, the construction of the Icelandic landscape marks a collective identity, while the individual farmers and others may have completely different notions of their livelihood and relative fortune.

The original journey towards Iceland marked a discovery, not unlike Columbus's discovery of the Americas some five centuries later. For the Vikings, too, the discovery of the New World (which included their discovery of Vinland, that is America), was based on a 'knowing the unknown' (Paine 1995: 47ff.). From their oceanic practices, the Vikings 'knew' the unknown shores before they left home, and the world they 'discovered' was readily incorporated into previous understandings. The Orkney and Faeroe Islands, Iceland, Greenland, and Vinland did not have to be 'invented'; they could be 'lived' immediately in the Viking or Norse way. It was part of the Norsemen's canonical knowledge that new territories existed and could be colonized without profoundly affecting the Nordic cosmography. In a smaller way, the process was repeated when emigrants from Iceland established New Iceland in Canada (Winnipeg) in the 1870s, which has been recast as yet another *landnámssaga* (Jackson 1919). The New World is not ontologically new, just another place in the same Old World.

Another important point worth making in connection with the constant reference to the settlements, and the landscape's being redolent with memories, is the paradoxical fact that by fixing the ancestry of Icelandic society in the land, it becomes a timeless reference point. As in Australian Yolngu ontogeny (Morphy 1995: 188) place takes precedence over time in Icelandic notions of the 'Beginning'. Without actually claiming that the Icelandic landscape is 'totemic', it does articulate a distinctive comment on society, by way of a historical poetics.

The poetics of history is found more ready at hand in the place names of Iceland. In both Suðursveit and Snæfellsnes, which framed the landscapes of my fieldwork, pastness was evident in the naming practice. Some will be elucidated as we go along; at this stage it suffices to note that place names in Iceland are relatively transparent, precisely because it was populated only on the verge of historical times. There is consequently a remarkable presence of the past tied to the landscape. History in Iceland is often understood through a spatialization of time, as is known from other parts of the world (cf. Rosaldo 1980: 55). Such understandings represent active engagements in the landscape; individual biographies are formed in dialogue with particular places. On the surface of it, farmers have a more extensive relationship with the land than the fishermen, but at closer inspection this is only true if we take the actual exploitation of the soil to be primary in the social relationship to the land. This is just part of it, however. The historical poetics not only by itself extends to the sea, as we shall substantiate shortly, but the sea itself provides a particular perspective upon the land. I did not realize this until I had personally gone fishing on the North Atlantic; after the gales at sea, approaching land gained new, even heightened significance, because of the contrastive experience. If wildness reigned at sea, land was the ultimate source of safety and a manifestation of familiarity. The domesticated space ashore, thus has no less 'totemic' meaning for the fisherman gaining his livelihood from the untamed sea than it has for the farmer, tilling the soil. What differs are individual experiences and memories, but the grand historical narratives are shared.

The three farms at the site had a shared well which had allegedly been in use ever since the time of the settlements. It was called Gvendarbrunnur, 'Guðmundur's well'. The historical content was explicit, when my friend said 'you know there are many Gvendarbrunnar in Iceland, and it is told that they have been blessed by bishop Guðmundur, but I am not altogether certain that he actually blessed this one.' Truly, the name is widespread and the tradition of Guðmundur (1161–1237) wandering about blessing the sources of water is extensive and bears witness to the way in which place names reflect tradition. Meanwhile the editor of *Guðmundar saga* at the Manuscript Institute attempts not only to give an accurate transcription of the manuscripts, but also to place Guðmundur in a broad, if strict, historical narrative (Karlsson 1983). Wells of wisdom like this again point to the fact that shared images of the past do not reflect similar thoughts about it. Guðmundur's well may relieve everyone's thirst for water, but at the same time differentiate their thirst for knowledge.

Whether seen through the lens of primordial Icelandicness or lesser histories, there is one remarkable feature of the Icelandic landscape which has in all likelihood deeply marked people's sensation of its historical magnitude—the feature of visibility. Unlike, for example, the ever-impeded vision of the larger world in the dense forests of New Guinea in which the Umeda live (Gell 1995), the Icelanders live in an open space. The lines of the land are vast, and no trees impede the vision. There are mountains and valleys, ridges and canyons, of course, but one is always close to a grander view. Around the corner, the horizon expands infinitely. The vastness and the barrenness of Iceland, combined with the clarity of the air, create a sense of emptiness within which the observer has difficulties in measuring distance and height. There seems to be no scale appertaining to the Icelandic space, save for time. The ethnographer arriving from lesser places, like myself arriving from Denmark, is constantly taken aback. And this evidently plays no small role in my tracking down the paths of Icelandic history. The very exposure to this landscape marked my own impressions vividly.

Walking in the rocky landscape in Suðursveit is a journey in collective memory

F IG . 5. Appropriating the vastness of nature: the church at Ingjaldshóll.

and narrative. Once in the mountains to round up sheep I ventured far afield with the farmers and virtually every top and turn, every rock and cave had a name, and on my inquiry the names could all be explained. At Staðarfjall I was told that this had originally been Papýlisfjall, indicating that there had been *papar* (Irish monks) when the settlers first arrived. They had a church there, and when the newcomers arrived from Scandinavia they fled further into the mountains and dropped the church bell in a ravine of about 300 metres depth that was still named Klukkugil, the 'ravine of the bell'. Another version of the origin of the name was that it was owed to the troll Klukki, since trolls had been known to reside there. The ravine was impressive, and one understood that it had caught the interest of the mountaineers. Close to Staðarfjall is Helghóll, and *þar er huldufólk*, and there are 'hidden people', as I was told and for which I was referred also to an authority, Þorsteinn Jósephsson, whose work *Landið þitt*, ('Your Country', 1967) was part of the farm library and gives such detail on places. In this view of the landscape, Irish monks and trolls belong to the same register of previous inhabitants; they left their mark in legend—words being prime among Icelandic monuments.

At a more general level, 'a journey along a path can be claimed to be a paradigmatic cultural act, since it is the following in the steps inscribed by others whose steps have worn a conduit for movement which becomes the correct or "best way to go"' (Tilley 1994: 31). Paths create relationships and the more people have walked there, the greater the significance attached to the relation. The paths created by generations of people structure the experience of subsequent walkers, and the historical marks left by predecessors form the conceptual space of present-day travellers. One significant example is provided by the two-dimensionality of the terms of orientation almost all over Iceland, and certainly at my fieldsites. Chasing the stray sheep, or driving towards more distant goals from Suðursveit, invariably was conceived of as taking one of two possible directions: *suður* or *austur*, south or east. 'South' covered a varied field of directions, largely towards the south-west, but due to the rocky and crumbled nature of the land actually covering the entire compass; 'east' likewise, if generally heading towards the north-east. The point is that due to the topography, and the ancient political geography of Iceland, most locations are *en route*—towards somewhere else. The route, invariably, consists in a line connecting two or more points on a circular path, ultimately linking the four quarters of Iceland, established *c.* 965 as a judicial division. Thus, the recurrent reference to what appears to be a two-directional space is owing to the nature of the Icelandic world having of necessity been built along the coastline, and to the fact that the line thus created was punctuated by a political decision to subdivide the country into four smaller judicial units. They lasted only briefly, but they deeply marked the representations of the landscape in all quarters, where orientation generally is two-dimensional (Haugen 1957). In Suðursveit (and elsewhere), *suður* today refers to Reykjavík, capital and centre of the ancient southern quarter, or to the direction towards it; *austur* is the other way, towards Höfn in Hornafjörður, and farther (north, actually) towards Egilsstaðir, the 'capital' of the Eastlands.

In addition to the original landtakings in Iceland, the domestication of the landscape consists in this kind of appropriation through a naming practice that leaves a lasting imprint on space, as do the thousands of cairns indicating old paths in the wilderness—that is thereby incorporated in the social space.

Nature as History

Place names, when reflected upon, are immediate partners in the intertextual appropriation of nature by those people who move about in it. Nature itself is as deeply historicized as history is naturalized. Whenever nature has to be dealt with as a category, we cannot separate objective and subjective knowledge, matter and idea. They are deeply implicated in one another, once we take the human point of view. There is no way of experiencing nature from outside history, and vice versa. The material and the ideal are experienced as a unity. Therefore human beings stand neither inside nor outside nature; the social and the natural are not reflections of each other, of which first the one and then the other is assigned reality. They make up a natural unity—one world—in which there is not sufficient distance for talking about a relationship at all. The farm people's looking up the rock slope behind the farm, sometimes with binoculars, spotting the sheep and also commenting on the birds, is not an exemplar of 'man looking at nature'. Once the gaze is directed against something, the seen becomes party to the world of the beholder.

By implication, the map we may draw of any place is filled out with names that are human-made, and which therefore is so much more than an abstract means of orientation in geography; it is also an orientation in a social and moral space. On a visit to the Arhuaco Indians of Sierra Nevada in Columbia some years ago I was told in slightly sneering tones about the new tourist attraction in the mountains, *la ciudad perdida* (the lost city). It is the remains of a city from the period when the ancestral people of the Arhuacos, the Taironas, had a highly developed agriculture in the area with terraced fields and irrigation. The city had been abandoned and had become overgrown with dense vegetation, but had now been rediscovered, by the Whites that is. As one Arhuaco woman told me, 'for us the city has never been lost. It has always been there, and we have always known about it; it is part of our history. They could just as well call it "the discovered city", because the truth is that *they* have just discovered it now.' This wise woman taught me a lesson which has some bearing also on the Icelandic world, where so much history is known, even if embedded in nature, and thus somehow recedes from the view of the passing visitor.

The lost cities of the Icelandic landscape hardly amount to more than moss overgrown ruins of individual farms, originally built from stone and turf, some with wooden gables, but all of them very modest by continental European standards. There are no castles, churches, or feudal mansions standing from the Middle Ages.

Every building in the country, except one or two eighteenth-century stone buildings in Reykjavík, since 1800 the adminstrative centre of the country, was made
from nature itself, as it were, and once abandoned it was swallowed back into
nature. Timber was extremely scarce, and recycled until left for the fire. Therefore,
words are the most significant remains of the past, as we saw in the previous chapter;
they are the ones that carry the message of antiquity, as attached to little knolls,
rocks, ruins, and cairns that are often barely visible. There is no immediate appearance of antiquity or age, only a sensation of a timeless nature. The looks of history
are stubby, implying that the awareness of things past cannot readily be anchored
in either visible antiquity or conspicuous decay (cf. Lowenthal 1985: 125). This,
probably, is one reason why space takes precedence over time in the recollection of
history in Iceland.

As for the space, the map is ever-changing, not only because of the natural
changes in the landscape but also because the meaning of the words and images of
pastness is emergent and changing. What at one point in time is a 'deified' sign of
nature, may at another be simply a source of water; landscapes are always contested
(cf. Bender 1993*b*). In other words, even ecology is deeply historicized, as the
growing discourse on 'historical ecology' testifies.

When moving about the landscape, people mark it deeply; they are by their own
nature 'architectonic' (Harré 1978). In the landscape, boundaries are drawn between the cultivated and the wild, between inside and outside, and everywhere
these boundaries are more than lines on a map. They are also social markers; people
cannot be on both sides at the same time. Similarities and distinctions are created
by way of borders that are projected as natural; territories are social spaces rather
than geographical places. What gradually dawned upon me during my own
meanderings through the landscape on foot is that nobody ever walks completely
alone, not even the lonely wanderer like myself on my many excursions; by way of
words and implicit knowledge the landscape is always already populated—if sometimes by absent figures.

The landscape is something *seen*, but it cannot be seen from 'nowhere in particular'. It is seen from the point of view of particular human agents, whose perspective
is also historicized and directed by tradition. Thus for example in Iceland petrified
trolls are a part of the landscape in the shape of huge approximately 'troll-shaped'
rocks. Even though they are mostly referred to in folk tales, they have a certain
material reality in the collective scheme of things. At the time I worked in Iceland
I was told by a number of people that 'trolls are extinct', implying their one-time
reality (cf. Chapter 3). By contrast, *huldufólkið* (the hidden people) were still in
evidence, albeit mostly hidden as a matter of course. They are not totally absent
from view, however, as testified by a recent map of Reykjavík made by the town
planning department (Borgarskipulag Reykjavíkur, 1988) where the known dwelling places of *huldufólk*, *álfar* (elves), *ljósálfar* (light elves), *gnómar* (gnomes), and
dvergar (dwarfs) are marked for the planners to respect. Rural or urban, the
environment is a participatory field of many kinds of beings. Seeing nature as

human territory, our consciousness of hidden and visible features inevitably becomes part of it. We have no possibility of stepping out of it; like the petrified trolls
we have no choice but to stay in place.

One feature of the territory has a deep impact upon life, namely the feature of
movement. In the case of Iceland, we note how nature has changed, often abruptly,
in the course of history—and because of it, and with major consequences. The
domestication of the land early entailed heavy soil erosion, as did the cutting down
of the primary forest of low birch during the first century of settlements. Volcanic
eruptions, ash falls, glacier torrents, and so forth all contributed to a shrinking of
the arable land, and an increasing dependence upon the sea. But also smaller
movements have been noted, such as today's farm people noting how the amount
of birds, especially *fýll* (fulmar), have increased in the nearby mountains, with an
increased fertilization of the rock shelves as one of the consequences. These, then,
have become more attractive to the grazing sheep who often land themselves in
deep trouble when they jump down for green grass and find that they cannot get up
and away from the shelf again; in spite of the promise of food, they land *í svelti*, as
it is called, 'in hunger'. They will have to be rescued by shepherds whose binoculars
are constantly monitoring the rocks. For Þórbergur (1981: 133ff.) as well as his
relatives living at the farm today, this monitoring of the *svelti* is highly regarded: it
is exciting, important, and fundamentally challenging,

*Flest sveltin höfðu nöfn, og menn þekktu þau neðan frá bæjunum og vissu, hvort kindur kæmust
sjálfar úr þeim eða ekki. Ef þær komust ekki sjálfar, þá varð að síga eftir þeim niður í sveltið
eða klöngrast í það án sigabands. Þetta var misjafnlega erfitt. Einstaka svelti voru svo slæm, að
það var enginn vegur að komast í þau, og þá urðu kindur, sem í þau fóru, að deyja þar drottni
sínum, en sá dauðdagi var sjaldgæfur í Suðursveit.* (Þórbergur Þórðarson 1981: 134)

(Most *svelti* were named, and people [lit.: men] knew them from the farm below and knew
whether the sheep could get out of them by themselves or not. If they could not get out by
themselves, one had to be lowered down to the *svelti* for them or climb down without ropes.
This was varyingly difficult. Some *svelti* were so bad that there was no way of getting to
them, and sheep who went into them had to die in their stronghold, but such deaths were
rare in Suðursveit.)

The naming of *svelti* and the shared recollection of sheep's fates on various shelves
are still an active part of the collective memory of the local landscape, and the
noting of shifting propensities to go in *svelti* by the sheep is an example of the way
in which nature is historicized.

Another example could be the fishermen's comments that the number of seals
had vastly increased recently, with some drawback to the cod fisheries as a consequence, and certainly with some influence on their quality, if my workmates in the
fillct factory wcre right in assuming that the 'ringworms' (codworm) we had to
evince from the fillets were due to the seals' waste. This view is probably substantiated by biology, but it is also related to the general negative attitude towards seals
which are believed to consume or destroy a great deal of the potential catch (N.

Einarsson 1996: 53). At the level of immediate production we can thus see how nature's movements are translated into changing historical conditions. This also plays a role at the level of geography. Thus, at Snæfellsnes *utan* Ennis it was clear that within living memory the principal landing-place or port had had to move between three different places, with each their socio-geographical consequences.

It is in this sense that nature becomes a social agent in its own right. In the case of volcanic eruptions creating islands offshore where none was before (like Surtsey in the 1960s), or destroying other islands in whole or in part (as happened at Heimey, one of the Westman Islands, off the southern coast of Iceland, in 1973), or laying large tracts of arable land waste due to currents of lava or a downfall of ashes (as happened to the famous Þjórsárdalur in the Middle Ages), the agency of nature seems unquestionable. Yet, the point is that on some smaller or greater scale this is always the case. All over the place, nature's movements are registered as history, affecting the everyday.

The point is that whenever people are dependent on natural resources they will know all too well that these are not stable and given once for all. They are ever changing. Some changes are small and appear insignificant except, perhaps, in the long term, while others become markers of major historical shifts. Sifting through the Icelandic annals, of which there are a number right from the Middle Ages until today, provides rich evidence for the historical impact of nature. There are endless lists of natural calamities befalling the Icelanders during the centuries. Significantly, commentators upon these natural calamities do not separate them from history in general. One example is provided by the seventeenth-century natural scientist Gísli Oddsson, who wrote two treatises on Icelandic nature in 1637 and 1638, respectively (Hermansson 1917). Both deal with what he calls the *mirabilia islandiae*, the 'wonders of Iceland', but their perspectives are complementary, also from the author's own point of view.

In the first book he gives a historical documentation of natural events from 1106 to 1637. He tells of floods, volcanic eruptions, hard winters, ghosts, and the occasional appearance of certain sea monsters. In his postscript the cautious Gísli relates that he has obviously only included the information about natural events which could be viewed as truthful, and which could be backed by authoritative sources, such as his own observations, as far as the last part of the period was concerned (Hermansson 1917: 27). The book is, in other words, a veritable natural history, the truth value of which is backed by recourse to tradition and learning, as we have seen before.

The second book has a spatial frame of reference; nature is described as geography. The first chapter deals with the position of Iceland on the world map, a question with which European scientists were deeply concerned at the time. The second chapter concerns the drift ice surrounding Iceland, which was particularly remarkable in the seventeenth century due to what has sometimes been called the 'Little Ice Age'. Chapters follow on meteors, that are signs of impending catastrophe, on sea monsters, whales and fish, birds, insects, and mammals (which did not include whales, then). Clearly, geography is more than topography, it is also a set of resources. This is even clearer in his chapter on hidden valleys and their inhabitants, who, in contrast to the rest of Iceland's population at the time, live in plenty. This theme, which we have already encountered in *Grettis saga*, appears over and again in natural histories of Iceland, and today still many Icelanders would tell me how such secret valleys of abundance were part of their childhood consciousness of the landscape—if no longer entertained.

This feature of the 'hidden valleys' points to a peculiar feature of any landscape: the feature of potentiality, of background possibilities, as contrasted with foreground actualities (Hirsch 1995: 4). 'The purest form of potentiality is emptiness itself, and it is interesting that sacred sites and places are sometimes physically empty or largely uninhabited, and situated at some distance from the populations for which they hold significance' (ibid.). The valleys of plenty are empty, in the sense that they are actually unknown or absent, but they are filled out imaginatively; abundance becomes part of a virtual reality, relating both to the secret and the sacred—the literally unknowable. The vast emptiness of the Icelandic landscape is pure potentiality.

The early twentieth-century editor of the above-mentioned books on the Icelandic wonders seriously doubts their documentary value, either because the events cannot be verified or because they are simply 'fantastic' (Hermansson 1917: p. vi). He claims that for these reasons the works cannot have had any significance for the history of Iceland. This I would contest; the imagery Gísli Oddsson presents is historical, whether or not we are able to ascertain the appearance of a particular monster in Lake Lagarfljót and take it as an infallible sign of approaching evil. Positivism had not yet been invented, and even if it had, ghosts and plagues were part of seventeenth-century experience. It was upon this experience that Gísli Oddsson built his treatises, among the first ones to deal scientifically with Icelandic nature and in the process to cement the image of secret valleys, mineral riches, and a society of abundance amidst an ever-changing nature, imposing 'history' from the outside, so to speak. Nature in this sense was uncontrollable like everything else from the outside seems to have been, be it merchants or rulers, plagues or new household orders.

Today, this idea of nature as consisting of not only a given framework but also a string of events is very much part of the Icelandic idea of nature, as I have encountered it. As Gísli Pálsson has so extensively demonstrated for Iceland with particular reference to fishing, there is no opposition between the ecological and the discursive in the appropriation of nature (Pálsson 1987, 1991). Just as Collingwood in *The Idea of Nature* has argued that the natural scientific facts are just one class of 'historical facts' (Collingwood 1945: 177), so the people with whom I spoke of this in Iceland implicitly related that the facts of nature were part and parcel of Icelandic history. We can add that the opposite also holds true when we take the point of view of the social agent in Iceland as elsewhere. 'Time and space are components of action rather than containers for it' (Tilley 1994: 19). The landscape is a total social fact.

Stones that Speak

In his chronicle of Suðursveit, Þórbergur Þórðarson uses the image of the speaking stones for his reminiscences of family and local history. It is an apt image in Iceland, where rocks and stones are named monuments of bygone life. They are not equal in this respect, because they are part of a political economy of the landscape, reflecting not only people's movements but also the structure of authority.

The first among stones in Iceland is the Lögberg, the Law Rock, standing majestically at Þingvellir, the site of the ancient Althing or people's assembly. The Althing was inaugurated in 930 and was in use until 1800 at the same site. Thus for close on 900 years, the Law Rock was the centre of political attention and decision in Iceland. From it, the Lawspeaker would announce laws and verdicts that for the first couple of hundred years had to be memorized and orally transmitted. Whence the Law*speaker*. Today, Þingvellir is a site of veneration and festive celebration. It is also a camping site, giving anyone the possibility of resting in the vicinity of pastness—as I have done with my family, hoping to inhale some of the political beauty of it all. Before the camping site was inaugurated, there was (and there still is) a hotel on the spot, which was also a great place of merriment. Listen to our travel companion W. H. Auden once again, in a letter to E.M.A.: 'I've been to Thingvellir, the stock beauty spot, which is certainly very pretty, but the hotel is full of drunks every evening. A very beautiful one called Toppy asked me to ring her up when I got back' (Auden and MacNeice 1985: 108). So much for Þingvellir, in Auden's view.

Close to the place from where the Lawspeaker would announce the law are remnants of booths where the travelling *þingmenn*, representatives to the Althing, would dwell. They are modest structures of low stone walls around a hollow in the ground with room for two or three persons to sleep, over which the *þingmenn* have probably raised temporary hide-roofs. This is all there is left in terms of human-made structures and they date not from the Saga Age but mostly from the seventeenth century. By comparison with Versailles or Persepolis the scenery is austere and architecturally very modest; yet the whole place is tremendously im-pressive and symbolically loaded with Icelandicness. The Althing is a condensed symbol of the original society, of independence, and of the will to order amidst the demanding and rather chaotic nature of Iceland. A most impressive part of it is the Drekkingahýlur, the drowning pool, where adulterous women and suchlike were drowned (men were beheaded in the case of capital offence). The pool may have changed shape and position during the centuries, as the roaring stream and water-fall down the rock are said to have done, but the name and wildness of the present pool leaves nothing wanting in terms of its manifestation of the horror inherent in past punishment.

In the Nordic countries of the early Middle Ages, laws were generally connected to 'landscapes' (see e.g. Olwig 1993). These were localized socio-political units. Land and law were one, as evidenced by the proverbial entry to the earliest Nordic lawbooks, *með lögum skal land byggja, en eigi með ólögum eyða* ('with law shall the land be made inhabitable, and not with unlaw laid waste') (cf. Hastrup 1985*a*: 205ff.). Law was deeply rooted in the landscape and, conversely, the landscape was deeply politicized. There was no 'country' apart from the 'land'. The First Stone of Iceland is major evidence of this. It also provides testimony to the point made by Tilley on Swedish megaliths that their role in social reproduction resides in the authority structure able to raise them in the first place. However much the megaliths or the Law Rock seem to be born of nature, they reflect a society's view of itself, and 'personal biographies are formed through encounters with particular places in the cultural landscape and the recognition and understanding of the panoply of codes constituting their meaning' (Tilley 1993*a*: 82). In Iceland, Þingvellir is encoded with Icelandicness as embedded in landscape and history, and to which individuals may relate differently.

Locally, other rocks and mountains tower over daily life and due to their magnitude, both in terms of sheer enormity and of impressive beauty, they are almost personified and seen more as social than natural features. The 'troll'-rocks and other named and categorized stones are reminders of nature being on the edge of the social, wild yet also impinging upon social life. People are engaged in a never-ending conversation with nature in Iceland, and it is in that sense that we may say that the mountains speak, and speak back.

Lesser stones than the Law Rock may also speak of Icelandic history, and of the encounter between biography and place, such as Björnsteinn (Björn's stone) at Rif on Snæfellsnes. A local teacher first showed it to me when I had just arrived at the fishing village. It is a relatively small stone protruding from the earth some 30 metres from the seashore, and allegedly the stone where Björn *ríki* (the rich), was killed by Englishmen in the fifteenth century (1467). Then, I was told, the stone had been right on the border of the sea, and it would have been a dramatic sight with Björn standing on the top of it fighting fifteen Englishmen, the teacher said while enacting the drama himself. Afterwards, 'they cut him to goulash upon the very stone', where a small hollow still indicated where the blood had been. The tale has become more important than the stone, somehow. When I asked a young workmate of mine whether she had seen the stone, she had not; she had heard of it, though, and she knew about Björn *bóndi* (farmer), and his having been killed there. She then volunteered that 'he had a wife who said that one should not cry over his death, one should revenge it. And so she did.' Clearly impressed by this woman (Ólöf), whose name she did not know, her way of appropriating the tale was one of attributing to Ólöf the strength that she herself did not have. The male teacher stressed the rich man's fight with the Englishmen, the holding off of the foreigners, while the woman labourer emphasized the social bond within the farmer's family, and female power. The point is that the stone does not just 'speak'; its tale is transformed and interpreted according to individual perspectives, all of which are, however, part of a larger social space, built not from stones but from human relationships.

FIG. 6. Björnssteinn: a stone that speaks.

The perspectives are intertextually constructed, however 'oral' the account given to the ethnographer. In this particular case, Björn *ríki* Þorleifsson is a historically well-known figure, and one with a certain prominence also in the local lore at Snæfellsnes. In the legends about Snæfellsnes collected by Clausen (1968: 8ff.) Björn *ríki* and his slaying is recorded in some detail; his courage in facing up to the English merchants on behalf of the distant (Danish) king having imposed an unpopular toll on their commerce, with the aim of banning them from their trade, speaks to his honour. Again, historical facts blend with performative features when Clausen tells the dramatic story of the actual killing on the rock, of which now only the top is seen, and relates the cutting up of Björn's body, and the famous words of his wife: *Ekki skal gráta Björn bónda, heldur safna liði*, of which we heard a distant echo in the words of my workmate.

Other stones speak of the everyday, but even then the authority structure and the political nature of the landscape leave their trace. At Fiskbyrgi, 'fishing sheds', on Snæfellsnes we encounter that rare feature in Iceland of age-old house structures, here on the border between the lava field and the coastal area leading down to the rocky landing place known to have been here since the fourteenth century. They are situated less than one hour's walk, or about ten minutes' drive, from the village where I worked, yet few of the inhabitants had been there and some had never heard about it. I walked out there several times, in wind or snow, and each time I was moved. The structures were little rounded shapes built entirely from lava stones, erected as domes over fishermen's resting places. Possibly once covered by hides, and with small entrance holes, they would still have provided a very modest shelter against the cold and the snow—given that the fishing season was February to May.

In Hellisandur there is a general acknowledgement of the site being an age-old fishing place, but there is little specific knowledge about the various landing places and previous dwellings such as those just mentioned. It is different in the world of scholarly works where the singular remains of the fishing abodes are readily acknowledged. Thus, by an authority on 'the folkways of the sea', Lúðvík Kristjánsson, we are told that already in the fifteenth century there was a big *verstöð* at the site, remaining in use until the early nineteenth century when the landing place was more or less bankrupt and people moved. Nowhere in Iceland are there more or older remains of the past than here *undir jökli* (under the glacier) (L. Kristjánsson 1982: 47–9). Yet ten minutes' drive from the place people could not care less, and do not bother to go and see the place—even if increasingly provoked to do so by the growing tourist interest. Tradition does not always make sense in the everyday. Yet, new ears from elsewhere may draw renewed attention to the stones that speak in the wilderness about previous lives.

The Ways of Water

History not only connects to stone or other solid features of the landscape. In Iceland, as supposedly elsewhere, water is prominent. The island floats in the ocean, as it were, an ocean which both separates and connects Iceland to the rest of the world. Iceland was settled across the water, so the sea is not only a medium for present-day island life, it was also the original medium of history. As such it features as the way towards whatever Iceland has become.

It has also been the way of the waterborne plague, the Black Death, first reaching the Icelandic shores from an English merchant vessel in 1402, and upsetting society for centuries to come. It is estimated that in the years 1402 to 1404 between one-third and one-half of the population succumbed to the plague (Bjarnadóttir 1986). It was the first catastrophe of the kind to hit Iceland, and thus to unify it with the rest of the world through disease (Ladurie 1981). First-hand evidence of the Great

Plague (*plágan mikla*) is sparse while a little more contemporary information on the Later Plague (*plágan síðari*) hitting Iceland 1494–5 is available (Steffensen 1975: 320–40). There is no doubt, however, that both of these and the recurrent *drepsóttir* (killer diseases) ravaging the island intermittently for centuries, were thought to have come from overseas. In Fitjaannáll it is told of the Later Plague that *sú plága er sagt komið hafi úr bláu klæði, sem út hafi komið í Hvalfirði, (en sumir segja í Hafnarfirði við Fornubúðir)* ('The plague is said to have emerged from a blue cloth, which had come to Hvalfjörður, (but some say Hafnarfjörður at the old booths)' (*Annálar* ii: 27). The two best-known ports of Iceland are mentioned here as the passageway of the plague.

Epidemics of other kinds, notably smallpox and measles, came and went with ships from outside, adding disaster to poverty during the centuries of crisis, and together with the plagues emanating from various ports, the killer diseases were generally seen as externally imposed. The Great Plague itself left an imprint upon Icelandic memory for centuries; such was its effect that it marked the landscape by leaving fields to waste, by emptying farms, and destroying age-old patterns of family subsistence. Not only plague but also foreign merchants and rulers came across the sea, relating the waterways to the ways of domination and exploitation. Even pirates from 'Turkey' capturing slaves were all too well known on the Icelandic shores during the sixteenth and seventeenth centuries. Small wonder, then, that 'overseas' was interpreted as impending danger by the Icelanders, feeling for good reasons prey to the 'others'.

Added to this danger, relating to the sea as a waterway for others, there was the inherent uncertainty of the sea as a natural resource, exploited by the Icelanders since the earliest times. 'Icelanders belonged to the land, but their fate was largely shaped by two kinds of uncertainties relating to the sea', namely the uncertainty of the catch and the danger of the sea itself (Pálsson 1991: 97). Fishing implies the hunting of an invisible prey, yet the 'blind date' with the sea was no random venture, but relied upon the fishermen's *eftirtekt* (attentiveness) to natural signs (ibid. 88ff.). The apppearance of particular birds, for instance, were indicators of the arrival of fish. There was thought to be a special bond between different species, such as the seal and the black-beaked gull; the former provided the latter with food, such as the intestines of fish while the latter would give cries of warning when the seal slept ashore. To seal hunters this bond was simply a matter of experience (Kristjánsson 1980: 449). The exploitation of the natural resources of the sea was not simply the individual hunter negotiating the uncertainties; fishing was deeply embedded in a social system of collective wisdom, including also an elaborate folk meteorology. This wisdom was solidly based on local experience.

Today the fisheries are deeply embedded in a global capitalist economy which has meant a shift in the folk model of fishing from the household producer engaged in a struggle against the elements, to the model of the modern skipper competing with others (Pálsson 1991: 103ff.). Still, hunches and dreams play an important part in decision-making (Pálsson and Durrenberger 1982); the sea becomes memorized

in the subconscious, as it were. The official record of catches is everywhere comple-
mented by a local recollection of relative *fiskni* (fishiness), or the ability to get fish.
Such recollections play an important part in the mapping of the sea, and the
evaluation of particular fishing places. At another level an inversion between humans and fish seems to have occurred, in that before the fish were seen as the
active ones, those responsible for human life, while today with the industrial
(over-)fishing, humans become responsible for the maintenance of fish (Pálsson
1990). The main point is, however, that in the social history of the Icelanders the
sea has always been both prey and partner.

Landing places would shift, according to catches and according to the changing
nature of the coast itself. Thus, Magnússon (1990) has witten the history of two
communities on the southern coast, demonstrating the fluctuations within a relatively short period of time. On a lesser scale a similar history could be written for
almost any possible landing place around the island. Thus, on seeing one of my
friends cleaning and folding up nets after having caught trout in the *lón* (lagoon)
below the farmsite, we engaged in one of many conversations about local lore. He
told me that 'before', people had also gone fishing at sea from this place, between
March and June, and 'that was the best time of the year'. The landing had become
too difficult and the catch too meagre to run the risk. Also, with roads to other
places, however much dirt roads they still were, and with trucks at every farmstead,
subsistence had become far less localized during the last generation. The memories
of offshore fishing at the place would soon lose interest.

Even bigger landing places would survive only marginally in local tradition, such
as a local *verstöð*, some 15 kilometres to the east of the farm, of which there were
frásagnir (tellings). I was told that the place had evolved into a veritable *kauptún*
(field of trade), to where northlanders would come every year across the glaciers.
They were ill looked at and generally thought to be ungodly. Allegedly, the place
fell into disuse in 1573 ('but we do not know for sure') when fifty-four fishermen
had drowned in one day ('maybe owing to whales'). In popular legend, the
rauðkembingar (red giant whales) were often blamed for misfortune of this scale,
because 'they were the most wicked ones'. It is an often noted feature of the
Icelandic discourse that whales are mentioned for their intrusion into human
history (Hastrup 1990*a*: 269; N. Einarsson 1996).

The uncertainties of the sea were not only tamed in discourse, they were also
framed in particular notions of territoriality. In the earlier days, access to sea
resources was largely governed by landownership; rights in fish and strandings
were derivative of rights in land, at least as far as fishing within the limit was
concerned. The idea of *almenningar* (commons) was an idea of limited practical
application; it only applied beyond the *netlög* (net area). Even if this gave everyone
access to the sea at some distance from the coast, at the time of limited technologies
it still prevented common people from much gathering and hunting on the beaches.
Today, the territoriality is not only internationally regulated, there are also internal
regulations relating to individual skippers acquiring customary rights to particular

areas. Fishing has also become restricted in time; the *róðratími* (rowing time) was restricted for individual communities, allegedly with a view to equality (Pálsson 1982: 7). The ten cod-wars fought between Iceland and other 'nations' since the fifteenth century (Björn Þorsteinsson 1976) are by no means the only signs of sea fishing being deeply territorialized, as a consequence of the sea itself being socialized. As argued by Gísli Pálsson, the territoriality of fishing is not so much an attempt to control the appropriation of the resources as it is a wish to regulate the conduct of the hunters (Pálsson 1982: 11).

At sea the territory is represented in various ways; there is the depiction by coordinates—providing a map—and the presentation of *fiskimið* (fishing banks), which provided the fishermen with an itinerary. Maps and itineraries relate differently to human movement; maps serve as charts of an overall orientation, while the itinerary gives a sense of direction. The latter, therefore, is much closer to social experience than the former, and surfaces in the the poetics of history in a quite literal manner. Such poetics may direct fishing practices. An example of a verse attaching to a particular *fiskimið* off Snæfellsnes Lúðublettur ('Halibut-spot'), will give a sense of this:

> *Þott langt sé fram á Lúðublett,*
> *legið hefur þar bátur:*
> *Bjarnarfoss í Búðaklett*
> *breiðan Gölt í Látur*
> (Kristjánsson 1983: 197)

(Although there is a long way to Lúðublettur, boats have been lying there: [where one sees] Bjarnarfoss [a waterfall] in Búðaklettur [a rock], and the large Gölt [a sea-rock] at Látur.)

Even though the translation is somewhat hampered by the fact that we do not know the place names, the general point comes through, I believe: The cognitive map of the sea is supplemented or even constructed by features of land. In that way, land is as much context of sea as vice versa.

If the sea virtually frames the image of island life, other waters colour the picture from within. The spring torrents will stop people from moving about, as described by Þórbergur Þórðarson in his short story 'Vatnadagurinn mikli' ('The Day of the Great Water'), which is an account of a real event. Unlike the great rivers of ancient civilizations, such as the Nile or the Tigris, the torrents of Iceland have rarely been conceptualized as arteries of fecundity. In modern times they provide energy for the welfare state, thus supplementing that which steams out of the volcanic interior.

The hot or thermal springs have reached mythical proportions in some narratives, but they have also had well-established historical use, such as the still visible bath of Iceland's greatest medieval chronicler Snorri Sturluson, to which Auden alluded. Visiting the bath, a slightly 'edited' natural pothole with stones to sit upon in the warm water, one receives the impression of stones and waters speaking together of the past in a multivocal narrative of nature and history. Today, the thermal springs warm up the city of Reykjavík—giving a distinct smell of sulphur to every bath one takes, and blackening the silverware—and supply Icelanders with vegetables from distant hothouses. If not sources of fecundity, they are at least sources of much-needed heat in the subartic.

By contrast, one might claim that the area swept by the tide is an area of richness from water. The tide, relating the very concept of time (*tíð*) to the rising sea, meant changing access to the resources of the beach, and they were plenty. In medieval registers as well as in living memory, *fjörunytjar* (the usufruct of the beach) are extensively described. Seaweed, strandings, driftwood, shellfish, and hosts of other material and edible items were important supplements to a marginal economy (see Kristiánsson 1980 for elaborate detail). Since I am not here primarily concerned with the economic assets of the beach but its position in the practical construction of space in Iceland, I shall just suggest from my own reading and direct experience that the beach constitutes a liminal space between land and sea, between private and common property. The ways of water make this space as well as others and thus deeply affect the lives of people who cannot be separated from their environment.

The Times of Ice

The colder form of water, ice, also deeply marks life in Iceland, symbolically and practically. The ice defines time and history in many subtle ways. First of all, Iceland owes it name to the occurrence of drift ice in the fjords, as experienced by one of the first would-be settlers, Flóki Vilgerðarson. Drift ice is a well-known phenomenon on the north coast of Iceland, and quite apart from the inconvenience caused to the traffic at sea, especially at earlier times when boats were smaller, the drift ice has also caused peril ashore, when starving polar bears landed and went foraging in nearby farms. Although a rare event, bear hunts were a popular theme in tales of manliness and strength.

Ice, however, is not only a phenomenon of the sea, it is also a remarkable feature of the landscape in Iceland, where glaciers take up a large proportion of the land. As it happened, both of my fieldsites outside Reykjavík were hovered over by glaciers, Breiðamerkurjökull (being part of the huge Vatnajökull) and Snæfellsjökull, re-spectively, covering vast volcanic structures. Rain and fog, snow or sleet would often block the view, but the glaciers were more impressive when the view was clear. From their position in local conversation I gathered that, in both cases, the *jökull* was not an inanimate thing, it was a friend or, sometimes, an enemy. Which-ever, it was a living force, and one which potentially spoke back to people.

As Þórbergur Þórðarson (1981: 196-7) has it about the place under Breiðamerkurjökull:

Many hundred years ago, when there was more sunshine in Iceland and the weather was better and the country ready for feasting, when elves played in the woods and fairies drifted

FIG. 7. *Undir jökli*: the port of Hellisandur at Ríf.

in the air, then there was a big farm under the mountain [this farm was called Fjall, and apparently it was a major place with a prominent history to its name. However, things deteriorated, and people had to fight poverty, famine, and all kinds of trouble, and] the weather was destroyed, the sunshine became less, the downpour more, the cold harder, the woods disappeared and the elves fled into the rocks, and the fairies disappeared from the air, and Breiðamerkurjökull woke from its long sleep and began to slide down on the plain between Fjall í Öræfa and Fell í Suðursveit, longer and longer, towards south, east and west, until Fjall fell waste and the glacier covered the mountain and everything around it, and nothing was left which reminded one about people living there, except a coldish place name.

The movement of the glacier will be noticable in a long-term perspective, but at any point in time, its threat 'to wake' and to contest people's claims to space, makes the *jökull* an icy companion.

This is no less true for Snæfellsjökull. As the writer of the yearbook of Snæfellsnes from 1982 has it about Neshreppur *utan* Ennis, the commune outside the mountain Enni: *Yfir henni gnæfa Snæfellsjökull og Ennisfjall, bústaðir hinna góðu og illu vætta* (H. Kristjánsson 1982: 125) ('above her tower Snæfellsjökull and Ennisfjall, dwelling-places of good and bad landspirits'). In Ennisfjall itself lives a troll woman and the *jökull* is permeated by living forces, as we shall see later. The point is that while few people in 1982 (and later) 'believe' in trolls and landspirits, such beings still provide a vocabulary for speaking about the animate nature of mountains and rocks. People are engaged in a never-ending conversation with nature in Iceland, and it is in that sense that we may say that the mountains speak, and speak back.

At Snæfellsnes, this 'life' of the glacier is conspicuous also in another way of speaking. I was repeatedly told by people that the glacier evaporated *straumar* (streams) of good or bad influence, much like the *vættir* (landspirits) referred to above would be good or bad. Individual life histories were thus deeply affected by this extremely beautiful, cone-shaped glacier that was nowhere to be hidden from in the area. In the literature, the entire area which ever since the fourteenth century has been a prominent fishing site as was mentioned above, is known as *undir jökli* (under the glacier), as we have seen before (in Chapter 2). According to one of my interlocutors at the place, the area *undir jökli* is 'that place in Iceland to which most *þjóðsögur og sagnir*' (folktales and legends), are attached. Whether statistically verifiable or not, the lore of the glacier and its people is pre-eminent in local discourse—as it is in the landscape.

The glaciers are 'historical' in another sense as well. Vatnajökull, of which Breiðamerkurjökull is one of the tongues reaching down towards the sea, had always been what separated the northern farmers from the rich sea resources of the southern coast, and they had known how to traverse it, if sometimes in great peril and with fatal losses, to be able to take part in the season's fishing (February–May). Many stories were still told about people who had been lost in the ice; some had fallen into clefts and had been heard singing hymns from within the ice for decades after. With such stories we are in the field of reminiscing the (im)possible, rather than in the field of actual memories. Yet even such stories, of which there were plenty, were prefaced with the old verbal entry into historical space: *svo er sagt* (it is told thus). The stories need no other authority; once 'said', they have their own. After this, the question of whether the Icelanders 'believe' in these stories is as nonsensical as the question of 'how wide is a Dreaming track?' within the discourse of the Dreaming (Layton 1995: 213).

One recurrent if unpredictable feature of the glaciers which has marked the Icelandic landscape as well as individual histories is that represented by the glacier bursts, *jökulhlaup*, where water that has been stemmed up beneath the glaciers bursts out and ravages vast areas of land. In 1996 the world was able to follow a glacier burst on the south-eastern coast of Iceland on television, and thus to get an impression of the frightening power inherent in the glaciers should they choose to wake up. In nearby Suðursveit, glacier bursts would be an all too well-known phenomenon; as we know, it is neighbour to a *jökull* of prominence. In the sandy area close to 'my' farm where some of the sheep strayed were the remains of an old mighty farm, Fell, which had been inhabited since *landnámsöld* and until 100 years ago, when it had been devastated by a *jökulhlaup*. Allegedly, it had been one of the biggest farms in the country, and it had housed *sýslumenn*, local officials, but even they did not have the power to subvert nature. They were powerful in other respects, and I was told that, when in 1720 a popular *sýslumaður* was to be buried at the church of Kálfafellsstaður and was carried eastwards towards the church, the bells began to ring all by themselves, 'just like they did in the case of Jón Arason, Hólabiskup'. This is no insignificant comparison, since Jón Arason was the bishop of the North who resisted the Reformation for fifteen years until he was finally beheaded in 1550. In confrontation with the *jökull*, however, even the inhabitants of Fell came out losers.

My local chronicler knew that Fell had been a *höfuðból* (main farm), and had had four *hjáleigur*, four cottages attached, but all had been destroyed in 1869 when the Breiðamerkurjökull had burst, 'devastating some of the most fertile *tún* land in the country'. With 'the fall of Fell, destruction was complete', as Þórbergur Þórðarson (1981: 197) continues his saga of the awakening of Breiðamerkurjökull. An attempt to move the farm had been unsuccessful, because the fields were beyond redemption. I was told that a similar fate had befallen the farm Sléttaleiti (due to avalanches of stone rather than ice), at some other 'unknown' time. People had also attempted to move it, but had to abandon the new site again shortly after. Farms were built from stone and turf until well into this century, and leaving a farm meant giving it up to nature again, with just small traces left in the landscape that would set it apart from the landscape in general. One of my friends at the farm had attempted to rebuild the smithy of Sléttaleiti, mostly for the fun of it, but admitted to having 'cheated' a bit with the roof, where he had felt forced to use timber beneath the turf: 'I do not know how the old people made it; it must have been witchcraft' (*galdraverk*), he suggested half-jokingly.

The time of the ice, then, is both the beginning of Icelandic history, and the long-term history of the slow withdrawal or progress of any single glacier, measuring small changes in average temperature over generations and leaving their mark upon the conception of the landscape, as well as the immediate results: giving or taking of possible grazing lands, blocking or opening passages between farms and friends, and bursting in upon people's lives in torrents.

Liminal Spaces

In the discussion of the Icelandic landscape there seems to be a degree of ambiguity adhering to most features, a double nature, as it were, of familiarity or companionship on the one hand and unpredictablity and adversity on the other. This general feature is all the more conspicuous at certain places that are marginal spaces by common consent.

An early example of this is provided by the saeters. As elsewhere in the Nordic countries, saeters were a prominent feature of the economy from the time of the settlements in the late Viking Age until sometime in the sixteenth or seventeenth centuries. Prominence seems to have been matched by real economic importance, and the abandonment of the practice of transhumance begs explanation.

The Norse settlers in Iceland brought with them a pattern of transhumance from their distant Scandinavian homelands where it was absolutely vital to the farming economy, at least in the northern parts where arable lands were scarce. In the medieval Icelandic lawbook, *Grágás*, saeters are simply referred to, not explained. They are referred to by a specific Icelandic term, however, namely *sel*. In spite of the Nordic origin, the Icelandic notion was not derived from the Old Norse word in use elsewhere, *sætr*. The basic meaning of *sel* was a small hut, used for temporary dwelling, and only later did it come to include the pasture around the hut; there is a distinct Icelandic centre of gravity here, being the dwelling place rather than the grazing. As such it was private property. It was part of the farm and bought and sold with it, if the boundaries were often open to dispute—as were potentially all boundaries in the rugged landscape. In laws and verdicts from the Middle Ages and onwards, the *sel* is rigorously distinguished from the commons, *almenningar*, and the shared pastures of a local community, *afréttir*. It was explicitly forbidden to establish a *sel* within the *afréttir*.

Although saeters were privately owned, the farmers could not use them at their own discretion. Rules about proper usage were given and upheld by the community. The law stated that livestock had to be brought to the saeter 'when two months of summer had passed', and to be returned to the home fields before the month of *tvímánuður* (*Jónsbók* 1904: 172–3). This makes a total of about two months (mid-June to mid-August), but doubts can be raised about the actual duration of the period. The ancient month name, *selmánuður* (the month of the saeter) may indicate that saeter time was actually less than two months.

In the early literature, it is related how sometimes the entire household would move to the saeter during the summer, and in some sagas the saeter was explicitly contrasted to the winter dwellings (e.g. *Laxdœla saga*, ch. 35). Generally, it was only a proportion of the household that went to the saeter in order to keep up with the tasks of herding and milking. In addition to the Icelandic lawbook—and I am thinking here particularly of *Jónsbók* which framed Icelandic society from 1281 until the nineteenth century—a distinct 'household law' stipulated the rights and duties of the farmhands. This *Búalög* was first composed in the early fifteenth century, after which it was reproduced and amended successively until the eighteenth century. In the earlier versions it is presupposed that three women had to be at the *sel* in addition to the housekeeper, *matselja*, in order to milk eighty sheep and fifteen cows (*Búalög* 1915–33: 22, 34, 61). In the seventeenth century the work rate seems to have gone up; now three maids were supposed to manage ninety sheep and fifteen cows besides *heimavinna* (housework) and *heyvinna* (hay-work) (ibid. 191).

There are at least two significant implications of this. First, the practice of transhumance was a feature of large-scale farming; it is doubtful that more than a few landowners would own this amount of cattle in the seventeenth century. Second, the idea that *sel* women were supposed to do 'housework' besides saeter work indicates that the *sel* was within easy walking distance from the farm. This pattern is generally confirmed in the material (Lárusson 1944: 99–101). A large number of place names with the suffix -*sel* are found all over Iceland, suggesting a widespread practice, yet with the breaking up of the larger farms, the saeters seem to have generally become fewer during the centuries dealt with by the *Búalög* and have been taken over by the emergent class of *hjáleigur* (cotters). In the eighteenth century the saeters had completely vanished, much to the regret of Enlightenment observers who generally lamented the poor state of the Icelandic economy (Eggers 1786: 120; Ólafsson 1772: 178; Olavius 1780: 247–8). In 1754 the Danish king issued a decree explicitly reinforcing traditional rule about saeters in the old law (*Lovsamling for Island* III: 191). It seems that by then, all that was left of the rational economic practice was the word. The *selmánuður*, which is still listed as a month name in 1780 by a British observer (von Troil 1780: 117–18), had become an empty category, just like the saeter had become an empty space in the landscape. In spite of all attempts to refill the category, saeters never reappeared. Economic progress had to wait for the upswing in fishing in the last part of the nineteenth century.

If we accept that 'economy is rather a function of the society than a structure' (Sahlins 1974: 76), we shall have to seek the reason for the abandonment of what seems to have been an absolutely rational economic practice in the wider social order. Generally, the Icelandic economy declined during the centuries from 1400 to 1800, and the pressure on the infields (*tún*) increased considerably. There was no shortage of land, but there was often a perceived shortage of labour; this perception was related to the fact that by self-ascription the Icelanders saw themselves as farmers. For *society* to survive, farming had to be continued at all costs; it was part of the very definition of Icelandic society. Everybody had to associate with a farm; the *bú* (household) was at the centre of the universe, reflecting an age-old cosmological model of concentric circles, the inner circle being the controlled, human, space, the outer circle being the uncontrolled and largely non-human space, as we saw above (in Chapter 1). No one could live outside this structure; wandering day-labourers were condemned as criminals along with vagrants. With increasing poverty, it seems that the people with power to make a choice concentrated their energy in the centre of the social universe, the *bú*, on behalf of society.

The *sel* was ambiguously classified. It was part of the farm, yet outside the fence. It was both social and wild. It also contained another anomaly related to the gendered universe. Generally, women were closely associated with the farmstead, while men were associated with both the social and the uncontrolled wild (see next chapter). Like the sheep wandering in the mountain commons, the men regularly crossed the boundary between the social and the wild. At the *sel*, however, the distinctions were blurred; here the women found themselves in a marginal space of the social. The ambiguity of the *sel* meant that it was associated with danger, in the classical sense of Mary Douglas (1966). When the dairymaids left the well-bounded social space of the *bú* and its infields, they were under no small threat from the wilderness, mainly in the shape of *huldumenn* ('men of the hidden people'). These men were known to seduce shepherdesses at the saeter, and children often resulted. This is a common theme of folklore and legend, and also (earlier) of lawsuits seeking to establish human paternity in spite of mothers insisting on their children having been sired by *huldumenn*.

The point I want to make here is that due to the ambiguous classification of the *sel*, the women were called home when society started to disintegrate. While the economy would have improved, Icelandic society could not afford to have its women roaming in the liminal space between the inside and the outside. Characteristically, the saeters disappeared when the boundary was already crumbling. When almost every bit of life takes place in a marginal space, there is no need to go for it elsewhere.

While this problem now seems to have resolved itself, there is still a sense of liminality attached to certain places or areas of the Icelandic landscape, as I have experienced in the company of Icelandic farmers and fishermen. They are rocks or caves known to have been inhabited by *huldufólk* or outliers, and to some extent the notion of liminality itself attaches to the sea, being on the margins of the inner circle.

When the economic base changed from farming to fishing in the last century, the image of Icelandicness remained centred around the land practices—at least by people in power or in structural dominance. Fishing was not only regarded as a less noble mode of livelihood, the fishing communities were also presented as 'devoid of culture', and a source of degeneration, alienation, and deficient language (Pálsson and Helgason 1996: 61). I would argue that this is related to a view of the sea as (literally) marginal to the island community; this probably is by no means an exclusively Icelandic feature.

The sense of marginality is still echoed by people living in the fishing villages. While certainly at the centre of their own history, and in earning both wages and respect for their hard labour, the fishers' community is also marked by an ambiguity—at least when they enter the contact zone and have to see themselves through the eye of 'another'. In this zone, one of my women workmates at the fillet factory would stress over and again how she had grown up 'in the country' (*í sveit*) and how that was to be generally preferred. No less significant, during conversations over coffee at the factory, the ideological asymmetry between the rural areas and the fishing villages would often be alluded to in subtle ways. I shall relate a brief example.

Christmas was approaching and we discussed eating preferences for the festive meal. Some would have grouse, and this made the aforementioned *sveita*-woman embark on a lengthy talk about different species of birds in Iceland and their habits and ways of life, their relative edibility, and ways of catching them. After some time another woman listening remarked to me: 'She is so wise (*fróð*)' and she repeated it. The first speaker immediately answered that 'it is because I grew up *í sveit*, and not in such Ólafsvíkurmylla [lit.: mill or grind of Ólafsvík, the neighbouring and slightly bigger village] as you.' It was not unkindly put, it was a statement of fact, and it was accepted by both parties. In the grinding mill of the fisheries, wisdom was in strained circumstances. In no man's land on the shores of the sea it is difficult to truly *know*. This, of course, is not a statement of fact, nor is it a key to understanding a fixed semantics of space. It is a clue to particular modes of orientating within the practised space of the Icelanders.

The inside–outside dichtomy, which may be seen as relating to the discourse of farming and fishing, is possibly better seen as a tertiary construct. There is no absolute boundary between what is native and integral to the community and what is foreign and alien to it. There is only a marking of something marginal, a liminal zone. Within it, the community stages itself in an extensive repertory of social and discursive performances, and without it people are largely on their own—temporarily irrelevant. Yet in between is a transitional space, an ambivalent staging ground of the contradictions within the community itself. Such a space is found in the fishing villages, epitomized in the *verbúð*, where the repressed feeling of a class-society and the opposition between the sexes etc., are staged. The marginal space of Icelandic society is not totally unlike the margins of the renaissance city of London, defined as the London Liberties and stretching up to one mile from London on the south of the river (and containing both theatres and leper hospitals) (cf. Mullaney 1992). It is a space in which the community dramatically set its own conditions at stake.

Clues in Place

In this chapter I have implicitly argued, following Yates (1992) and Radley (1990) among others, that remembering is something which takes place in a world of solid rock and other *things*, as well as in the world of *words* dealt with in the previous chapter. When particular objects or sites are selected for preservation and awe, they turn into monuments of a shared past, which thenceforth govern the politics of remembering. The First Stone or the ruin of a local farm freeze the images and link remembering to ideology. By making monuments, or by turning particular objects into museum pieces, in short by commemoration, other interpretations of the past are silenced (cf. Middleton and Edwards 1990: 8). This leads on to the other side of remembering, namely forgetting. Like other areas of attention, memories are selective; something is forgotten, either by being silenced or repressed, or just by being deemed irrelevant. What makes the collective remembering so important is that it gives a shared sense to individual feelings—much in the way that tradition produces a set of shared images, which one can then attach to and interpret individually.

The act of recalling, whether in spatial or some other social practice, constructs the past. Yet it cannot be constructed in just any way for it to make 'sense' in this profound way; it must be grounded (cf. Shotter 1990: 133). In the Icelandic world, this grounding of the collective remembering must be taken very literally. Remembering Iceland, and thus to perceive it in the first place, is not to retrieve its history in accurate detail, but to move in the space of momentous pastness, along ancestral paths, and in a shared sensorial field of tactility, sound, smell, taste, and vision. Within this space the individual is constantly reminded of the collectivity; the past is not a 'foreign country' in this sense (cf. Lowenthal 1985). Quite the contrary: the landscape is a well-known history.

What I am arguing here is that history is not just a trace left in the landscape, or an external sign left by the ancestors for people to memorize and read. To comprehend the Icelandic space, we should not aim at 'decoding' the landscape. There is no code to be deciphered, no signs to read. There are clues to be understood, clues that connect people into a unified orientation in a space, where the social and the natural world are not seen as constituting a duality but a whole, of which people cannot have an external perspective.

Thus, memory and landscape, history and nature, or even more generally, time and space are mutually implicated in this vision of the world. In Iceland, stones speak, ice grinds, and the water plays a symphony which the attuned ear may understand—not as a representation of history—but as a composition of practices, past, present, and future. This composition is what unites individual sensations of Icelandicness, and it is achieved not by way of reference but by way of resonance across time and space and between people. The landscape is a major vehicle of collective memory, that part of historical consciousness that is brought to bear on contemporary life by literally grounding it in space.

6

Community and Honour

From the preceding discussion of space and spatial practices in Iceland we shall now turn towards the people practising. The attempt is to understand how people, and here Icelanders, contribute to history through their daily practices, and how the world becomes embodied in them, on the assumption that there is a relation of mutual embeddedness between people and their world. It is the dynamics of this mutuality within the local community which is in focus in the present chapter.

The traditional notion of society as a bounded, empirical unit has lost momentum in a world of flux, and we have come to realize that society is not solely the context of actions, but also the result of actions—and certainly not a *thing* (Barth 1992: 31). This will be the implicit viewpoint taken in this chapter, where whatever unity we may perceive is at any time corrigible from individual action; society is but a temporary, institutional, form of historical events analytically inferred. Such historical events, or individual actions, are always without precedent, yet within a particular space they are deemed either 'mad'—that is incomprehensible—or (most often) sensible. The social space within which one can make such a judgement is where one is 'at home'. This, it will be understood, is totally different from suggesting that people live in cultures that give a priori meaning to, or inherently determine, social action.

Judgements, like meanings, are passing. This may be seen as the rationale of another recent suggestion about society as a network, globally forming a network of networks (Hannerz 1992). While this notion has some merit in stressing the likelihood of cumulative change and enduring diversity by pointing to the chain-like, multi-directional flows across the world, I still think it falls short of the most critical feature of societies worldwide—empirically and analytically—their localizing propensity, their 'homeliness'. As Hannerz says, in dealing with the global 'ecumene' in network terms 'we abstain from an *a priori* privileging of local social relationships over those operating over greater distances' (Hannerz 1992: 51). It is precisely this privilege I want to maintain, since from the point of view of the experiencing social agent, the local relationships of necessity take precedence in the feel for community, quite irrespective of how many internationally produced items or television shows people are exposed to (cf. Olwig and Hastrup 1996).

What I am saying is that even if there are global or transnational flows of goods and images, for the individual they are experienced locally; even modernity hits the world in diverse ways (Sahlins 1993). In the present chapter, I want to investigate how social life in Iceland has been framed by and frames a community which is glued together by distinct values, relating to notions of locality, production, kinship, and gender. What seems to be pre-eminent is a shared (more or less implicit) notion of honour or respectability, which is closely linked to both gender and work. As I said before, the idea of a 'shared notion' does not entail that all Icelanders think alike; it only means that there is a standard by which individuals may measure the relative sensibility of particular actions. Social action is interwoven with local discourses on the social. The sense of community starts in common sense.

Since the social and the discursive cannot easily be disentangled, any discussion of social groups and categories will contain an element of social stereotyping. Social stereotypes are the effects of metonymical reasoning, implying that a subcategory has a socially accepted status as representing the category as a whole (cf. Lakoff 1987: 79ff.). Social stereotypes are the result of what Rosch has called the prototype effect (Rosch 1978); in another phrasing, they represent semantic densities within particular identity categories relating to frequency and materiality (cf. Ardener 1982, 1989a).

Before embarking on a tour of selected groups and social boundaries in Iceland it is worth staying a little longer with this notion of stereotypes. In the social sciences they have generally been dealt with as erroneous representations, usually made by outsiders (to the category), and with little bearing on anything except the prejudice of the observer. As recently argued by Maryon McDonald (1993), this is only part of the truth. Surely, people do say nasty things about minorities which may have no bearing on reality, and nobody is free of prejudice. Yet, in anthropology we cannot afford to relegate stereotypes to accidental matters of classification since they have real effects, which cannot be explained solely by reference to historical malice. I agree with McDonald that even Said's well-known work, on orientalism, which purports to dissolve the alienating discourse upon the East, has played an active role in the moral construction of two central categories—'Europe' and 'the West'—which seem to have become metaphors of blame (McDonald 1993: 222). It seems that most attempts to overcome dualisms tend to freeze them even more.

Stereotypes are always to some degree embodied; like an adjective qualifying the noun, the stereotype qualifies action for the social agent. Being an 'outlaw' is being banned, but it is also a licence to certain actions, as we saw for Grettir the Strong. The position occupied in the social space, be it central or marginal to the categorial system, deeply marks one's actions. If it does not determine these actions in any absolute sense, it frames the perception of them, both by the agent and by others. There is no way totally to free oneself from categorical adjectives within one's home society.

What is 'home' and what is not is a matter not only of ability to act sensibly and to engage in meaningful conversation, but also of scale. Scale cannot be taken for granted, analytically. This is one reason why the discussion of the local and the global is twisted from the outset; these parameters are measures of scale and they cannot be real or conceptual opposites (Strathern 1995). The life worlds of people are in a very fundamental way centred; the body is the locus of agency and the zero point of perception (Hastrup 1995*a*: 77ff.). 'The human body is at once highly local, in the sense of being a basic part of any interactive "here", whether face-to-face or mediated, and at the same time equally general in so far as values, orientations and features of the social field are inscribed in the body and realized through it'—whence 'corporeal field' (Hanks 1996: 1). Emphasizing the centrality of the body means taking the agent's point of view in the study of 'locality' and its significance in different parts of the world. It also means taking a practical perspective upon the world, not a detached semantic one. The corporeal fields extend differently in different areas of social organization, production, and values. In what follows we shall investigate the extensions of Icelandic fields of orientation, questioning scale along with practice. We should not worry about reducing the corporeal practices to words, because in 'general terms language is a means of both grounding practice in the body and suspending the link to bodies' (ibid. 1). This is why local notions of the interactive space can and must be appealed to in the course of our investigation, without, thereby, reducing it to categories and prisons of 'culture'.

Locality

Taking the notion of corporeal field as an effective point of departure into Icelandic society means starting at home in the narrow sense of the word. In Icelandic, 'home' is a space of intimate life, of domesticity, as opposed to a more or less unfamiliar space of wilderness; it will be recalled how Þórbergur Þórðarson perceived everything but Hali as 'outlandish'. Home is the household in which one lives, and most often it is centred around a nuclear family, although in earlier times, and in many farms today, the family often consists of three generations, and possibly lateral relatives as well. However constructed, 'home' is a unit of production and consumption, a space of shared interests—in principle. Occasionally, there are conflicts of interest between men and women within the household, even of more or less separate economic lives (Skaptadóttir 1996) or domestic violence (Gurdin 1996). Yet, generally, at the core of individual life worlds is one's home, *heimili*. Homes are areas of domestic pride, and as such they are to some extent 'public' domains. Unlike the Mediterranean area, for instance, where public life unfolds outside the homes, in Iceland homes are where people meet and communicate. There are practically no village squares or outdoor bars, where one can expose oneself to the gaze of others and thereby see oneself, even though café life seems to be growing in Reykjavík. There is only the home in which to display oneself 'as another', as I had ample opportunity to experience during my eighteen months of Icelandic becoming.

After Sunday service in *sveit*, I was invited along with the rest of the churchgoers, where I had gone with my friends from the farm, to the vicar's home. Service takes place in the local church about once a month (less frequently in summer), and it is as much a social as a religious occasion. I had been told that 'in the old days' people always went to the vicar's home after mass, but that this had become rarer. However, in 'our' *sveit* it was still done and it was much appreciated. Even my socialist woman friend and others, who could not be called 'believers' in any traditional sense of the word, went for the occasion. For me it opened new doors of understanding. We were lavishly provided with 'buttered bread' (with spreads of various kinds), cakes, biscuits, and the thinnest possible pancakes with whipped cream (thinness being highly praised and cream always being a token of wealth), and I realized the truth of what I had been told about the traditional 'coffees'. 'We' automatically dispersed into three groups: the older men, the older women, and the younger women. Young men were conspicuously absent. It was this absence, explained by themselves by a lack of religious faith, which made me realize why the young women came. It was not faith, either, which made *them* leave home on selected Sundays, it was sociability. If the older segment of the population possibly were believers, the younger women with whom I debated the matter explicitly went for the being together. They enjoyed getting out of their homes, which were generally far apart, dressing up a bit, and talking, quite apart from the singing in church. In short, the church provided a place where one could practise the communal space.

The vicar's home was a 'fine' one, according to my woman friend. The coffee (including the food) was lavish, and the rooms were beautifully equipped. There were embroideries, crystal vases, and silver chandeliers, etc. all over the place. On the armchairs, the elbow-rests were covered in real lace, which also adorned the framed photos of children and grandchildren on display. In short, the home testified to the industry and skill of the vicar's wife. She was the homemaker, as the women generally are. My companion on the occasion, then aged 30, told me with some sadness how she always felt her own home to be empty and even drab when she returned from the vicar's coffee. Having visited scores of Icelandic homes, I can see how the theme of the nice home is played out in various ways, and even if academics in Reykjavík generally display less lace and silver, there is still some pride taken in the 'home-made'—whatever it is. It could be private beer-brewing, as I had the pleasure of experiencing at a friend's house.

The main point here is that the home is the centre of private as well as public life. Its interior testifies mainly to the woman's success, but its size and exterior is closely linked to the man's economic abilities. In earlier times, this notion of 'home' was closely associated with the farming household, the *bú*, which was a notion that embraced both the place and the domestic community. Today, the notion of *heimili* has replaced it, and 'home' has been cut loose from a particular way of living and become acknowledged as the innermost sphere of relevance in anybody's corporeal field.

Homes are located in a wider circle of significance, however. Generally, the main distinction in Iceland as elsewhere is between rural and urban areas. In contrast to many other places in the world, what counts as urban in Iceland is of a small scale, the capital of Reykjavík having some 125,000 inhabitants, while the second town, Akureyri, numbers only *c*. 20,000. From there, towns or villages go down to only a couple of hundreds, yet they are still set apart from the rural areas. The fishing villages or 'sea places' (*sjávarpláss*), or just 'places' (*pláss*) in daily talk, are by definition set apart from the countryside, where farms are scattered and rarely cluster into anything like villages, although obviously distances between them vary. In the fishing village where I worked, there were about 600 people, forming *c*.100 households in as many individual houses, while the neighbouring village, with which there was some local competition, numbered some 1,200 people. Urbanity is thus very much a matter of local scale and definition, and in Iceland it seems that until recently, town or village life was negatively defined by its *not* being farm life. This is one reason why it seems appropriate to start by a discussion of the space of farming life.

This space is linguistically embedded in the notion of *sveit*. It could be translated as 'tract', but it also has a definite aura of 'countryside' as opposed to 'town', of 'tradition' as opposed to 'modernity'. It is where one's roots are, and often where one's parents or grandparents live. It has a sense of local community, with the emphasis on both the local and the communal. I recall a vivid conversation that centred around this in the home of one of the families in the fishing village that had particularly welcomed me and to whom I have returned several times over the years. There was a small party going on, and one of the villagers asked me if I had not found life in *sveit* very *einfaldur* (monotonous or drab). He thereby implicitly invoked the notion of *fásinni*, referring to a place where there is a lack of events and usually alleged about the rural communities. I denied the allegation and said that quite to the contrary I had found life in the countryside very rich and fascinating; there was always something to talk about and much knowledge behind the talking. My hostess was very glad to hear that, and entered into the conversation by stating that it was a general mistake to believe that life in *sveit* was tedious and uninventive; if one knew it, it proved to be everything but monotonous. There were always lots of people, who cared about each other, who knew and helped each other, in contrast to city life where nobody cared. In *sveit*, she said, 'it is impossible to keep outside'. She had grown up in *sveit*, and confirmed my feeling of life in *sveit* celebrated as the warm 'inside' of Icelandic society, at least when seen from there or from the well of tradition. Unlike the hinterlands of many other countries, in Iceland the *sveit* seems to be collectively celebrated as the source of proper Icelandicness. This, of course, is mainly so when seen from the core of the dominant discourse upon Icelandicness, from where 'proper' Icelandic speaking is also defined.

Iceland is more than farming and *sveit*, it is certainly also fishing and village life. And, contrary to what I was led to expect (having started my fieldwork in Reykjavík and in *sveit*), there was also a sense of pride attached to the village. In my attempt to internalize that part of life in Iceland, I took residence in a fishermen's barrack (*verbúð*), as I related above (in Chapter 2), and started to work in the fish industry. My workmates and other aquaintances in the village talked a lot about life here and there, and made their cases by way of explicit contrast. The contrast was not only made between *sveit* and *sjávarpláss*, but also between different 'places'. This came home to me when one evening I sat drinking with my barrack mates, three young fishermen, who in many ways really were prototypical of the category, in the sense discussed above. We talked—or rather they did most of the talking while I did the listening—about the neighbours, about other people in the village, and about life in general. They also talked a lot about the place as such. They were quite fond of it, and from their extensive experience of various fishing ports of Iceland they concluded that Hellisandur was one of the best 'places' (*pláss*) in Iceland. It was certainly far superior to neighbouring Ólafsvík, which might be twice the size (1,200 inhabitants), but which had a much poorer *félagsheimili* (communal house), a much older school, and much uglier houses. Furthermore, Ólafsvík was completely 'filled out'; there was no more space to build on or live in, while in Hellisandur there was plenty of room for expansion. One of the guys had previous experience of Eyrarbakki and Stokkseyri on the south coast. These were truly miserable places: only old houses, almost all of them in a state of disintegration. No new houses at all. Deplorable places, indeed.

The 'places' are centres of sentiment, as are the rural tracts. From the brief rendition of my house mates' opinion of the local place, we can see how part of their sentiment was anchored in the relative newness of its houses and other buildings. They had to be modern. While I would not claim this to be the view taken by other Icelanders, such as for instance the inhabitants of Stokkseyri, I still think that it is significant that for the wage-workers in the fisheries 'the good life' has less to do with tradition than with material progress and economic expansion. The quality of the locality, the *pláss*, is both the medium through which this is expressed and its measure.

Within the fishing villages there are several social domains centring around the port, the freezing-plant (*frýstihúsið*), and the homes, of course. The domains are gendered; the port (and beyond, the sea) is primarily a male domain while the freezing-plant is predominantly thought of as female. In practice both sexes work in the freezing-plant, yet there is a clear sexual segregation in work and in recreative areas, quite apart from the distinction in terms of relative wages (see also Skaptadóttir 1996: 97). One certainly has the feeling of working in an almost all-female domain when one works in filleting and packing the endless amounts of fish during the season; the men are evident only as a backdrop, delivering the fish, and steering the heat and freezing system, etc. One of the notable differences is related to the fact that the women have to go home and provide lunch for their children during school breaks; even though they are for the most part employed in wage work in the fishing industry it is either part time, or at least it involves a shifting of place during the day, between the plant and the home. The men are under no such compulsion, it appears.

Across other boundaries related to the practice of place, there was a notable distinction by class and social status in general; in 'my' village, this was partly expressed in terms of membership (or non-membership) of the Lions Club. Once a party was going on in the Lions Club, and I had naïvely assumed that it was an open party, since it seemed to be much talked about also at the factory. On closer enquiry among my mates, it was only for a select group of people: it was only for Lions-*fólkið*, not 'us'. The explicit distinction between 'them' and 'us' was an acknowledgement of an inherent distinction by social status. Theoretically, one could work oneself 'up' to Lions status, like the wealthy skippers, but labourers and ordinary fishers were a far cry from that. The groups were marked by their occasional gatherings, for parties or cultural events, rather than by a distinct code of conduct, dress, or general aspiration. Aspirations were shared, but success was differentiated, and it found an outlet in the creation of a community of the success-ful, which would manifest itself only occasionally, 'occasion' here being defined both in terms of time and place. As far as I could tell, this community was also a prime element in the local church life, including the fine church choir, which again served as a social marker rather than a religious one.

A black hole in the village was found in the *verbúð*; a 'black hole' because it appeared in many ways to be the negation of the social space, empty of pride and grace, yet full of energy and the will to survive. Part of this energy was fuelled into extravagant drinking (on nights off, only; not during workdays), partying, and a certain amount of sexual licence. All of this was very much part of my own experience from living in the *verbúð*, as I have related in some detail elsewhere (1985*b*). Through my position in the village I also became subject to a certain amount of sexual aggression by half-drunken youngsters who apparently felt li-censed for all kinds of pleasure at this place. This was not particularly pleasant for me, of course, but I realized that I had become victim of 'the force of locality', as it were. I was classified, and had classified myself by my coming in from nowhere and asking for work, as a migrant woman labourer and, furthermore, by my choice of dwelling place I had unknowingly announced myself a 'free woman'. This recollec-tion of mine, which served to make an analyical point, made Níels Einarsson jump to his pen, claiming that my story was

comparable to the experience of a stranger spending a few nights in a brothel and then coming to the conclusion that the people of the town are immoral. Hastrup is generalizing about the culture in a fishing village (and Icelanders' conceptual world) from her fieldwork in a subculture of migrant workers. This subculture has a code of values and conduct which is in no way typical for Icelanders; extreme machismo behaviour (sexual and physical aggressiveness), extraordinary consumption of alcohol and very little respect for the existing norms of the hegemonic culture. The young people who work as migrant-workers (some of my friends have done so) often have not finished compulsory schooling, feel rejected by society and are disillusioned and sceptical towards society at large. Very often these people have hostile attitudes towards academics or intellectual [*sic*] which probably does not help the ethnographer in her fieldwork. (Einarsson 1990: 74)

I actually was not asking for 'help' in fieldwork. I knew perfectly well, as most fieldworkers do, that I was an intruder, and I never expected people to engage in *my* knowledge project. I did try to enter their experiential space, however, by taking up their kind of work and by locating myself among them—on the assumption that this is what 'helps' fieldwork. There, I experienced and have recounted just what Einarsson states as a fact, that there is a society of anger and rejection centred around the *verbúð*, only I would never have phrased it as a socio-psychological feature. My talk of categories relates to images and stereotypes, and it was part of my experience, and of the story to which Einarsson refers, that the conduct was linked to the locality, not to the people, who next day or elsewhere were neither violent nor drunk.

After one more paragraph questioning a couple of my suggestions concerning matters of gender and sexual conduct on the basis of personal experience in the field, Einarsson adds that 'I do not know if Hastrup knows, but it may also be of importance that Danish women are commonly considered somewhat more promiscuous in sexual matters than for example Icelandic woman. Thus the fact that she was a Dane may have been equally as important her being a woman' (Einarsson 1990: 75). Although intended as a rebuke, this claim actually confirms the points I tried to make about the *verbúð* epitomizing the anti-social, and about a shift in modes of conduct between generally accepted social propriety and revolt. When Einarsson states as a matter of fact that the migrant workers have a special opportunity and encouragement to take off the straitjacket of following established rules, I cannot but agree; and all I hear is an echo of what I myself wrote about the fishing villages:

Violence, drinking and low moral standards are conceptually associated with these places. The migrant labourers' barrack epitomizes it all, and not without merit. The *verbúð* is a condensed symbol of the non-social, as opposed to the farmstead which is the social writ small and concretized . . . A consequence of this position of the *verbúð* is that women who take up residence there have 'gone wild', as it were. In the barrack they are not so much an object of seduction for the 'hidden people' as they are appropriate game for the local hunters—or fishermen . . . Women may object to this status as individuals, but as a category out of place they cannot escape the position. (Hastrup 1985*b*: 61)

According to Einarsson, my own experience of aggression was partly due to the fact that I was Danish; here is then another spatial category, if not imprisoning the individual Dane, then at least accounting for the aggression against her. Einarsson is right in pointing out, of course, that not all persons living in the fishing villages see themselves as either 'outside' or 'wild'. When I claim that violence and drinking are *associated* with life in the fishing villages, this may be a view from outside, but then again, this is based in an understanding of the inside point of view. I believe that when it comes down to it, Einarsson and I share a good deal of the understanding of the *verbúð*, even if we have opposed gender experiences within (and without) it. The general problem that we are all facing when analysing social stereotypes is that outside representations feed back into insider's views, as we have seen in the idea that people of the fishing communities speak bad Icelandic. The licence to machismo behaviour in the barracks of the back of Iceland is another example. The point of relating it here is not to claim it as 'typical for Icelanders' (as implied by Níels Einarsson in his parable of the brothel), but to offer it as a token of the 'force of locality' in the Icelandic world.

Beyond the home, and beyond the *sveit* or *pláss* to which one belongs, there are other local divisions, such as the *hreppur*. This is a formal, administrative unit, where the sense of belonging is less emotionally charged. The *hreppur* is often mentioned as one's place of origin or dwelling, and it embraces both *sveitir* and *pláss*. The unit was already introduced in the Commonwealth period where it coincided with the function of the local *þing*, popular assemblies, from where local issues were either decided or transferred to the *alþingi*, the national assembly (Björnsson 1972: 47ff.). When, in 1281 a new constitution was adopted following the introduction of Norwegian reign in 1262, the *löghreppar* (law-communes) were confirmed and rules for their scope and their functioning were stipulated. Among the more important functions were the keeping of population registers, the distribution of paupers among the farmers, the collection of tithes, keeping up with the requirements of the land, and the securing of collective rights in the *afréttir*, the communal grazing lands. Thus, the *hreppur* was clearly an administrative unit with wide significance for the daily economic practices of the the Icelanders. Today, the old names persist, as do some of the functions, but as a practised place it relates to the ordinary lives of people in a hierarchical fashion, as it were.

If one does not practise the *hreppur* as such, it may still frame a series of communal practices in addition to those just related, such as activities related to sport and schools. Both function as areas of collective attention, and have integrative functions in a local life, which in spite of its local feel may be rather dispersed over wide stretches of land. As implied in the brief exposition of my visit to the vicar's home, the church and its services may also function as a kind of local social centre.

Beyond and above all of these localities and centres of local sentiments is the Icelandic nation. The nation is the overarching local community of Icelanders— and it is deeply rooted in both tradition and landscape. We shall return to that at a later stage. Here we shall consider other practices within the social space of the Icelanders, practices that are significant parameters in the orchestration of community and honour.

Productive Practices

In the month of May, the lambing season takes place in Iceland. During one of my revisits to the farm where I had originally worked, I experienced some weeks of intense activity, night and day. Everyone was up and about most of the time, and

FIG. 8. Checking the earmark: grandmother and grandson.

a system of communication between the houses was set up, so that any one could call for help from the sheep house if alone and a difficult delivery occurred. Apparently, today an increasing number of ewes give birth to two or even three lambs at a time (where previously one was the norm) and close observation is demanded—quite apart from the ordinary feeding of the sheep who are all of them indoors for the season (in this case the stock was of $c.300$ ewes)—bottle-feeding the tiniest lambs and those rejected by their mothers, removing and skinning the stillborn, and putting 'third' triplets up for adoption with ewes who had had only one or a stillborn. Successful adoption is achieved by washing the adoptee in soap and subsequently 'dressing' it in the skin of a stillborn lamb to cheat the mothers who have milk to spare.

Meanwhile, the local talk on sheep and lambs is as intense as are the practical matters. The attention is acute; from the grandparents and downwards every family member owns his or her own sheep. The main stock is collectively owned by the joint family, but every individual, including the young children of the family and long-since moved grown-up siblings of the parental generation, have some sheep as their private property. They dispose individually of the earnings when their sheep are sold for slaughter and wool. The children take great pride in their own small stock, and watch the lambing with acute awareness—not only of the lambs' frailty or beauty but also their economic value. One day the 8-year-old was violently jealous because his own *mórauða* (referring to the colour: maroon or brown) gave birth to only one lamb, while his 10-year-old brother's ordinary white one had three. The non-white, and especially the spotted ones, are most highly praised, not only for their beauty and distinction but also for the greater economic value of their wool or skin. Pride and general sense of value came together in the remark of relief made by the 10-year-old at the advent of a spotted lamb, only the second of the lot, *loksins kom annað flekkótt* (finally another spotted one came). Beauty and economic value are not easily disentangled, and everybody has his or her own interest in the lambs.

Sheep are earmarked almost immediately after birth, and are given an individual name. Each individual sheep-owner has his or her individual earmark: in the one ear the mark of the farm, in the other the mark of the individual owner. With three generations and many children in each of them, the earmarks at currency at the farm were numerous. Some of them were inauspicious; it seemed that in each generation one or two of the (individual) earmarks turned out to be ill-fated for the sheep; they would disappear, die, or prove barren. Some of them are so 'bad' that they are simply given up, and the lambs born to the owner of the inauspicious mark are marked by the mother's or somebody else's mark. Or, and that was a solution offered to me by one of the young farmers, a deliberate 'mistake' is made in marking, so that no one really recognizes the mark, except, of course, that the mistake is publicly known. I witnessed it happen one day when I was the one helping to hold the lambs for marking. The point was to cheat 'fate' into letting the lamb live. Experience told everybody that it worked. There was no explanation for the ill-fate of some marks save for noting a parallel: 'it is just as some families are always unlucky, and it is not possible to tell why', I was told. The actual marking of the lambs was painful to the animals but also very revealing for the anthropologist: the symbolic marking of the livestock with 'culture' and ownership was much more than that. It was also domestication turned into fate, or earmarking into 'luck' or 'un-luck' as the case might be.

Once during the days of intense labour in the lambing season, an 11-year-old boy of the joint family sat lazily in a wheelbarrow while everybody else was running to and fro, and his grandmother quietly urged him to work with the others: *svona sitjur enginn í sauðburðinum* ('nobody sits like that during the lambing'). She thereby struck one of the recurrent themes in the orchestration of Icelandic society: the value of hard work, to which we shall return below. For her, and for others, the lambing season was the most wonderful time of the year, *because* it was the busiest and the most important for next year's income.

Adding to the pleasure of hard work at this season, the same grandmother said, is the advent of the *kría*, the tern. It arrives and nests on the coastal strips of land at this time, and from it one will later collect the eggs—under heavy attack from the angry birds. The sound of the tern in the air at this time gives people great pleasure, I was told. The wild geese also arrive and land on the shores of the *sveit*, exhausted and hungry from their long trip across the sea. They are shot (and eaten) partly out of the habit of hunting and collecting whatever is edible, and partly because they are a nuisance on the *tún*, where they damage the emerging grass. In general, the domestic production includes extensive gathering of 'natural' resources: eggs, plants, birds, berries, etc. Earlier, a lot of seaweed was also collected and used for firewood, porridge, and for the making of 'salt' from the ashes. As I recall from my own expeditions to the lower slopes of the hills beyond the farm, this kind of gathering is very much a women's venture. On the appointed day, and in reasonable weather, we—who were women and young children (and a visiting anthropologist) who could be spared even during the autumn peak of sheep collection—formed a little troupe of berry collectors, and made quite a day out of it, bringing sandwiches and coffee. The grandmother headed the expedition, and her patient teaching the children (and me) about nature's gifts and the value of everything belongs to my fondest memories. This woman, who had given birth to nine children and worked hard to make ends meet long before roads connected the place to the rest of the island, and before electricity brought light to the long winter evenings, once taught me the most important lesson: 'the day is long enough to comprise everything.' No one could tell what was going to happen, but days were patient; let come what may, and let people make the most of it.

Productive practices in Iceland are closely tied to time or season. Of course, with cows and foxes (which have been introduced recently for fur production) each day seems more or less the same, and this is precisely why it is not very highly regarded. But with the hayfields, the sheep, and the fishing, seasons are all important and the year is structured around them; cows, etc., are subsidiary to these basic activities. Each period poses its own demands on people, and on labour. Earlier, during the centuries of decline, started by the Black Death in the early fifteenth century, there was a felt shortage of labourers to keep up with the requirements of the land. This was the reason why the fishermen were 'called home' to the fields from the emerging villages in the first place, and why the government of the *hreppur* had to see to it that each year the seasonal fisheries were brought to a halt before the hay harvest. Generally, the feeling of shortage possibly was less 'real' than imagined, as I have argued elsewhere (Hastrup 1990*a*), and a consequence of the construction of the Icelandic identity as based on farming. This did not make the problem less pertinent, of course.

Today the pendulum swings the other way; there is an incipient unemployment, if still on a modest scale by comparison with other European countries. Interestingly, an explanation for this is now constructed in terms that are a kind of echo of my own analytically based proposition about earlier times. According to one of my interlocutors, the emerging unemployment is 'home made'. 'It need not be there at all, because there is enough work in fishing, but the Icelanders do not want to work in the fishing; they are too snobbish,' he claimed, 'even though fishing is the basis of the Icelandic economy.' Whether generally true or not, my friend struck a theme of strong discursive power, the theme of cultural devaluation of the fishing, while also acknowledging its paramount economic importance. Its value is, so to speak, suspended between culture and practice.

Such statements generally refer only to the male labourers because of the still strong feeling that women are primarily housewives. This again is an ideological construction, because the fact is that most women now work outside their homes even if on a part-time basis that allows for child-caring as well. The women are, and always were, a source of cheap labour in the incipient class society emerging in the wake of large-scale fishing (Magnússon 1990: 121; Skaptadóttir 1996: 91). Many households have been temporarily split up during the fishing season ever since fishing became a specialized profession.

Farming and fishing never occupied equal positions in the discourse on Icelandicness. They represent two different strategies for relating to nature, as we have seen. Farming is based on the logic of harvest, while fishing is based on the logic of hunting. Farming involves long-term considerations and requires a certain social organization of access to and transfer of land. Fishing, of the earlier small-scale kind, invokes a more immediate relationship between people and prey. The result is that 'nature' is portrayed differently in the discourse: farming involves a domestication of nature, while fishing takes place in untamed nature—even if landscapes and seascapes are equally 'culturalized' by the very discourse that differentiates them. The domestication of nature, that is cultivation, implies an integration of farming and the social system. The relationship is one of inclusion. Conversely, there is a relationship of externalization between the social system and the environment of fishing. I have argued at length about this structure for the earlier periods (Hastrup 1990*a*), and suffice it to repeat here that at the centre of the social universe in Iceland was the *bú*, the household, around which the rest of society was discursively organized.

The *bú* was conceptually equated with permanence, stability, and social order; apart from 'household' it also denoted the permanent dwelling of the *búandi*, or *bóndi* (farmer), whose defining feature was one of having settled down on a particular plot of land. In contrast to the stable *bú*, the seasonal fishing populations at the landing places lived in temporary abodes, or *búðir*. The *búð* represented non-permanence, instability, and, as a consequence, social disorder. Even today, social disorder is still epitomized in the *verbúð*, as we have seen.

It is important to note that individual Icelanders could, and still can, move between the categories; farmers could become fishermen during the season, and women who would normally not be expected to participate in the precarious hunting at sea, could actually be seen to do so. In spite of this individual transgression, there was and is a clear symbolic boundary between land and sea and the related activities of production. It is vividly demonstrated by Finnur Magnússon, who tells the story of a farmer-fisherman who was despised and ridiculed by his tenants as their landlord, but who earned their respect whenever he acted as their foreman on boat. 'The man who is at one moment seen as embodiment of everything evil is transformed to a hero and model figure the minute he puts on seamen's clothes' (Magnússon 1990: 106). Evidently, the clothes are not the issue, but they cover the practical skills for which the landlord is recognized.

Today the productive practices include a number of industrial enterprises, primarily related to fishing, as we have already discussed, but also chemical plants, transforming some of the natural wonders into cool cash. A parallel kind of transformation takes place in the growing tourist enterprise, marketing the unspoiled landscape for consumption. The service sector is also expanding, and there is a notable academic community. In such quarters, there is less concern with productive seasons and local weather, yet there still seems to be a collective awareness of the old productive practices, and in the traditions connected to the seasons, as testified by the revival of *þorrablót*, discussed in a previous chapter.

Gendered Worlds

By way of introduction to the gendered world of the Icelanders I shall relate an experience from my fieldwork, where I once had the pleasure of attending a ram exhibition. As we saw above, social life in *sveit* is carried forward by a sense of community, relating both to the fact of extensive kinship links within the locale and to shared work experiences, such as the rounding up of sheep from the mountain commons, a task in which all and sundry must participate.

The rounding up of sheep in the *sveit*, where I worked, was followed by a kind of ritual event, expressing the community in another way. It was the annual ram exhibition, which took place in the biggest sheep house (*fjárhús*) in the area, and which attracted almost all the adult male population of the *sveit*. It soon occurred to me that not only was the ram exhibition (*hrúta-sýning*) a feast celebrating the successful recovery of sheep from the mountain pastures, it was also a feast celebrating maleness.

The air had been loaded with excitement for several days, and it had been endlessly discussed among the men of the farm which rams to select for the exhibition, and guesses were made as to who else in the *sveit* were going to exhibit which rams. With some fifty farms, each exhibiting one to three rams out of their much larger stock, there were a good many possibilities, but as far as I could tell the men were relatively familiar with the stocks of the entire *sveit*. Rams, of course,

FIG. 9. Collecting the sheep is a communal task.

were far fewer than ewes, but the men's knowledge was still very impressive. On the Sunday morning of the exhibition, the young farmer, who was responsible for the cows, and I, who was temporarily engaged as a milkmaid, rushed out to do the morning milking with a speed and at a time which contrasted sharply with the ordinary leisurely pace of this (downgraded) activity. The man could not wait to join his brother and father who had already left with the chosen rams of their joint farm. No sooner had we finished milking, and he had seen me and the cows off to the pasture, than he drove away to the exhibition.

If I hoped for an invitation, I was disappointed. The event was 'male', and it never occurred to the men to invite me. Eventually, my young woman friend at the farm who sensed my strong wish to go, and who perfectly understood my professional interests, offered to drive me there. In this rugged landscape and with huge distances between the farms there was no way of just walking to the place. I arrived there, then, dutifully equipped with notebook and camera—the material expressions of the anthropologist's second thoughts and third eye. There were no women in the sheep house, but plenty of men and a mass of huge rams. A committee went about (hand-)measuring the size and weight of the rams' testicles, and noting their general impression of the animals in terms of size and beauty. The air was loaded with sex, and I realized that the event was literally and metaphorically a competition of sexual potency. The men competed in the name of their rams, but the

FIG. 10. The ram exhibition: a men's world.

meta-message was perfectly clear. Sexual jokes and very personal remarks were incessant; the bursts of laughter followed by side glances at me conveyed an implicit question of whether I understood what was going on.

I did; and I left early out of embarassment on my own part. A few other women had peeped in briefly during the time, and no one prevented them or me from staying. But a sense of being completely out of place finally made even the anthropologist evade. There was no question of being or feeling like an honorary male, as has been claimed for female ethnographers elsewhere. As everybody knew, I was an anthropologist and *fjósakóna* (stable woman) at the well-known farm, and my femaleness was conspicuous even though I was dressed much like the men, in jeans, wind-breaker, and rubber boots.

This was not the only instance where transgression of the gender boundary was felt embarrassing rather than honorific. This is in part an implication of doing fieldwork in a society much like one's own, where gender markers are also much alike, and not easily subsumed under other and more conspicuous differences, such as skin colour. However, my own explicit gender marking produced some revelatory instances as far as the local images of gender were concerned, images that, again, were just images, not prisons of categorial prescription of behaviour for individuals.

I shall relate another instance, which in a previous publication has given rise to a kind of criticism, which, I believe, is misguided by an allegation of precisely such categorial ascription to my suggestion of gender stereotypes. Once, I had been allowed to join an expedition up into the mountains to collect some of the last stray sheep. When seeing me off together with the rest of the party, the senior farmer expressed a degree of disbelief and almost sadness when he exclaimed: *ætlarðu fara í klettarna?* ('do you intend to go up the mountains?'). Upon my affirmative answer he asked whether other women (*kvenfólk*) were going. If not out of place in any absolute sense, it was certainly unexpected. His son, who was leading our (lesser) expedition, confirmed that on the longer expeditions there had never been women in the party. Off we went, and well underway, the men talked endlessly about sheep, and about last year's problems of getting them all down before winter, and they named a number of distinct *svelti* (hunger shelves), the nature of which will be recalled from Chapter 5. The hardships were real, yet the discourse was extremely joyful; I clearly got a sense of the emotional attachment to the sheep, and via them to the land. Every autumn, the men go to the mountains eight to ten times for sheep, I was told, and it is *mjög skemmtilegt* (very joyful). Significantly, once in the mountains, my leader not only pointed out to me all possible features of the landscape and of the magnificent view towards the sea, he also stressed the way expeditions had remained unchanged, and he referred me to the description given by Þórbergur Þórðarson in his chronicle of Suðursveit. The sense of spatial and productive practices is intertextually constructed to a remarkable degree within this highly literate community, literate not only in the sense that people read and know a lot of *sögur* (stories), but that stories *matter*.

On our way towards the mountains, I experienced a shift in my own categorial affiliation, when at the first really difficult slope, I became embraced by the category of 'youngsters', instead of women. When the ropes that were going to aid the novices up were in place, the man called out, 'come on *krakkar*' (youngsters or guys). It seemed that in some way we had reached a point beyond which women could not proceed, and which made the men classify me with the young and inexperienced boys, who also had to be taught. Women could, and did, participate as persons, but they were designified with respect to gender. Another way of phrasing it would be to say that the gender difference was immaterial, once in the mountains.

In a critique of this, Níels Einarsson suggests that I am overinterpreting and picking out utterances to suit my theoretical bias (Einarsson 1990: 73). While he is absolutely right in his claim that the word *krakkar* is very often used, and need have nothing to do with gender, he is wrong in assuming that I just picked the word to suit my aims. To me, it is not a matter of the word—and this of course may be seen as a theoretical bias, if not the one that my critic suggests. What is at issue here is, first, something which I *experienced* (not simply *heard*) as a key, not to a fixed set of semantic properties relating to individuals or categories, but to the practical orientation in the social space of the Icelanders. In this space, women were never alienated from society and relegated to 'nature' as elsewhere, as I have argued (1985*b*), and as Pálsson confirms (1995: 63). His claim that they were not, as a consequence, excluded from the men's wild, is surely correct in that they did go up the slopes and did participate in the fishing, as I myself did, and a fact that I may have downplayed earlier in my concern with the categories of male and female. My preliminary analysis of these categories opened with the phrase: 'It will be understood that the opposition itself is the origin of the qualities attributed to these categories; they are certainly not rooted in the individual characteristics of men and women' (Hastrup 1985*a*: 49). Yet, because statistically there were always fewer women than men in the mountains and in the fishing, the material experience tended to favour social stereotypes that associated women with the farmstead, and men with both farm and wilderness, including the sea. It was this *material*, even statistical, content of the stereotype that I experienced. The word was just a signal, a way of summarizing what to me was a long-term, intense experience of the materiality of gender categories in misty mountains and elsewhere in Iceland. It is one of those episodes that conveys a feeling of 'sudden' understanding, a highly personal experience or 'event' that nevertheless makes a distinctive difference to their comprehension. Who can objectively assess, let alone prove, that this or that event is significant, apart from the participants in the event. It is part of our professional predicament that personal experience must count as evidence. I fully applaud Pálsson's suggestion (1995: 11) that fieldwork can be seen as as a progression from the margin of the discursive community towards the centre. This is exactly what I felt, and what I hoped to convey. For me one step was taken in the mountains.

Níels Einarsson's lesson to me is ethnographically informative, however. He repudiates my conclusion that women are out of place in 'the wild', and maintains that I am 'jumping to conclusions, perceiving and interpreting as her theory tells her' (Einarsson 1990: 73). And he continues: 'The reason for saying this is not only because I know of my own experience that untrained people should not participate in such strenuous activity, but also because she herself admits that she could not keep up with the men (or her stronger female friend). The old man was warning her that she would be a burden to the group, which turned out to be the case . . . It is common knowledge that these gatherings can turn out to be dangerous and therefore not suited to novices' (ibid. 73). Inadvertently, he confirms my view that the 'unpractised' had better remain at home; as it happens, statistically this category consists mainly of women, who are likely therefore to abstain from the 'danger' of the mountains (symbolic as well as real).

Interestingly, when I came back to the *sveit* the following spring to take part in the lambing season I was greeted heartily by an older man of a neighbouring farm, who recalled with a smile our joint trip in the rocky mountains. He recounted the tour and my participation with no little pleasure; it had left an imprint in his memory, which was far from a memory of my having been a burden. Rather, it contained pride and joy in having been able to show me the landscape and to demonstrate his own agility in moving about on the slopes. Also, they knew when to leave me behind; at a certain stage I was left waiting on a small platform, holding an ewe, while the men continued upwards and inwards for more. I had asked to join on the assumption that the expedition members knew what had to be done, and when. Surely, Einarsson cannot mean that they did not, nor can he overlook the fact that even the most experienced mountaineer was once a novice, and that the passing on of the skill—in practice—was part of the adult men's obligation.

In my discussion of male and female I had suggested that women were not expected to take part in the actual fishing, and I was repeatedly told by friends in the village that this was one reason why no vessel would take me out. My ethnographic ambition included such a venture, and, as told before, I succeeded. Einarsson is sceptical about my conclusion that women are to some degree at least out of place at sea, and he rightly points out that there is historical evidence of fisherwomen in Iceland, referring to the work of Pálsson (1987) in particular. He then adds 'I have personally witnessed a woman breaking new ground in working as a small-scale fisherman. There was no talk referring to anomalies, boundary-crossings or inappropriateness. Quite the contrary, this was looked upon by the fishermen I talked to as an interesting initiative rather than a case for disapprovement' (Einarsson 1990: 75). Einarsson's witnessing a woman *breaking new ground* gives full support to my suggestion that women are or were not normally expected to go fishing for themselves; there is little to disagree about, yet criticism continues, and gets an even stronger tinge in Pálsson's work, when he says on the same issue:

Again, Hastrup seems to overinterpret what she sees and hears in the field. In this case, much ethnographic and historical evidence runs counter to her claims. It is true that, during the period of peasant production, Icelanders defined membership of the category 'inside' in terms of both the territory of the farmstead and the social relations of the domestic economy. Hastrup rightly points out that in peasant society female muteness did not exist, in the sense that women no less than men participated in the discourse of the 'inside', the realm of culture as opposed to nature. But while women were insiders in the peasant economy, in Hastrup's sense, they were definitely not excluded from fishing in the realm of the 'outside'. Even though women's roles and responsibilities within the household, particularly in relation to pregnancy, breast-feeding and caring for young children, often ensured that they stayed home while the men went fishing, there were no clear-cut categorical barriers preventing them from joining fishing crews on their expeditions into the wild. Indeed, both men and women participated in fishing. (Pálsson 1995: 63–4)

It strikes me that what is at stake here is less a factual disagreement than a terminological one (cf. Hastrup 1990e). I for one cannot but agree with Pálsson on this matter which he himself has dealt with so eloquently. But even his disclaimer of the gender barrier confirms it *in practice*: there are limits to women's participation. And the point I am trying to make here, I hope more clearly than before, is that categories are not mental prisons, they are 'summaries' of practice. The differentiation of gender in practice is also a division of labour, and it is this experience which in turn produces the stereotypes that we all have to live with, whether we belong to the statistical 'centre' (majority) of the category or to the 'margin' (minority). There are centres of gravity in all identity labels: some are 'better' examples than others when it comes to spelling out the prototype. Since anthropologists cannot spell out individual behaviour in detail or write metrical history, we have to some degree to rely upon 'summaries' of the kind that I have just described. We then arrive at statements like this one:

There is a clear division of labor between women and men and [*sic*] Icelandic fishing communities. This division has become more clearly defined with industrialization. . . . One can almost say that there are men's work places and women's work places. Going to the sea is a man's job, except for a few women who go as cooks. (Skaptadóttir 1996: 97)

Whether the distinction between men and women is described as a division of labour or as a matter of categories, in both cases it is the material, or experiential reality that provides the evidence, not any abstract theory.

The above polemical sketch serves the ethnographic purpose of saying something about the gendered world of Iceland. However, the reason for citing details of the debate is also my wish to clarify my view upon categories and concepts not as entities or prisons, but as summaries of practice that are firmly grounded in material or bodily experience, including my own. My general point is that gender plays a significant role in the productive and spatial practices of Icelanders, even today when most people have become 'urbanites' in the sense discussed before.

Muted Characters

In spite of terminological discrepancies, there seems to be a general agreement that since the Middle Ages, women have been firmly defined as within 'the social' by their being at the centre of the farming households. Conversely, the men seem to have been living also partly in 'the wild', as it were, by their rounding up sheep in the mountains and their being engaged in *veiðar*, that is hunting and fishing. From the sagas an image of strong and independent women has been transmitted, and on the whole one has an impression of Icelandic women being firm characters, perfectly capable of speaking for themselves. It may therefore seem paradoxical that the women's movement is so vital in Iceland, where several waves have taken place this century (Kristmundsdóttir 1989). In 1982 a women's list (*kvennaframboðið*) was established and has since then had great success in the general elections. In 1975 all Icelandic women took part in a one-day strike, and this was repeated in 1985, when even the woman President refused to sign bills.

Why would such manifestations be felt necessary if women have their rightful social influence in perfect complementarity with the men? The answer, of course, is that even if the image of the independent women is tenacious, historical reality has changed rapidly, and women have faced new problems. A largely urban, or at least non-rural, condition has replaced the old peasant life for most of the people. Only about 10 per cent of the population now live on farms while about 75 per cent did so at the turn of the century. Thus, within the range of living memory, farm life has become limited to the few. And even on the farms, the women are now perfectly conscious of their services often being just 'taken for granted'. It is as if some of them at least feel confined by the very domesticity that is the hallmark of farming life; while not muted within the social, some seem to want access also to the wild. Individually, they may go in the mountains or set up a fishing enterprise, they may even be elected to the Althing; but by their being defined partly by the men's view of them as central to the household, they experience restrictions.

If the farm was always conceptually associated with permanence and order, the fishing villages that emerged last century were marked like the old seasonal fishing places, or *búðir*, and remained associated with instability and disorder. Thus, towns grew at the margins of society, and there is a sense in which even Reykjavík is part of the wild. I argue, thus, that there is an implicit association between towns and the men's wild, where women do not (yet) have quite a 'natural' place. As women they are marginalized in the urban surroundings. The regular 'pilgrimages' made back to *sveit* are journeys back to rightful positions, yet few women have or make the choice of reclaiming that. They want equal opportunities in the town, where they have not been seen or heard as equal with the men. In short, the women have become muted as a result of urbanization and changing economic conditions in Iceland as elsewhere. When society itself has 'run wild', meaning that it has in fact departed from the traditional farming basis while still emphasizing it discursively, it should not surprise us that the women's movement is of such importance in Iceland. What is more, Icelandic women have an image of strength and independence much readier at hand than most other women in Europe, and that again may account for the success of the movement both within the community of women and within politics in general.

The process towards success has been a process of capitalizing both on the historical 'centrality' of women, and on the symbolic capital inherent in their new marginal position; marginality, as we know, has a greater symbolic potential than the commonplace (cf. McDonald 1989).

There is no question that Icelandic women's movements have succeeded in giving their actions a sense of authenticity and thereby forge a new identity of the social group to which they appeal—women. One of the reasons for their success is precisely that their notion of women as social beings, underlying and defining the movement's activities, was that of the outsider. All the movements [in this century] saw and presented women as socially marginal and politically alienated because they lacked established authority, were outside the authority structure, and they all strove to change this situation by using this alienation to obtain for women rights that would give them access to the domain of authority, an important 'inside' of Icelandic society. (Kristmundsdóttir 1989: 95)

What is at stake for the women's movement, then, is not simply a matter of getting access to the men's world, but redefining the 'inside' of the shared world, as located, not in the household, but in the wider, urbanized society. In conquering the male wild, the women domesticate it.

While conceptual boundaries are never fixed, and while their meanings are always emergent, in the actual 'wild' of the fishing world there seems to be an image of the man as 'provider' at work. In the fish plant, my women workmates would endlessly discuss not how much their men earned, but how efficient they were to 'provide' (*skaffa*). I was astonished to hear how these strong and independent characters saw themselves as subjects to their men as providers. They quite clearly did, however, and we may now suggest a reason in the fact that men were still the main characters in the wild. The women's talk revealed, I believe, that they some-how conceived of themselves as 'out of place' in the fisheries, even as they worked endless hours and had always been a labour reserve.

Muted though the town women may be, they still are characters in a story that speaks of a society of hard-working women and men, now as before, and of a high degree of self-consciousness in matters of sex and gender, partly as a consequence of a strong tradition and a collective memory of their import.

Unsettling People

One evening after the milking I sat down to one of the recurrent conversations with the young farmer. It was among my favourite situations; the conversations we had were always packed with knowledge, and it was such a pleasure listening to the man who did most of the talking. That particular evening we talked about literature. Some days before I had been given a book to read written by his father's father's brother, the often quoted author Þórbergur Þórðarson; the young man wanted to know how I liked it. Upon my acclaim, I was told that he wrote in a very good Icelandic and that he was the first one to bring politics into Icelandic literature. He then ventured the information that between the sagas and the nineteenth century 'there is complete emptiness. There are simply no books; *ekki neitt*, save Bibles and a few stanzas related to the Church.' The first piece of literature to appear after the sagas was Bjarni Þórarinsson's *Piltur og stúlka* (*Boy and Girl*) in the nineteenth century, he told me. And he went on:

The fact that there is no more is partly due to the fire at Skálholt [the diocese]. I don't know when it was, but the entire library (*bókasafn*) burnt down. There would have been some notes there. Another reason is the fire at Árnasafnið in Copenhagen [in 1728], when a large proportion of the manuscripts burnt, and we don't know what they were. Skálholt was most probably set on fire by *flakkarar* [vagrants]. Skálholt was one of the richest farms in the country, and *flakkarar* often went there in the hope of getting something to eat. They never got anything there, though, and to revenge themselves some of them would burn down Skálholt.

We went on talking about the permanent problem of vagrancy in Icelandic history, and from there to the almost fixed end-motif: life in Suðursveit, our favourite topic.

My friend, if I may call him so without taking his attitude for granted, was and is a very knowledgeable person. Like all knowledge his knowledge is historically situated, and the little tale told above relates a recurrent motif in Icelandic tradition: the conflict between farmers and *flakkarar*, between settled and unsettled Icelanders. The conflict is not only social, and related to degrees of wealth and poverty; it is a much more profound conflict of values. The *flakkarar* don't care whether they set fire to the entire cultural heritage of the Icelanders (as possibly the Danes don't do either in the local view, somehow conflating the fire at Skálholt and the fire in Copenhagen). They have no sense of value beyond the immediate satisfaction of their basic needs.

The discourse on *flakkarar* epitomizes an age-old feeling towards the unsettling amounts of migrants and others who have threatened the self-definition of the farming population, being in structural dominance since the age of the settlements and until this century. Migration is a movement of people in space. Sometimes the movement has a straightforward purpose, or intention, yet the meaning of migration is rarely reducible to a spelling out of this intention. The settlement in Iceland in the ninth and early tenth centuries has been understood by the intention to gain freedom and land, but the meaning and the implications were the creation of a new history and a new society. Similarly for lesser migrations within Iceland. Their intentional meaning is not all there is to them.

In the previous chapter I dealt with the Icelandic saeters as liminal spaces. In the terms of the present chapter, we can see the practice of transhumance as a modest pattern of seasonal migration that was abandoned in the face of history, even though it was still economically rational. Rationality had to abide by implicit motives about which we can only conjecture—if within a larger systematic approach to the semantic densities of social categories.

In the domain of fishing there was also a certain migratory pattern. Until last century, when a full-time fishing population emerged, it was the farmers who engaged in fishing. It was a vital, subsidiary means of income, not to say survival. Sea-fishing, in contrast to the small-scale fishing in lakes and streams, involved smaller or greater migrations. It will be recalled how in the fourteenth century fishing seems to have outweighed farming in the national economy, with the result that fishing villages began to emerge. This only lasted until the early fifteenth century, when it was made illegal to winter at the landing places. Henceforward, fishing was defined as a temporary activity, and the fishing grounds in the south and west attracted scores of men from all over the country only during the *vertíð*, lasting from February to May. Walking huge distances across wastelands and even glaciers, the migrant fishermen were a recurrent feature of the winter landscape. The annals and other contemporary sources provide details about the hardships of their lot. The work was dangerous, and quite a number of people perished at sea or when landing their small rowing boats on the rocky coast. But it was the principal means of earning cash for such necessities as grain, timber, and metals, all of which had to be imported.

From the perspective of the farm, the seasonal migration meant the depletion of male labour, and at several points in history people had to be reminded (by royal decrees) that they were to return for the hay-work in early summer. Fish meant cash, but farmwork was essential to the upkeep of (the image of) the social. The various regions were affected differently by the seasonal migration. As discussed earlier, there are two broadly defined ecological zones in Iceland, one affected by the Arctic Current and consisting of the north and east, and one touched by the Gulf Stream and connecting the south and west of Iceland. In the latter zone, fishing was a much more direct asset to the economy, since the fish came to spawn in the warmer waters of the Gulf Stream. In the north and east, the decision to participate in fishing activities was more radical and involved seasonal migration on a larger scale.

The implicational meaning of seasonal migration was connected to the conceptual definition of *veiðar* (hunting/fishing). *Veiðar* took and take place in untamed nature as differentiated from the domesticated social space. The migrants were men (even if women are known to have taken part in fishing), and the category of maleness (consequently), became associated with excursions into nature. The *verbúðir* were seen as dangerous, not because they were placed in nature, but because their inhabitation was counter to the idea of the social, as centred around the *bú*.

The (negative) semantic density of notions of mobility and migration in Iceland is further sustained by the analysis of other movements of people in the Icelandic space. Some time during the fourteenth century, a category of wandering farmhands (*lausamenn*, 'loose men') emerged; it was quickly followed by legal attempts to settle these people, making vagrancy a capital offence. The laws were at first explicitly directed against the *lausamenn*, but gradually this category became the category of *flakkarar*, whom we met above. During the fifteenth to eighteenth centuries, many decrees and laws were passed with the aim of combating vagrancy, which was generally seen to be the cause of most social problems in Iceland.

There is no doubt, then, that traditionally mobility was negatively evaluated, at least uncontrolled mobility. It was associated with a transgression of boundaries, and in the social choreography this was permitted only if a return was part of the migratory pattern. 'No return' signalled an uncontrollable association with the wild, inhabited since time immemorial by outlaws, outliers, supernatural beings, and magical forces. The women of the saeters were the first ones to be called home when the social order was under threat from the outside. The seasonal migration to the fishing grounds could continue only if the fishermen returned home; a temporary habitation of the wild was acceptable. By contrast, nomads and wandering laboureres were socially and legally completely out of order. Since the times of the settlements, taking land and defining the social were two sides of the same coin in the Icelandic world. To some extent, this is still the case, as evidenced by the discourse on *flakkarar*. In the 1980s, a rock band by the name of *utangarðsmenn* ('men from outside the fence', that is outlaws) made an attempt to counter the negative attitudes to the work in fishing by giving voice to the migrant labourers.

Foreigners, who in a sense are but long-distance migrants, were not always welcome in Iceland; at least they were not welcome to stay. There were explicit rules about the latest time that foreign merchants had to leave the island, so as to avoid wintering. In only a very limited number of cases were foreigners allowed to stay, either because they could be of use because of their (medical) profession, or because they were prevented from leaving by their having broken their legs or some such thing. In all cases, the ban on foreign wintering was lifted on condition that people learnt Icelandic. While the rules are no longer so strict, there seems still to be an immanent scepticism towards foreigners who come to Iceland, including the growing number of tourists, whom we shall return to at a later stage. It is in the nature of proper Icelandicness that it is settled and confined to the inside.

Practising Memory

At this stage we shall recentre the argument around a particular practice of community related to both kinship and friendship, and pointing to a wider sphere of public recognition of the individual. The interconnectedness between biography and national history in Iceland has often been remarked upon, for instance by W. H. Ker, who in 1923 wrote that in Iceland, 'there is no sense of those impersonal forces, those nameless multitudes, that make history a different thing from biography in other lands. All history in Iceland shaped itself as biography or as drama, and there was no large crowd at the back of the stage' (Ker 1923: 315). The intersection between private and public domains evidently is an implication of scale; by comparative standards, Iceland is small among nations, and the Icelanders are few. Yet it is also a consequence of a particular way of practising social relationships, as epitomized by the writing of obituaries (Koester 1990: 114ff.; 1995a).

In Iceland, obituaries constitute a particular genre, by means of which the memories of individuals can be maintained. The obituaries are written for the daily newspapers, *Morgunblaðið* in particular, which in a country of 250,000 people prints *c*. 75,000 copies. They are peculiar in that they can be written by anyone and about anyone; they are not solely written by journalists and about the élite as is the case elsewhere. In Iceland, kinsfolk and friends may submit their own obituaries, and several commemorations of the same person may be published simultaneously. Often they are accompanied by a poem, written either by the author or by a known Icelandic poet; the poem may be all there is, like the following *Kveðja frá systur* (greetings from sister), from which I shall relate the first two (out of six) stanzas:

> *Sæli bróðir sefur þú við söngsins óma.*
> *Kirkjan öll í ljósum ljómar.*
> *Ljúfir heyrast orgelhljómar.*

Hingað mamma bar hjarta barnið til skírnar,
mjúkt á sinnar möðurörmum.
Mild þá léku bros a hvörmum.

(21–2 Jan. 1984, p. 19, *Sunnudagsblaðið, Þjóðviljinn*)

Blessed brother, sleeping by the sound of song.
The whole church shines with light.
Wonderful organ tones are heard.

To here mother carried her bright child to christening,
softly in her mother-arms.
Then, at everybody's face played a mild smile.

The point in relating these two stanzas is their conveying an important feature of
the entire genre; the point of departure is the fact of death, and in this case the
scenery is that of the church where the burial service takes place. The second stanza
goes back to the beginning of the life that has now terminated. From there the life
history unfolds, until once again we reach the inescapable fact of death. At one
level, the burial itself presents us with a synchronic picture of the life-course of the
deceased; the people present reflect various stages and various social roles held by
the person. At another level, the commemorative practice of writing obituaries
amounts to an archival practice (Koester 1995*a*). And this is the key thing: the
obituaries turn biography into history. It is a history that truly conflates the private
and the public and makes relatively insignificant and individual happenings into
eventful stories for everybody to read. Generally, the obituaries are chronologically
ordered and centre around the work life of the deceased, who may be a housewife
having struggled hard to hold poverty at bay for her family. They are also senti-
mentally arranged, however, around key words of praise, like *gestrisni* (hospitality),
gjafmildi (generosity), or *gleðja* (joy).

'On the morning of 22 December it was clear and beautiful weather at Borgarnes;
more and more Christmas lights had been put up as Christmas time approached.
Our thoughts were full of expectations and joy. Then broke the news that a friend
had died, on board his boat in a foreign port' (*Sunnudagsblaðið, Þjóðviljinn*, 31
December–1 January, 1984, p. 29). The piece continues by a recasting of the birth
and childhood of the deceased, and the point at which the two authors came to
know him. His talent as a fisherman is praised, *hann var góðu veiðimaður*, and his
glistening of joy when he strode through the waves with his boat. More generally
he is noted for being *gætinn og athugull sjómaður* (a level-headed and attentive
sailor). This is significant in the context of the following rendition of a previous and
severe accident that he had at sea, from which he had nevertheless recovered, and
the recounting of the final death on board. Any assumption of bad seamanship has
to be done away with.

Without pushing the evidence further, this obituary confirms the genre's construction of life histories, and its literary propensity towards plotting and foreshad-
owing or counterbalancing the end. Within even the shortest obituary, the life

history is interpreted and evaluated according to a general scheme. The public thus once again becomes personal. The interpenetration between the two domains is complete.

The writing of obituaries is a practising of memory. As individuals are remembered in writing, their biographies are frozen into fixed memories. They also connect individuals to a larger national ideology of a respectful life, of the beauty of nature, and the use of poetry as a popular medium for the expression of emotion. It is a historicizing communication which contributes to the creation of a social space.

If lifting biography into a paradoxically timeless history, the obituaries also reflect the significance of kinship and friendship in Iceland. In the two examples quoted above, the authors are sister and friends respectively, and I believe that there is no obituary written which does not contain information about parents and place of birth. The naming practice in Iceland by itself makes at least an identification of the father immediately pertinent, since the system is one of patronyms. There are no surnames (except a few 'survivals' from the Danish period) apart from being son or daughter of so and so. Pétur Jónsson, is Pétur, son of Jón, and Pétur's first born son is very likely to be Jón Pétursson. While daughters will also be identified by their patronym, the eldest daughter is likely to get her first name from the mother's mother. Second sons and daughters may get the other grandparents' first names, after which the game is open, even though there seem to be a number of names that are considered to be 'in the family'. Somehow the name conveys its own message about kinship and belonging. Today, it is increasingly common for parents to give their children two 'first' names, as it were, maybe to add a more individual mark of identification.

On the whole, kinship is bilateral, and if any system prevails it is that of a cognatic kindred, placing any individual at the centre of his or her own kin group. The kinship terms are purely descriptive and extend in both directions. However, given the naming practice there seems to be a favouring of the paternal line, and in fact some anthropologists have suggested that the bottom line of Icelandic kinship is a pervasive patrilineal descent principle (Pinson 1979, 1985; see also Rich 1989). On the surface, there is very little 'system' to kinship in Iceland. What there is, and always was, is a keen genealogical interest that seems to extend in all directions, and in relation to which 'friends' are defined. Both kinsfolk and friends belong to a circle of close relations that may become activated at moments of feast and at moments of sorrow, as we saw in the practising of memory.

The practising of memory not only links the individual to society by publicizing his or her 'belonging' and personal character, it also links individual fates to a nationalist imagery of an all embracing order:

Memorials to drowned fishers found throughout the island are Iceland's equivalent to the unknown soldier, which Anderson [1991] suggests is integral to nationalist imagining. Through the image of the fisher/soldier (doing battle with the sea), the nation can imagine itself in a struggle for survival, transcending death to achieve immortality in national memory. (Brydon 1996: 40)

The soldiers in Iceland are the hard-working ordinary people, who gain respect from their struggle with nature and from their ability to keep families together, to entertain friends—in short their individual power to function as a centre of attention in community. The practising of memory is a celebration of the individual at the centre of a world that transcends all biography.

Respectability

The commemorative writings serve the purpose of passing judgements on people, judgements that have always been part and parcel of the evaluation of individual character in Iceland. Commemorations in this sense are not limited to obituaries, they are also found in extensive autobiographies, and in the literature, ancient and modern. It is tempting to cite the (always much cited) passage from *Hávamál* (from the earliest times in Iceland):

Deyr fé,	Livestock dies
deyja frændur,	relatives die,
deyr sjálfur ið sama.	oneself dies.
Eg veit einn	I know one thing
að aldrei deyr:	that never dies:
dómur um dauðan hvern.	the judgement of each dead person.

The memory of the deceased is not simply a recollection of biographical events but more importantly his or her reputation rendered in narrative form. The power of reputation is a structuring principle in the practising of community; the obituary is just one genre among others in which this is expressed, and one which is particularly explicit in its linking people to the literary tradition.

In the medieval Icelandic literature, honour is a central issue (see Sørensen 1993 for detailed analysis). It was a function of a social order with weak central powers, but with a strong sense of personal integrity. Contemporary notions of honour were based on an assessment of what was proper conduct for the individual, and as such it was firmly integrated in a system of relative prestige. Just like *Hávamál*, which is often referred to in modern Iceland, the sagas still are important vehicles of tradition, and a brief venture into their world is not a detour to the past but a way of historicizing present notions of individual respectability.

In medieval Iceland, the constitution was based on a fundamentally free position of the individual. Structurally, all people were equal (except the slaves, who disappeared in the early eleventh century), yet in practice social differences were created according to power and status, amounting, in fact, to a class society. The classes, however, were open in principle. Everyone could aspire beyond his or her class; there were practical limits to exercising this freedom, but the key point is that in the world of the Icelandic sagas, it 'is in his relations with other persons, and not as part of a collective, that the individual is responsible and is put to the test' (Sørensen 1993: 336). Every free man has the right and duty to defend himself and his kin group; it is a matter of honour. Honour is what makes social life work, because it is what operates personal integrity in the absence of a central power. Honour is gendered; men and women both possess honour, but they maintain it in completely different ways. The woman's honour is a function of a man's honour, either that of her kinsman or her husband, but she gains independent status as mistress of the household, and by influencing men's conflicts. When individual conflicts are cast in terms of honour, they often produce tremors in large parts of society because kinsmen all over the place will (have to) take sides, and the women will be split between brothers and husbands. However, what remains is a society in which everyone is endowed with an inherent marker of mobility: a changing and negotiable honour.

In this century, we have a similar case. Now it is work that brings about respect, and anyone can change his or her prestige by being skilful and hard-working. In a thorough analysis of Icelandic fishing communities from 1880 to 1942, Magnússon (1989, 1990) demonstrates how respect falls to the hard-working and the clever. The two are seen to be closely interrelated; cleverness accounts for better worksmanship in general. In addition to this, physical strength and endurance are highly praised, but also—and significantly—the task's position *vis-à-vis* nature: the closer the task is to nature, the better it is (cf. ibid. 130). A millennium after the saga code of honour was established, it seems to have been transformed into a notion of respectability, mainly as a function of skills and proficiency in work. No less interesting, the evaluation of individual character is closely related to the nature of work. By this standard, it seems that once again it is the original modes of livelihood that would be favoured, not the new wage-earning pursuits in construction or industry.

The social honour of present-day fishermen is closely related to their relative success. Skippers are evaluated on the basis of their performances. Truly, their relative success is partly a consequence of their *fiskni* (fishiness), their ability to catch fish, which is independent of actions and simply distributed unequally among the fishermen like 'luck' in general; yet there is also, as in all discourses on fate, an individual ability to exploit whatever luck one has, and thus to influence fate. As for the skippers, their individual capacities for tracing and catching fish is the basis of their reputation, and thus the foundation for their attraction of good crews. The 'skipper effect' is self-affirming (Pálsson and Durrenberger 1982, 1990).

Reputation and honour, however, are also democratizing functions in a society of incipient classes. Prestige or social status is not tied to birth but must be achieved by individuals. Whether we look at the medieval code of honour or the modern distribution of respectability, it is for the individual to earn reputation in practice. In both systems, reputation or respect makes a transgression of social boundaries possible.

Thus, I would argue that although 'honour' is no longer on the lips of the Icelanders, as a principle it seems to be at work. It accounts for both personal integrity and mobility. Within the community of Icelanders, honour or respectability in this sense seems to be what motivates people to action and binds together the individual with the nation, biography with history.

The Vitality of Identity

The main implicit theme in any discussion of honour and respectability is the nature of social relations. Respect is fundamentally a relational fact; it connects people in a web of evaluations, and while apparently ascribed to individuals as a kind of 'essence' it has no substance; all it has is a shared referent that is part of a shared imagery of good and bad in social life. While apparently either natural or self-evident, kinship and friendship are not exempt from the strong evaluations that are embedded in notions of honour or respect in Iceland. Even within families and between friends, evaluations take place all the time.

In closing this chapter on community and honour I would like to quote Anthony Cohen, who in terminating his discussion of the symbolic construction of community says that 'whether or not its structural boundaries remain intact, the reality of community lies in its members' perception of the vitality of its culture. People construct community symbolically, making it a resource and repository of meaning, and a referent of their identity' (Cohen 1989: 118). In Iceland I think we have seen that, indeed, the community members do perceive their culture as vital. The referent of identity may be anchored in a distant past, but this past is drawn into modern life, whenever the value of this life must be grounded.

In individual and collective memories of departed members of the community the personal and the public fuse. In any obituary, the individual life history is measured and formed by the heritage from the past, and not least the literary heritage. If not consciously invoked, this heritage nevertheless functions as a repository of shared images, to which people may attach their own understanding, and which closes the cleavage between individualism and communality. Honour is individually gained, but collectively acknowledged, and as such it lends emotional texture to community.

PART III
Themes

7

Time: Uchronia

We have reached a point where we may generalize some of the dominant themes in the Icelandic world, as they relate to time, space, and people, seen also as forceful elements in the contexture of that world *as lived*. Regarding time, the ambition is to discuss some of the ways in which time and history are salient features in social life and discourse. I am not primarily concerned with matters of classification or ways of explicitly conceptualizing time; my focus is on the role played by Icelandic views of past and present in practice. In other words, the idea is to show how an implicit historical consciousness embraces current notions of selfhood and collective identity.

In a recent book, Alfred Gell (1992) has proposed new ways of seeing time in anthropology, breaking away from the classical discussion of whether time is an objective or a subjective category. As he points out, this discussion has contained implicit notions of 'us' living in (modern) objective time, and 'them' in a (pre-modern) subjective time (ibid. 290–1), notions that we will have to shun once we have realized that time is always constructed with reference to practice. Thus what differs between pre-modern and modern temporal regimes is not that the one is 'lived' time and the other is 'represented' time. In practice they conflate, and may be differently measured on a potentially shared time-map; they have perhaps less to do with being either pre-modern or modern than just reflecting different social spaces and practices. The 'great divide' between us and them dissolves when we study the multiplicity of histories that people live.

Local action becomes history with time, and the link between time as lived-and-represented and history as told-and-interpreted is close. As discussed elsewhere (Hastrup 1992*a*) Western scholars have largely been victims of a Eurocentric view of history as something linear and continuous. Consequently, our sense of history has been defined as a particular mode of consciousness, which assumes social change to be homogeneously progressive (Lévi-Strauss 1962), and even in anthropology 'the others' seem to have been excluded from 'our' history and placed in a different, non-progressive time (cf. Fabian 1983). Before anthropology became truly 'historical', whatever history 'the others' had was prone to be seen as an implication of their being part of 'our' history (e.g. Wolf 1982). No society, of course, is without history, but some may do fine 'without Europe' (Davis 1992). Even European history is far from a unified progressive road of social change; Icelandic history for one is abundant evidence of 'other histories' also within Europe.

The unified sense of history seems to be a discursive rather than a social fact and the product of a highly literate Enlightenment heritage. If as a mode of consciousness it has become objectified in a particular historical genre (cf. Sahlins 1985: 52) favouring the linear and the continuous, analysis reveals the non-synchronicity and discontinuity of social experience. Such also in Iceland, where long-term history is thematized as three different 'ages' (cf. Chapter 1), and where short-term history is but little distinct from biography. 'History' has become adjective to different living conditions and the three ages represent different quality spaces. The 'first times' are presented as a primordial golden age, while the 'old days' are seen as poverty-stricken and hard. 'Today', history is dominated by a sense of expansion, and of opportunity, if no longer, perhaps, for all and sundry. In short, the sense of history relates directly to social experience, which is not therefore set apart from the time of maps and models, but rather forms an integral part of it. The choreographical possibilities in the practical lives of people depend on the combined forces of time-as-lived and time-as-represented.

The Sense of History

People are literally habituated by their experiences; in turn this habituation implies different ways of literally *sensing* history. One of the important lessons from historical anthropology is that the modes of producing 'history' differ from one context to the next. There are obvious differences in environment, economy, and social organization. But the making of history is also in part determined by local ways of thinking about history, or by kinds of awareness of change. The conceptual and the material form a simultaneity in the experience of the world. This implies that there is more to time and causation than chronology and sequence. It also implies that a single society may construe its history in a way which seems to blur the Western historical genre.

These points have been extensively substantiated by the history of Iceland. This history displays a remarkable long-term vacillation between a highly structured, well-organized autonomous society in the Middle Ages and a disintegrated, dependent, and crisis-prone condition from the early fifteenth to the nineteenth century, succeeded by a redressment and a final move towards autonomy and self-sufficiency in the twentieth century. If this development has given rise to distinctive periods in the social history of the islanders, it also lies behind contemporary modes of thinking about history.

Through the centuries there is a conspicuous coherence and unity in the image of 'Icelandicness' which—and that is the point—has had a decisive influence upon the actual course of history in this North Atlantic community. Evidently, part of the framework was already given; we cannot and should not overlook the role played by such objective features as subarctic climatic conditions, geographical isolation, political submission, or integration into world economy. But even such features are subject to particular local interpretations and to social reactions which transmute objectivity into relativity. The irreversible is not the same as the inevitable, and the sequential is not conterminous with the causal.

The sense of history finds itself *in between* history as lived and history as represented. In the Commonwealth period (930–1262) there seems to have been a general sense of conflation between these two areas, or between action and awareness. The sources do not allow us to generalize much about actual social experience, but it seems reasonable to suggest that at least in the beginning of the period, actions were what made awareness—Iceland being virgin country. The normative and literary sources that have been handed down were produced at a time when a cleavage between the 'proper' and the 'real' conditions was beginning to be felt, and contributed to the idea of an original 'free' society, governed with what had been sensed as freedom, statesmanship, and ultimately honour. While possibly not totally anachronistic for the time described in the sagas, we should not forget that the sagas are literary texts, conveying images of proper Icelandicness that may be summaries of an ideal, but which need not reflect the actual state of affairs, neither in the story time nor the writing time.

In the centuries following the writing of the sagas, which took place mainly in the thirteenth century, the discrepancy between life and representation seems to have grown to a point were the actual sense of of history may have had little likeness to those representations that were still in currency. Action and awareness were torn apart. While we cannot envisage the Icelanders having no consciousness of change and even decline, their collective awarenes, which I take to be an explicit or articulate form of consciousness (Hastrup 1995*b*), parted company from actual history. This had rather sad consequences for the people, which were later aggravated by the colonial policies. A key example is provided by the development of the modes of livelihood of which there were always two supplementary kinds in Iceland, farming and fishing, as we have seen. Although recognized as complementary at the level of consumption, farming and fishing as two distinct systems of production did not occupy equal positions in the minds of the Icelanders. They were never simply alternative ways of making a living, because they held asymmetrical positions in the (social) system of classification.

The domestic unit was based in farming ever since the first settlements in the ninth century, when Norse immigrants took land on the virgin island. Landrights were specified in detail, and distinctions between infields, outfields, and commons were strictly adhered to. There was a fine balance to maintain between arable and stock farming; grain was grown in the early period, but mostly hay, the latter being vital for the livestock. Natural grazing was adequate only from June to September; for the rest of the year the animals had to be kept at the farmstead on stored hay. The balance between animal numbers and labour input in the fields was, therefore, delicate. Grain-growing was soon abandoned, however; it is mentioned for the last time by Oddur Einarsson in 1589, when it is reduced to a rare occurrence in a small corner of the island (Einarsson 1971: 126). With it disappeared the plough. This means that 'in the old days' stretching almost up until the Second World War, farming was principally a matter of hay growing and animal husbandry at a simple level of technology. Due to this, and to the soil erosion following the rapid cutting down of the primary forest, the Icelanders became more dependent on another natural resource: the sea.

Fish had always been plentiful, and provided an additional resource for the farming households. During the fourteenth century fishing became a necessity; it also became favoured by new external markets. The Hanseatic League replaced Norway as Iceland's main trading partner, and a new market for dried fish opened in Europe. The net result was an economic upswing which again favoured a separate development of fishing. The old trading ports which were nothing but temporary landing places now turned into tiny villages, and a category of 'professional' fishermen emerged. While earlier there had been no specialist groups at all, the late fourteenth century witnessed an incipient division of labour between farmers and fishermen. Nevertheless, fishing expansion was obstructed, as we saw in Chapter 1, to the point where even technological skills were repressed and then forgotten.

The decline of fishing technology had a parallel in farming, where a collective loss of skills can also be documented, as we saw. The collective loss of memory in all areas of the economy is a token of a repression of earlier awareness of how to fight off hunger in a marginal agricultural area like Iceland. Generally, in the second 'age' Icelandic society showed a failure to keep up with the implicit requirements of social reproduction. Increasing material poverty was correlated with a remarkable degree of collective amnesia as far as local technological skills were concerned. The result was that the Icelanders became increasingly prone to forces beyond their control. As time wore on, the experience of the Icelanders was one of increasing impotence in all domains of the social; survival had replaced influence as the most important item on the agenda. The idea of human causation in history, as embedded in old notions of fate, faded and gave way to ideas of external and largely uncontrollable causes of all changes. The economy deteriorated, the merchants exploited, and the distant Danish king subdued the people. 'The wild' approached from all corners, while the fences of Icelandic society disintegrated.

In modern times, the sense of history has recentred, as it were. In the nineteenth century, huge efforts were made to put Icelandic society on its feet again, partly by appeal to old virtues, and partly by a developing of the fishing potentialities that had so far been only subsidiary. In the twentieth century, fishing has become predominant, and forms a highly acclaimed area of economic and material progress, while also—it seems—still being seen as somehow marginal to proper Iceland as established by tradition. It is in some way still conceived of as a frontier area, not least in its embodying the national struggle against world powers. Fishing limits have become a matter of definitional proportion to the country. This can be inferred from, for instance, the historian Björn Þorsteinsson's deliberations on the last of the ten cod-wars fought by the Icelanders, which expanded the fishing limits (in 1976) to 200 nautical miles:

Ýmsar stofnanir íslenska ríkisins hafa unnið vel og mikið við erfiðar aðstæður, en stærstu afrekin hefur þó landhelgisgæslan unnið. Allir íslendingar eiga þar fáum, gætnum og djörfum mönnun óendanlega mikið að þakka. Gæslan vann það ótrúlega afrek að verða bakhjarl íslenskra samningamanna, þegar þeir gengu á hólm við fulltrúa stórveldanna. (Þorsteinsson 1976: 235–6)

(Various Icelandic state institutions have worked hard and well with difficult matters, but the greatest achievement has been made by the guard of the sea territory (*landhelgi*). All Icelanders owe these few, level-headed and brave men an unlimited vote of thanks. The guard won that unbelievable feat to be the back-up of the Icelandic negotiators when they went to single combat with representatives from the great powers.)

The rhetoric of the passage is revealing; the combination of (implicit) connotations to Churchill's comments on the Battle of Britain during the Second World War on the one hand, and the reference to the Viking practice of *hólmgangr* (single combat) on the other, points to a central feature of the modern sense of history, which can best be explained as a kind of suspension between (global) modernity and (insular) antiquity.

With an ever more marked integration into the world economy, and the correlated stress on modernity, this sense of suspension seems to gain momentum, and consequently the core of Icelandicness seems to be increasingly cast in terms of the frontier. 'Icelanders feel the need to define themselves more closely than ever before, because the island is getting more involved in the international scene and moving out of the periphery. They take pride in talking about how well they have adapted to the international scene without having lost their "ancient" identity and traditions' (M. Einarsson 1996: 231). This suspension is linked to previous visions of an Icelandic Uchronia, entertained by Icelanders of the second period and to which we shall now go back.

Uchronic Visions

If the production of history is related to the thinking about history, there is all the more reason to explore the traditional notions of history in Iceland. First of all we should recall that no conceptual distinction between history and story was made. The notion of *saga* referred to anything that was 'said' of history; as such it contained its own claim to truth. With the sagas, a one-to-one relationship between the words and the world was claimed. When the main corpus of Icelandic sagas was written in the twelfth and thirteenth centuries, the objective was to relate Icelandic history. Although certainly literary products, we may assume that they were also perceived as historical documents. This was true also for the reconstruction of the ninth- and tenth-century events and characters in the *Íslendingasögur* ('Stories of the Icelanders'). In these sagas, that have rightfully remained famous, the pre-Christian past of Icelandic society is recast in the shape of a *Freiheits-Mythos* (Weber 1981). The original 'free state' of Iceland is celebrated, and the entire literary activity of the thirteenth century may in fact be seen as an attempt to raise local consciousness about the Icelandic achievements in *terra nova* (Schier 1975). Freedom and the taking of new land are tokens of original Icelandicness.

One of the consequences of the original Icelandic conflation of story and history on the one hand and of the peculiar atomistic social structure on the other is a remarkable conflation also of individual and collective history, as we saw when we discussed present-day practisings of memory in the writing of obituaries. At another level, it made every Icelander the author of his or her own fate. During the period of decline, in which history as a whole was sensed as beyond control, the individual Icelander was likewise unable to control his or her own fate. The ability to influence the biography was always an integral part of the power to influence the larger history of Icelandic society.

The actual history (in the middle period) was seen as originating in a space beyond control, while at the same time the Icelandic dream was recreated in an Icelandic Uchronia, drawing upon traditional images of Icelandicness as embedded in the heritage from the Golden Age (cf. Hastrup 1992*b*). Uchronia is nowhere in time. If Utopia is a parallel universe, Uchronia is a separate history. It is a history out of time, so to speak. In Iceland, uchronic visions were part of the collective representations of the world, and as such they deeply influenced the response of society to its own history.

If modernity entailed a vision of history as linear growth in the European centre, this had little bearing on its margins (and these may well have been found all over the place, where the rank and file had become alienated from élitist notions of history). The experiential gap between ideas of progress and the sense of defeat made room for uchronic imaginations on the part of the people. Where this is found, and certainly where it achieves the proportions of the Icelandic case, it reveals a feeling of incapacity to influence actual history. It also points, however, to a failure on the part of the dominant historical discourse to incorporate the experience of ordinary people. The gap between the two histories left people in a void.

In Iceland, this observation is acutely relevant to an understanding of the sense of history during the second 'age'. With no experience of a progressive history, the Icelanders returned to myth. Like other marginalized peoples excluded from the power to define their own history (Samuel and Thompson 1990: 19), the Icelanders resorted to collective memory and tradition, thereby both reinforcing a sense of self and using them as a source of strategies for survival. The uchronic visions were at odds with present social experiences, yet they could not be corrected without a loss of self. Uchronia had its own reality, of course, but from our point of view this reality was hypothetical.

We cannot ask the Icelanders of bygone centuries about their imaginations, but we can infer them from a whole range of historical evidence. As a vision of another time, Uchronia connects otherwise disconnected elements and adds a level of comprehension to our historical narrative. The history out of time entertained by the Icelanders was informed by their view of the past. The past was over, yet in narrative form it was continuously reproduced and invoked by the Icelanders, in search for meaning in the void between two histories.

The reproduction of the old images of Icelandicness consisted in the strong literary tradition dating back to the Middle Ages being continually renewed. Young people learned to read from the old lawbook, and the saga–literature was consumed during the institution known as *sagnaskemmtan* (saga entertainment), which was a reading aloud of the old stories as a general evening pastime on the farms (Gíslason 1977; Pálsson 1962). We have heard Þórbergur Þórðarson tell how this was still done at Hali, when he lived there, and we noted how the present youngsters were the first generation to grow up without this reading tradition. The individual farmsteads represented society in miniature; there was no distinction between élite and popular culture as elsewhere in Europe, no urban populations set apart from peasant culture. Although mass literacy was not achieved until some time around 1800 (which is still relatively early compared with European standards), there is strong evidence that at most farms at least one person was actually able to read (Guttormsson 1983). What is more, the stories of sagas also formed the core of the *rímur* (popular verses) that were orally transmitted for centuries. The old images were thus continually reproduced by a recasting of the old myths of creation and of the past virtues of men. Through this recasting, the Icelanders were perpetually confronted with an ideal order nowhere in time. One could even argue that while other peoples invent traditions to match new historical situations (Hobsbawm and Ranger 1983), the Icelanders reproduced images of the past to invent themselves.

The uchronic imagination was concurrently sustained by this invocation of the past. Because the Icelanders had no real 'others' with whom to compare 'themselves', the mirror-image of themselves in the past tense had major social repercussions. Living in the imaginary world of Uchronia, the Icelanders lived between two histories, or between an empirical and experienced history of decline and decay on the one hand, and between an imagined Uchronia implying permanence and antiquity on the other. Rather than defining a new reality and shaping it in language, the Icelanders defined the present in terms of a past of which only the language remained real. Experience itself was discarded as anomalous because it no longer fitted the old language.

Liminal Orders

The uchronic vision of reality was in some way 'beyond' actuality. It was a manifestation of a liminal order defined not so much in space as in time. The disintegrating fences around the infields provide an apt metaphor of the actual development in the second period. Nature encroached relentlessly, diminishing the socially controlled space, and giving up the classical notion of a concentric cosmological dualism firmly distinguishing between an 'inside' and an 'outside' world. Inside, humans were in control; outside the wild forces reigned. As time wore on, more and more humans were alienated from the centre and merged with the wild, because of poverty, vagrancy, or fishing. An increasing proportion of reality was beyond control.

History itself became split into two: an externally induced and uncontrolled succession of movements, and an internally emphasized repetition of traditional values. The repetition owed its force to the reproduction of past images in a discourse which mirrored the negativities inherent in the contemporary Icelandic world. With no symbolic exchange with real others the Icelanders could engage in no relationship of identification other than with themselves in the past tense. In a manner of speaking, they became 'others' themselves. As such they were alienated from the larger history—and ultimately from their own present.

This alienation was correlated with a particular pattern of event registration. Events are happenings which are registered as significant according to a particular cultural scheme which is constantly subjected to risk by social action. But in Iceland the scheme persisted in a remarkable degree of cultural self-consciousness. The uchronic vision was intimately linked to the reproduction of the past in voice and in action. The literary image of the free farmer was proudly read out to everyone, and the image was confirmed in action by the Althing's decisions to concentrate energy in the reproduction of the farming households at the expense among other things of an enterprising fishing. Due to the reproduction of an outdated cultural scheme, actions became anachronistic, and contemporary happenings failed to register as events. In contrast to the event-richness of the past—as collectively memorized in history as conventionalized in the local genre—the present appeared event-poor.

Some social spaces or some periods always seem to generate more social events than others; this is not primarily a mensurational feature, but a feature of registration. For events to be registered as such, they have to be significant from the point of view of the definer. The Icelanders of the second period did not single out many happenings as significant social events, it seems. The social space was event-poor; movement, change, and innovation were relegated to a non-social space where events did not register. Iceland was in a state of event-poverty; it was *fásinni*, to invoke a matching Icelandic concept which we have encountered before. By comparison to the event-richness of the previous period, contemporary reality was marked by absences. While the Icelanders certainly *had* a history during the event-poor centuries, they only indirectly *produced* it. Poverty was both material and symbolic; the two levels merged in the experience of the people.

In the diachronic dimension, relative event-richness is transformed into relative historical density (Ardener 1989b). In the representation of history, historical density is a measure of the relative memorability of particular events. For events to be memorized and to become part of 'history' they must have been experienced as culturally significant. This apparently self-evident point covers a fundamental truth: the structuring of history and the selective memory are not solely imposed retrospectively. Contemporary event-registration always serves as the baseline for the trace of experience left in history.

For Iceland this implies that the event-rich period of the early and high Middle Ages was matched by a historical density in this period. This contrasts with the unmarked reality of the later period. The continuous attention paid to past events made the present seem insignificant. The comparative historical density of the past also made the present not look like history at all. The reproduction of culture impeded the production of history. Inadvertently, the Icelanders themselves contributed to the destructive course taken by the development. 'History' had become 'myth'—and therefore beyond influence.

If culture (here used as a summary of diverse practices) generally encompasses the existentially unique in the conceptually familiar (Sahlins 1985: 146), this had a particular truth in Iceland. The strength of the conceptual scheme actually entailed a failure to register the uniqueness of present existential conditions, and seemed to block the way for an altered practice. In other words, if 'culture' amounts to an organization of current situations in terms of the past (ibid. 155), in Iceland the 'current situation' hardly registered, because the 'terms of the past' were so vigorous. Having lost control of their own social reproduction, the people were left without a proper historical appreciation of the main cultural categories. The unreflexive mastery of the traditional conceptual system made the Icelandic 'habitus' the basis for an intentionless invention of regulated improvisation that was quite out of time (cf. Bourdieu 1977: 79; cf. Sahlins 1985: 51). The vision was refracted to the point where society itself became liminal to the proper world. This, of course, was no simple consequence of the Icelanders being imprisoned in a particular view of the world; it was also due to the fact that in practice the marginal Icelandic society was extremely vulnerable to external definitions and natural calamities. Also, one should not underestimate the effort it takes to keep things 'as they used to be'.

In modern times, a new sense of liminality seems to pervade, qualified by what I have called a suspension between pastness and the presentness. The force of tradition is unquestionable, and the power of literary images and of symbols deriving from the Middle Ages—and sifted through nineteenth-century romanticist vocabularies and visions—is testified to in all public addresses. Indeed, being 'public' by itself makes any statement, such as an obituary, link individual courses of events to national historical issues.

We can see, then, how the different sense of history that may be said to qualify the three periods to which contemporary Icelanders refer plays out the notion of liminality in different ways. In the 'First Times' people lived at the centre of the world (*veröld*), which was also history, meaning literally 'the age of mankind'. Beyond it, ordinary humans had little to do in the liminal space of outlaws and such like. In the 'Old Days' people semed to live on the borders of history; life was eccentric by the standard set by the old central perspective upon the world. The centre had become identified with pure pastness, while the present was pure liminality. 'Today' people live in suspension between past and present, stressing adaptability to modernity and preservation of antiquity at the same time. In contemporary life, the liminal order comprises both what was central and what was liminal before. The sign of Icelandicness incorporates a consciousness of history as being both continuous and ever-changing.

In this section I have dealt mainly with the past, but the point is that even today the past seems to be a baseline for thinking about proper Icelandicness. History has turned into a myth the Icelanders live by. And by being lived by, it influences present-day practice in the liminal time-space that is the now. Of course, what is liminal and what is not is a matter of definition, and in practice there are many ways of coping in the centre as well as on the margins of history. We shall return to that in the next chapter, when the issue is raised again from a spatial perspective. Here we shall terminate the discussion of the Icelandic sense of history with a brief recourse to the desire for duration.

The Desire for Duration

Motivation is not found in the disengaged mind or in utilitarian ideas of the right thing to do. The hunger-stricken Icelanders of the second period teach us that instrumental reasoning cannot explain the actions taken. There was a high degree of consciousness of the state of affairs, yet the Icelanders were caught in a web of illusions about themselves that were actually counter-productive to social reproduction (Hastrup 1995*b*). The traditional cultural models motivated action but somehow obstructed an awareness of the deteriorating social conditions. Amidst decline there seems to have been an implicit desire for duration, which was instrumental also to the reshaping of the national image that took place in the nineteenth century. Duration is what counts if at the cost of replacing the awareness of history with a construction of an uchronic myth of an Icelandic world somehow out of time, even when still floating in world history, and ready to enter at any point in time, but only on its own account.

The desire for duration takes us back to the musical allegory, enabling us to understand if not the nature of history at least the desire itself. In music, what are the relations between length and meaning, duration and effect?—asked Basil de Selincourt in his *Music and Letters* (1920, reproduced in part in Langer 1958: 152–60). This is another way of addressing the question of causation in history which we have only just begun to understand. The commonsensical model of 'temporal causation' which has dominated the historical discipline, identifying the cause in the most recent and most extraordinary precedent, has broken down because it leaves out what seems 'ordinary' and absolutely necessary at the time for the thing to happen (Bloch 1979: 191), and furthermore, it does not question 'time' itself. It remains an open question how much time one can allow between cause and effect and still speak of a causal process. Somehow, for the idea of temporal causation to be convincing, the time between cause and effect must be 'filled out', so to speak, by the causal process. In human history it is simply not possible to provide evidence for this. Causation is embedded in duration.

With music we are faced with a form of duration that may help us understand the implications of this. While certainly played in time, the composition itself defies time, and whatever meaning emerges from it is suspended in a way that relates to the non-temporality present also in the Dreaming. Song-lines and other ancestral paths turned into myths of origin and permanence demand the absorption of our whole time-consciousness. The continuity in our lives is lost in that of the sound to which we listen, and so is also our biography lost in the myth which we live. The sense of duration embraces whatever notion we might have held about sequence.

If we are 'out of time' in listening to music, our state is explained by the simple consideration that it is as difficult to be in two times at once as in two places. Music uses time as an element of expression; duration is its essence. The beginning and the end of a musical composition are only one if the music has possessed itself of the interval between them and wholly filled it. (Selincourt 1958: 153–4)

In the Icelandic world it seems that history has a comparable essence of duration. Although cast in three distinct ages, these are not more than movements within a larger composition, filling out the consciousness of history from the First Times until this day. The first movement was one of balance, in the second the cadence was more disturbed, and in the third a crescendo embracing both of them seems to have become a more or less generalized mode of consciousness.

It is with Icelandic (and other) history as it is with music; you cannot be inside and outside of it at the same time. You cannot be absorbed in one time and act in another. When most successful, ethnographic fieldwork—conceived of as participation—brings about the same sensation of total involvement and loss of 'objective' measurements. There is a complete merging of action and awareness. 'Absorption', of course, can be defined and analysed from an external standpoint, also by the historical insiders. In our case, this may contribute to the transgressive potential of Icelandicness.

Transgression is part of the dreamwork of musical performance, even when it seems also to be based in a feature of repetition:

The value of repetition in music belongs of course to the peculiar inwardness of the art. A musical composition must be content to be itself. The reference and relations into which analysis resolves its life-current need point to no object, no event; they take the form of the creative impulse which is their unity and they repeat one another because iteration is the only outward sign of identity which is available to them. Repetition is also a basis of form because, as we have seen, it balances retrospect by peopling imagination. (Selincourt 1958: 156)

The reference to pastness, and the sonorous repetition of traditional words and tales in Iceland point to the same feature, and show us what repetition really is: continuousness. Through changing sounds of history, a shared imagery keeps the Icelandic world (and other worlds) together. Icelandicness has to be reiterated for it to be real. The desire for duration is what motivates history in its supended, *lived*, form, between habituation and representation. The transgressive element in the historical consciousness of the Icelanders for a long time seems to have been mainly a feature of intensification, and of attaching itself to an increasing measure of words and things, images and events.

In the context of the Icelandic world as lived, a sense of historical duration is paradoxically sustained by a sense of transgression. This gives the theme of time a peculiar quality of liminality, a suspense of historical form amidst its reaffirmation.

8

Space: Remoteness

Culture and wilderness are categories of thought, not entities. They may not even be categories of thought, just blurry images of an operative distinction between the controlled or tamed on the one hand, and the uncontrolled or wild on the other. In earlier works I have often emphasized this distinction, or the equally abstract distinction between inside and outside, in the Icelandic world, using it as an analytical instrument in my coming to grips with certain practices and figures of speech. This has been criticized as part of a 'neo-orientalist' discourse on the Icelanders (Pálsson 1995: 62ff.). There is all the more reason to stress, therefore, that in social practice, of course, there is no boundary, no distance between 'culture' and 'nature'; living from nature as do fishermen and farmers means being at one with it, even if it also means being subject to hazards and unpredictabilities that cannot be controlled. As we discussed in connection with the landscape, nature is no stage upon which culture may perform itself.

Whatever status this distinction is given in various analyses, what is in focus in the present chapter is rather the analytically constructed 'tertiary zone', that is the space in between the tamed and the wild, the space in which gains and losses are made and respect gained. It is the spatial counterpart to the temporal liminality identified in the previous chapter. It is a space which incorporates both culture and wilderness and makes them into one whole horizon for motivated action. It is also the zone of conversation between people whose specification as selves or others is temporarily subordinate to a shared experience of taming the untamed, or simply understanding the incomprehensible. In this zone, the Icelandic world takes on a peculiar quality of being both modern and archaic, both unlimited and strictly bounded, both worldly and self-conscious.

This liminal quality is stressed by Icelanders themselves in their marketing of the island to tourists. Just as previously the Icelanders defined themselves in response to travel accounts, today they respond to the tourist gaze, and as elsewhere in the world this gaze potentially redirects the view of the self, as demonstrated by Magnús Einarsson (1996). As far as the image of the *place* goes, it is purity and tranquillity that is emphasized, as well as the vast and paradoxically accessible wilderness. 'Icelanders like to present a romantic image by emphasizing the idea of purity in all spheres of the country—environmental, historic, linguistic, cultural and culinary (unpolluted waters and food)' (ibid. 228). Purity is very much a function of antiquity as we have seen, yet at the same time, the Icelanders certainly also want to be taken seriously as parties to the modern world. In short, confronted with tourism and travellers to an unprecedented degree (in 1993 the number of tourists was 256,000, according to Einarsson, thus matching the number of inhabitants), Icelanders to an increasing degree have to balance on the edge between antiquity and modernity, that is find themselves in a liminal space between past and present, and between culture and wilderness. The nature of this space may be qualified in response to a certain measure of 'cultural compression', owing in part to the remoteness of the island.

Compression

Cultural compression is a consequence of subjection to outside forces, colonial, economic, or otherwise. The plasticity of the word suits the Icelandic case well. One can almost see how 'Icelandic culture' was pressurized into being what it is due to the colonial squeeze made by the Danes, and also how intensity increased within it, so to speak. This image can now be qualified analytically.

At several points I have referred to Iceland as a remote island in this work as in previous works (cf. Hastrup 1990*d*). A perfectly natural term, it seems, for an island in the far north of the vast Atlantic Ocean. Yet here I want to qualify 'remoteness'—following Ardener (1987)—as a conceptual quality rather than a geographical fact. It is a quality of particular social spaces, which from the outsiders' point of view may be 'far away' while the insiders do not experience any barrier to the external world. Quite the contrary, there is a peculiar sense of reachability and of vulnerability *vis-à-vis* the outer world. This is one of the paradoxes of remote areas (ibid. 42).

There are other paradoxes as well, one of them being that remote areas seem full of strangers, if nothing else because strangers are so defined for a longer period of time than elsewhere. The general point is that 'remoteness' is a specific quality attributed to a social space from outside; while from the internal standpoint people have their own (counter-)specification of local reality as the centre of the world. This line of thought fits my Icelandic experience well. Virtually isolated in the North Atlantic, the Icelanders have been gazed upon by innumerable visitors, of late including anthropologists, yet they may have scarcely *seen* them. Reduced to invisibility by strangers exploring their own exotic dream world, the Icelanders have counter-specified the dominant world as outside, uncontrolled, and wild.

In their own extensive communication with the external world, the paradoxically cosmopolitan Icelanders are constantly redrawing the boundary around their own world, internally specified in opposition to a negatively marked wilderness beyond the boundary. Remoteness is more of a state of mind than it is matter of absolute distinction, just as—in fact—cultural boundaries are. The distance between people is cast in words that reflect a distance between minds rather than between cultures (Cohen 1994: 123). The Icelanders are concerned with their identity, established as archaic and pure, to a degree which continues to mark them off as 'remote' from the external point of view. The point here is that by insisting on the singularity of the social space and on their individuality, and by conflating participation and interpretation, people contribute to that note of eccentricity which is specified by 'remoteness'.

Again, we should understand that it is a counter-specification made in a world which tends to define the remote people 'out there', so to speak. The substance of it, however, is home made. In Iceland, as we have seen, the singularity is conceived of in terms of the past, and of the textual tradition. To quote Gísli Pálsson:

In the textual life of Icelanders, language, culture and history are not only understood in terms of a glorious literary past, with reference to the continuous written records of Icelanders of their society and history from the time of the settlement in the late ninth century; many Icelanders, in particular the intelligentsia, like to apply a highly bookish approach to both contemporary realities and the past. (Pálsson 1995: 20)

This feature of the Icelandic world, as Pálsson also notes, has much in common with the world of the Greeks, analysed by Michael Herzfeld (1987); once beyond the Oriental embrace Greek 'otherness' was established in the nineteenth century by reference to the ancient past. Greece became fixed in time before modern history, and represented as the definitive locus of European aboriginality (ibid. 54). Interestingly, when we compare the Greek case to that of Iceland, the points of reference and the claim to excellence were textual in both cases. In Iceland the 'European' would be substituted by the 'Nordic', but the issue is the same. 'In both Greece and Iceland, the ambivalent combination of modernity and aboriginality motivated a persistent concern among the indigenous élite with the "language question" and the "textual heritage": a preoccupation with cultural purity and external threats and the exaggeration of linguistic unity and cultural homogeneity' (Pálsson 1995: 20).

The liminal order of time, established in the preceeding chapter as a suspense between antiquity and modernity, can now be explicitly matched by a similar feature of space which in many ways parallels the Greek situation, not least in the fact that in both cases the discourse of anthropology and the discourse of the society are analogues of each other. Local claims to aboriginal, Nordic (or European) identity have clashed with Nordic (or European) claims to Icelandic (or Greek) otherness (cf. Herzfeld 1987: 54). If the Icelanders have seen themselves as the Ur-Norsemen, the last surviving Vikings, by reference to their linguistic and textual heritage, they have at the same time been counter-specified as others, a remote people. The reference to past reality becomes an ideological trap: it takes so much effort to prove oneself as modern as well, or as co-present in the same space as the descendants of the aboriginals.

We can see how the feature of remoteness is consequential to the peculiar nature of the contact zone found between dominant and marginal societies. Even though both Greece and Iceland have re-entered world history at full force on their own, the nineteenth-century nationalist heritage continues to inform local notions of

identity. It is, therefore, part of the ethnography, but not the whole of it. As we
have seen, Icelanders live and work without having necessarily to specify their
aboriginality, yet within the space they act, golden memories continue to play a part
in motivating action. The reality of modernity at some level or other must accom-
modate the claim to aboriginality. Thus, while welcoming foreign tourists to
Iceland, the Tourist Bureau of Iceland at the same time felt compelled to tell the
natives: 'Preserve the Icelander within yourself' (M. Einarsson 1996: 232). Local
survival is cast as a need to maintain strong boundaries against the foreigners
washing over the pristine land.

The specification of aboriginality also works at a lower taxonomic level. In
Iceland, and correlated with the bookish approach to Icelandicness, it is no small
deal to live on *landnáms*-land (a settler's farm). Of course, modern farming is quite
independent of the original settlements, but the symbolic value of antiquity remains of import. When entering the contact zone of conversation with outsiders,
personified by an anthropologist perhaps, people do not hesitate to specify their
farm as situated on settlement land—if that is the case. Aboriginality itself is of
value, and it is a value which has tended to marginalize segments of the Icelandic
population itself.

If aboriginality seems at first sight to be a temporal notion, at closer inspection it
does prove to be spatially premissed. It is the very fact of compression which lends
relevance to declarations of aboriginality in relation to a particular place or territory. In a contact zone perceived mainly in terms of vulnerability to outside and
domineering forces, the conversation slides away from dialogue and into the world
of claims and counter-claims. There is no way in which appeal to aboriginality can
be met with counter-claims to less; 'history' itself will not do, unless it has literally
grown out of place. Aboriginality is closely linked to a conflation of nature and
nation.

Natural Nationalism

Icelandic nationalism relies to a high degree on features of place, that is on various
constructions of the natural world. Identity is naturalized by appeal to
aboriginality, and by reference to a symbolic landscape. 'Nature in Icelandic
nationalist imagining brings together notions of place and history, on the one hand,
and blood and kinship, on the other' (Brydon 1996: 39). The symbolic landscape is
constructed not only around ideas of beauty and purity, but also around particular
sites that are cast as 'sacred'. We have already mentioned the ancient site of the
Alþingi, Þingvellir, situated about one hour's drive from the capital of Reykjavík.
We have not finished with it, however, since we have not yet discussed how this
place can be at the same time sacred and profane, by indicating both antique
inspiration and modern recreation.

Þingvellir represents a unique geological area on the Atlantic Ridge that cuts through Iceland and accounts for volcanoes, earthquakes, and other thermal activities. In the eyes of the beholder, Þingvellir is an image of natural forces, beyond control. As such it is not only attractive to the Icelanders for recreation and fishing, it is also a vast tourist attraction. On the other hand, it is a historical site, where the most important national events took place for centuries, and which has inspired Icelandic poets. Þingvellir thus is a place 'where culture and landscape seem almost identical to Icelanders' (M. Einarsson 1996: 224).

In the eyes of Icelanders, tourists and other travellers can make only a limited sense of such sacred spaces. As has been said recently, 'the collective tourists' reputation is low because they are believed to be too "vulgar" to understand the essence of being Icelandic, the purity of culture, language, and landscape so dear to that image' (M. Einarsson 1996: 229). It will be recalled (from Chapter 3) how it is still thought also in some quarters of scholarship that only Icelanders can fully 'participate' in the world of the sagas, because only they have the landscape within daily view.

If representations of time and history in Iceland were fused with notions of space, the reverse is also true, then. The representations of sacred sites are imbued with time. At Þingvellir history and modernity combine to make of this place a located national image. 'Nationalist discourse re-embeds itself in place, by rearticulating its relationship to the experienced world using the symbolic landscapes of the past, present, and future' (Brydon 1996: 40). By itself, the site of Þingvellir represents a combination of culture and wilderness, a distinction which is thereby transcended. As such it is an apt metaphor for a social space that incorporates both dimensions into a whole view of 'Iceland'.

The Mountain Woman

To some extent it can be said that nationalisms in general are conceived of as naturally grounded; the romanticist discourse on nations made notions of nature and culture, of land and language, and of human life and natural powers conflate into one vision of legitimate political entities. It is not surprising, therefore, that the Icelanders should entertain similar notions, based as their nation is in nineteenth-century nationalist ideas. What is possibly surprising is the extent to which this naturalistic approach to the nation is still in force. This may again be understood by reference to the peculiar state of compression and remoteness.

The genealogical link between the land and the people that was established during romanticism, and which today lies behind notions of 'aboriginality' found its own peculiar symbol in *Fjallkonan*, or the Mountain Woman. *Fjallkonan* comprised both nature and nurture, as it were, and was seen as both mother and protector of the nation.

She was at the same time outside culture and part of nature, an almost fairylike being who belonged to the mountains, the most remote parts of nature. But she was also part of culture, civilized, tender, good-hearted, firm, and determined, encouraging patriotism, courage, peace, and unity. While she symbolized what Icelanders considered to be genuine and purely Icelandic, in her purity she reflected a deep-seated, but unattainable, wish of the Icelanders to be a totally independent nation. *Fjallkonan* is thus not only a national symbol, she also represents the national vision, the nation's ultimate dream. (Björnsdóttir 1989: 107)

The idea of a nurturing mother has played a key role in the discourse on the making of the Icelanders. During the nineteenth century, the idea of Iceland as mother became tightly interwoven with practical experience (Koester 1990: 106). The poet Bjarni Thórarensen (1786–1841) began his famous 'Remembrance of Iceland' with the words, 'Ancient Ísafold, love-dear foster-soil, fair mountain woman', and the national poet *par excellence*, Jónas Hallgrímsson began his celebrated poem like this: 'Iceland, glorious land and prosperous frost-white mother'. The point is, that although genealogy and nature were current images in romanticist Europe, in Iceland these abstract notions took root in a clearly visual image that personified a powerful, poetic link between mother, home, and nation (Koester 1990: 107; 1995*b*).

Although the image was mainly poetical, it was also used by the Icelandic independence movement in the nineteenth century; 'one of the crucial arguments for sovereignty was that they were born and shaped by a different "mother" than the Danes' (Björnsdóttir 1996: 109). At closer inspection, the conspicuously gendered image contains its own negation; the mountain is a masculine area, and symbolizes the woman's political power. It is probably this inherent duality that has linked the Mountain Woman to the modern presidency which was constructed in an essential non-gendered fashion. Like the Mountain Woman, the president represents sovereignty and national unity, permanence or immobility, and ultimately what all Icelanders have in common, their country, their language, and their culture (ibid. 109ff.). With the election of the first woman president, Vigdís Finnbogadóttir, in 1980 everything came together. Like the Mountain Woman, she was an independent mother, and unlike most Icelandic women, she had to some extent conquered the men's wild, by having had a higher education and long-term experience abroad. It seems that 'her non-domestic career made her better qualified than most other women of her generation to assume the role of the national mother' (ibid. 117). Obviously, one could question this analysis of the presidency on many accounts, one of them distinctly historical, namely the recent election (1996) of a male president who does not at all fit the above notions. I leave Björnsdóttir's imagery unchallenged here, because it is still good to think with, however.

On the less romantic side of the image of Iceland as mother was its being invoked against women who during the Second World War fell in love with American soldiers; out-marriage was considered sacrilege, and 'the ultimate violation of Iceland's sacredness was for an Icelandic woman to bring a soldier to Þingvellir, the national shrine and the "real" home of *Fjallkonan*' (Björnsdóttir 1996: 113).

The Mountain Woman is the image *par excellence* of the Icelandic world being situated between a timeless nature and a cultural present, where people balance on a sharp edge between aboriginality and modernity, or between non-touchability and vulnerability.

Recentring

To argue that the Icelandic world displays features of remoteness is not to revert to any exoticism of cultural islands. The ethnographic and theoretical implications of globalization have destabilized the traditional object, and have called for a recognition of any society's embeddedness in larger structures (Okely 1996: 3). Noting that the relative 'event-richness' of Iceland is a result of the local specification of more objects or events as 'Icelandic' or as packed with significance than perhaps elsewhere, is also noting the situatedness of Iceland in the world order. Compression is a feature of hegemonic relationships, compressed cultures responding to pressures from outside. Yet local history is always more than just a result of being implied in world history. People do not only react to events, they respond, implying that actions are taken within a moral horizon that accounts for the relative value of these acts.

The specification of Icelandicness in relation to land or to nature points to such a horizon of moral values that outlast individual Icelanders, balancing between culture and wilderness in their daily negotiations of living. With tourism there seems to be an explicit emphasis, once again, on wilderness as the more attractive part of Iceland, the least spoilt. It seems that in contrast to some other parts of the world, where the model of domesticity produced in the hegemonic order was exported and consumed (Comaroff and Comaroff 1992: 265–94), the Icelanders have succeeded in counter-specifying their world as a 'natural' one. The fact that at 'my' farm in Iceland, during the 1980s the cows were replaced, first, with foxes, and, later with tourists provides a striking illumination. As I have related, tending the cows was seen as somehow debasing by comparison with the sheep; the daily tedium of milking, etc. had no seasonal highlights, no excitement. It did bring cash, though, through the selling of milk to rather distant dairies that had become feasible with the roads built in the 1970s. Foxes were tried out as a kind of 'wild' replacement, but the most recent and successful idea was to buy a small boat and take tourists out on the nearby lagoon by the glacier, notable for its drift ice and seals. A camping-van was placed on the shore and the young woman sold buttered bread and coffee, while the young man sailed the boat. The couple that had previously been in charge of the cows, while the senior brother and his wife were in charge of the sheep, thus regained wilderness and could forget about the cows.

Even if the distinction between culture and wilderness, or between inside and outside, has some relevance for the understanding of the Icelandic world, it must not be reified in anthropological discourse. 'Inside' and 'outside' carry no essence; they are figures of speech or implicit images, organizing a host of blurry experiences in the borderlands of the partly understood. The idea of organizing *anthropological* understanding of the Icelandic world in terms of whether the anthropologists are insiders or outsiders to Iceland (e.g. Durrenberger and Pálsson 1989), is at best foreign to me—seeing all intellectual work as in some sense 'exiled'. What matters in the study of the Icelandic world is to see how Icelanders are naturally 'central' characters in this, their own world (as other people are). They may be specified as on the margins of Europe, or as prototypical Nordics, or both, but they remain grounded in their own corporeal fields—in some way extending to the entire space of Iceland.

'At home', Icelanders define and redefine the substance of their life-worlds in constant counter-specification to 'outlandish' gazes. This substance, and its intense motivating force, is partly shaped by the feature of cultural compression, making of traditional values an almost explosive power, spilling over into nature, because it cannot be contained within 'culture', so to speak. In this way, spatial parameters are as important as the temporal ones in thematizing Icelandic self-perceptions in the borderland between wilderness and domesticity.

9

People: Othering

It is in the nature of people to see their world partly through the (imagined) eyes of the other (Mead 1934). One could argue that this dual vision is the bottom line of any reflexivity which nevertheless implies the taking of a first-person standpoint (Taylor 1989: 130). Awareness and experience are always those of an agent, and reflexivity implies a kind of presence to oneself which is inseparable from one's being the agent of experience. Yet the very idea of a first-person standpoint, and the sensation of its uniqueness implies a consciousness of second-person standpoints as well.

At a collective level we know that cultures materialize in implicit contrast with each other (Boon 1982), even if today we also have to reconcile ourselves to the fact that contrasts are not simple, symmetrical oppositions. All over the world, cultures have been constructed from the gaze of others. Travel accounts and literature have portrayed others in ways that have subsequently filtered back into local self-perceptions (Pratt 1992; Said 1993). In other words, and as I argued at the beginning of this work, intertextuality plays a major role in shaping local images, even if their substance is drawn from the place itself. On the individual as well as the collective level, reflexivity and representation are mutually immanent categories. In Iceland, this is no less true than elsewhere, and due to the remarkable quality of the sources since history's beginnings, we can trace the the process of shaping local images and self-portraits in some detail.

At the time of the settlements, the Icelanders were still part and parcel of the Norse world, and it took some time before they saw themselves as distinct. But by the twelfth century a sense of distinction can be inferred from the writing of a specific 'Book of the Icelanders' (*Íslendingabók*) and a little later, the *First Grammatical Treatise* identified a particular language, in explicit contrast to other languages; with a separate history and a distinct language, the Icelanders could declare their specificity on the world-map (Hastrup 1982). From inside their own world they could then produce a literature that confirmed the specificity as an aboriginal feature. The world-view was manifestly centred, as we have seen, and anchored in place. This anchoring was made explicit by the composition of *Landnámabók* ('The Book of Settlements') from the thirteenth century and (in one version at least) explicitly targeting those foreigners who claimed the Icelanders to be descendants of villains and outlaws fleeing justice in other countries. The gaze of the other premissed the casting of the Icelandic self, and representation became the vehicle of reflexivity as a matter of course.

The centuries following the collapse of the Commonwealth were in many ways silent by comparison to the first, flourishing period. Yet with increasing amounts of foreign writings appearing in the wake of Humanism, Icelanders once again felt the need to specify themselves. Thus Arngrímur Jónsson in 1609 wrote his *Crymogæa* (Iceland) in response to foreign accounts, and in Latin so that it would reach the foreign audience. In his preface he is explicit about his aim to defend Iceland against ignorance and allegations of paganism; this is a remarkable, yet unacknowledged echo of the inducement to writing *Landnámabók*. Arngrímur's work then relates the history, life-ways, and language of the Icelanders within the context of Nordic history. One could say that Arngrímur Jónsson personifies the 'contact zone' at the age of Humanism, and responds to outsiders' ignorance by an act of local learning—in Latin.

The declarations of selfhood always entail a degree of othering. The first-person standpoint implies a second person, as we have said. This othering is part of the problem inherent in the definition of cultures. In the words of Anthony Cohen: 'one aspect of the charged nature of cultural identity is that in claiming one, you do not merely associate yourself with a set of characteristics: you do also distance yourself from others. This is not to say that contrast is necessarily a *conscious* motivation for such claims' (Cohen 1994: 120). In other words, othering is an implication of all self-declarations, while not necessarily their intention.

A case is provided by the world of the Icelandic sagas, where some stories engage in a form of 'folk Orientalism' (Pálsson 1996: 77), collectively exoticizing distant others on the basis of hearsay from foreign accounts. A contemporary counterpoint is provided by some modern literary scholars, who may not claim foreign scholars to be nine feet tall or have dogs' heads, but who do claim that by their not being Icelandic, they cannot participate in the Icelandic world. What these examples point to is the fact that although selves and others are mutually implicated, they do not form neat symmetrical oppositions. Such is the nature of othering.

Conceptual Asymmetries

It will be understood that the process of othering may take place at many levels. It is not solely a matter of cultures featuring themselves in asymmetrical opposition to one another. It may be a feature also of identity categories at a lower taxonomic level, and even a personal propensity. In the world of the Icelanders, we have experienced this in a number of contexts, where allusions have been made to the inherent asymmetry between categories, social and otherwise. We have noted for instance how farmers and fishermen were rarely conceived of as on a par with each other, the rule generally being that farmers were considered the prototypical Icelanders, while fishermen belonged to the blurry outskirts of the category. For centuries the fishermen were being presented as if 'devoid of culture' (Pálsson and Helgason 1996: 61).

Prototypes, by definition, take conceptual precedence over less good examples, yet the hierarchy can only be maintained ideologically. If ideology presents the world as it is not, then it certainly also contributes to making the world become what it is not yet. The ideologically marginalized may become actually alienated, but this in turn may subvert the ideological scheme. If we look at the farmers and fishermen again, not only has history outbalanced their relative economical and political significance, but the very fact of the fishermen being marginal has somehow lifted them outside the normal scheme of evaluation and turned their very maginality into a source of power. As Fernandez has convincingly argued, there is an inherent transcendence in herder and hunter, that places them beyond and above those interactions of the subject–object world held to be practical and normal (Fernandez 1986: 244–6). In other words, the downgraded pole of the opposition may reclaim power by the very fact of their being defined out of order. We also saw how Icelandic women, by capitalizing on their marginality, could regain access to the authority structure. The point to stress is that social categories and conceptual distinctions between 'us' and 'them' are not fixed. Their meanings are emergent and shifting, as are social stereotypes. At the core of them is an experiential reality which habituates people but does not imprison them. It is possible to learn from new experiences, as any ethnographer will know from fieldwork.

Prototypes may be the 'best examples' of any category, but even then the fuzzy edges of the category always provide a potential correction of the prototype. In terms of the people 'inhabiting' the categories, this implies that they pose a latent question to the established order, not in a semantic system of flat referential categories, but in a network of relations between the nodal points of each. Those that fall between the meshes of the net are not powerless; nodal points may shift within the categories. In the words of James Fernandez, 'those we domesticate have domesticated us and those we have not domesticated are still useful in measuring the achievements or excesses of our domestication. If life becomes too much a following about cows, men may be excused for turning a bit bearish' (Fernandez 1986: 6). Even if it would not be appropriate to replace 'bearish' with sheepish or fishy, to give it an Icelandic sound, I think we get the general point; there are limits to domestication. The sheer insistence on the importance of liminal spaces in Iceland, makes the local 'other' permanently present as a counterpoint to domesticized selves.

Sensing Community

In an often acclaimed work, Benedict Anderson (1991) has suggested the notion of 'imagined communities' for nations. One cannot know, only imagine that such a community exits. Of course, it is a matter of scale, and from some perspective one could almost claim that in Iceland it is possible to know almost everyone, if not personally then at least vicariously. Kinship and friendship link people to almost any region of the country. I want to raise a slightly different point here however, which has less to do with quantification than with qualification of the space, including the sense of history as embedded in the oral tradition and in the landscape.

Granted that in Iceland, the corporeal field of any one individual seems to expand to the limits of the nation, I would argue that in Iceland, at least, the community is *sensed*. It may still be imagined, of course, but it is in a very direct way materially experienced and *felt*. One could say that all societies by having an institutional impact upon people's lives make themselves felt, but I want to go a bit further here and suggest an actual bodily sensation of society. This is not least owing to the strong link between nature and nation. The nation is a natural community in more than one way, and no one is out of touch.

Nationalist sentiments are gendered and naturalized, as in the Mountain Woman, in a way that reinstates the externalized women and wilderness in the national community. 'Othered', perhaps, at lower taxonomic levels, the national community incorporates all. At the same time, however, it recentres women's position in absolute domesticity, in the position as mothers. Like the surface of the ocean, glittering in different shades of colour and light, so the image of the Icelandic nation is fascinatingly varied, and difficult to pin down in any one image, except an ambiguous one.

The nation is sensed not only at the overarching level of being at one with nature, it is also experienced in daily practice. Acts of speaking may be heard as national declarations, because the purity of the Icelandic language is another strong marker of the national uniqueness. Even here, an internal othering takes place, in the alienation of 'bad' Icelandic speakers from the core values of speaking. Poor speakers are poor representatives of Iceland. In the corrective radio programmes, one is made to sense that by ear.

Language is the vehicle also of storytelling, which again is a site of tradition and of nostalgia. As spoken or performed, Icelandic gives people a direct sense of belonging, and is one among other features that dismantle the opposition between self and society, so prominent in other worlds. Attention to the sounds of the language sharpens the 'feel' for Iceland. The community is not only imagined, surely, it is sensed. The supposedly inherent feature of the human condition, the opposition between self as a locus of experience and society as a category of thought has not taken root in Iceland.

The Icelanders possibly prove a good case against universalizing this opposition, which may be a theoretical construct anyway. As Cohen has it:

[T]he opposition of individual to society may well be a figment of the anthropological imagination, rather than a consequence of their irreconcilability. There seems little reason to suppose that sociality and individuality must be mutually exclusive, nor even that behaving in a 'social mode' requires a person to mask his or her selfhood. The axiomatic juxtaposition of these modalities might be seen to reveal an overemphasis on the superficial dogmas of cultural theory, neglecting the more substantial reality. I suspect it also has a good deal to do with the disinclination of anthropologists to acknowledge that the people they study can bear much resemblance to themselves, a disciplinary posture which has arguably denied self-consciousness to 'the other'. (Cohen 1994: 54)

This is not to deny, of course, that any society or nation may want to cast itself as particularly social, using all sorts of devices to distinguish the collective from the individual. In Iceland, however, collectivism and individualism are two sides of the same coin. They are inextricably implicated in each other. The homogeneity of the Icelandic world that is constructed ideologically may be challenged by individual actions and modes of speaking in practice, but it remains a challenge from *within* that world, of which one shares the feeling.

In the age of modernity, it still seems to be the case in Iceland that identity is strongly localized. Among the attempts to catch up with modernity in explicit connection to identity is the work of Anthony Giddens (1991). He deals with the construction of self as a reflexive project, continually engaged in a process of adjustment to the ontological insecurity following from the deconstruction of the traditional small communities. As pointed out by Cohen, his argument rests on a 'strangely atavistic evocation of long-discredited distinctions made in anthropology between "folk" and "urban" cultures, and between Great and Little traditions' (Cohen 1994: 21). What is more, society itself gets an improbable ontological status, beyond the individuals who are seen to react rather than respond to circumstance, in the sense given above.

Instead of treating the identity project in the age of modernity, which may be reflexive in Giddens's sense, as an abstract problem, we have to reinstate it in the empirical order of things. Modernity is transformed locally, as I have already cited Sahlins (1993) for pointing out; or, in the word of Geertz, whatever global flows may overwash any one society, they are 'indigenized' (Geertz 1995: 56). Local orthodoxy may be shattered, but singularity shines through in new home-grown forms. So also in Iceland, where modern individualism is still contained within a communal corporeal field. While certainly, 'every Icelander is a special case' (Durrenberger 1996), the case is still contained by a more comprehensive history— to which it also contributes.

Identity and otherness are mutually implicated, and in all cases they form a unified baseline for anthropological theorizing about worlds. In Iceland, 'travellers' at all levels have embodied the opposition, and even when studying tourism in modern Iceland, the anthropologist ends up by studying the hosts, who are 'the spectators of their own dramatization, the Icelanders' (M. Einarsson 1996: 234). And this is the point: in the very process of othering, a people dramatizes itself, and becomes spectator to its own self-objectification. In the world of the Icelanders the feature of self-objectification seems remarkably powerful: the representation of self in a language and a literature which is claimed to transcend history and to be almost naturally grown makes the dramatization of the Icelanders tenaciously exclusive.

We, the Icelanders

The exclusivity of Icelandic selfhood is matched by a remarkable propensity to generalize 'the Icelanders' in most of the conversations we had about local matters. This, of course, was partly spurred by the presence of the anthropologist, yet the standard opening of almost any volunteered or elicited piece of information by a 'we, the Icelanders' (do or believe this or that) was nevertheless significant. There does seem to be a local sense of generality to being Icelandic. A generality which is a feature as much of boundary-making as of essentialism. It shines through also in Níels Einarsson's critique of my approach to the Icelandic world when he argues that something has 'gone wrong when the "natives" [i.e. Níels Einarsson] do not recognize the factual basis of the story in which they are the main characters' (1990: 76). Although I would have been only too pleased to meet Einarsson in Iceland, I never thought of him, or any other generalized 'native', to be a main character in my story. The main characters are real people whom I met and came to respect and even love, and whose voice we have often heard in the preceding pages. It is their view of the world I have sought to understand both in their particularity and in their generality. My aim has been to generalize, as all scholarship must, since we cannot retell the world in living detail. But I have wanted to generalize not about *the* Icelanders, whom I take to be individuals, not types, but about the contexture of the Icelandic world and its inherent themes of directive force.

Individual lives are textured, and because this texture both surrounds and con-stitutes, the contexture of the Icelandic world is seen as a dynamic whole within which the meaning of Icelandicness is emergent. The assumption that all Iceland-ers should be able to recognize 'the factual basis' of my story points to a view of an objective category of Icelanders, sharing experience at all levels. What I have hoped to demonstrate here is that beyond detail and difference in actual practice and in thinking about Iceland, there is a shared imagery, and a shared vocabulary, which cohere a notion of 'selves' by furnishing individuals with a sense of communality. Beyond this notion, 'we, the others' can only admire the tenacity of the shared imagery of 'we, the Icelanders'.

In any contemporary ethnography there is an inherent ambiguity of the boundary between persons, categories, or cultures in a shared global space. Boundaries must be questioned empirically, they cannot be taken for granted; in other words, even if 'Icelandicism' is an ethnographic fact, we may not assume that 'Iceland' makes up an entity or a unified whole outside the image itself.

We know from the deconstruction of orientalism that by the noble act of deconstructing it, we may in fact contribute to its continuation. As for modern Greece, now 'occidentalizing' itself in response to previous orientalist colonization (Herzfeld 1995), so also potentially for modern Iceland. Instead of placing the Icelandic world firmly and rightly in the world order as one lived space among others, and reading present-day life as one version of modernity, the very attempt to shed so-called orientalist views of Iceland may lead to new essentialist assumptions. By discarding 'other' views upon Iceland as (neo-)orientalism, as Gísli Pálsson (1995) has previously discarded my own work, one risks ending in a kind of 'occidentalism' which is neither more laudable nor necessarily closer to reality, of course. Thus, when Pálsson goes on to suggest a post-orientalist discourse on Iceland, in which conversation can continue, I could not agree more. This does not pre-empt the nature of the possible generalizations, of course. In my view, the discourse on Iceland, as any anthropological discourse, still has to rely on general summaries of multiple practices which cannot all be portrayed.

Even if 'othering' takes place within any one society, in the sense that some people are seen as more representative of the society than others, anthropology must take a different view of the world. This is what I mean when I have claimed that it is for anthropology to take the 'other' point of view, and from there to perceive not only different selves, but also differing forces of motivation embedded in the reproduction of those selves that make the world. I have argued, and I hope also to have illustrated, that the self-objectification of the Icelanders is a major theme in their negotiation of the world. It is a cultural theme of directive force, which has gained further momentum by facts of compression and remoteness.

This point of view should be taken also when studying our home countries. As Marcus and Fisher (1986) pointed out some time ago, the West has all too often been treated in a superficial manner in anthropology, being so self-evident; the repatriation of anthropology requires not only that it addresses itself to matters of the world from where anthropology sprang, but that any anthropology of the home country must take the standpoint of the 'radical interpreter', whom I introduced before. All too often have anthropologists made 'banal occidentalists of themselves, when studying the west, not recognizing the multiplicity of the places from whence they came' (Okely 1996: 5).

In short, whoever we are, as anthropologists we cannot take short cuts to know-ledge by taking the road to home in order to see ourselves. What we can do is to enter a communicative space, in the field and in scholarship, and by the very process of filling out shared categories with diverse experiences contribute to the enlargement of that space. Whether 'we' are Icelanders or Tikopia, anthropologists or literary critics, what we discover on the road towards home, is not just oneself, but 'oneself as another' (cf. Ricoeur 1992). This, perhaps, is the most fundamental feature of othering in anthropology.

In the world of the Icelanders, othering is a continual force of alienation which in its own way, and on many levels of local practice, implies a stress upon Icelandic singularity, as rooted in tradition, landscape, and a sense of communality from which others are excluded. In all of these domains, othering maintains a distinct feeling of a self and as such it permeates the contexture of the Icelandic world. Ultimately, Icelandicness seems premised by an acute local sense of liminality being the normal state of affairs: with respect to time this implies a suspension between pastness and presentness, or between antiquity and modernity. In terms of space, the Icelanders live in a liminal area between culture and wilderness, a tertiary zone embracing them both. And, as far as the imagined community goes, people perceive themselves as if permanently living in a contact zone, a zone of mutually implicated self-objectifications. The visiting anthropologist is just one among other outsiders, whose gaze infiltrates the Icelanders' view of their own world, which I have sought to understand.

Finale

Finale

Having embraced us and made us forget the beginning, even music must come to an end. What is left is a sensation of having been elsewhere, in another time. The sensation of having been filled out by pure sound, or by abstract, non-linear potentiality, moves us towards another history. This is the feeling I have always had when I have allowed myself to become absorbed in the Icelandic world, where my own history has become suspended. In this book I have wanted to show the Icelandic world as one whole space of experience, of sense and sound, of stillness and action. Instead of providing the reader with a monograph, pretending to relate the objective patterns of culture and society, I have wanted to transmit my experience and analysis of the Icelandic world as a topological space within which all action is premissed. It is this space that I have attributed with musical qualities, not simply by analogy but also by its sensational duration. Within this space, my wish was to show the forces rather than the structure of the unending symphony, and to render a feel for the texture rather than the classification of local action and thought. The notion of 'contexture' was introduced as a comprehensive term for the whole I wanted to present, if not *re*-present.

In the preceding chapters, I have orchestrated the experience and the contexture of the Icelandic world in three different dimensions: time, space, and people. Between them, they make up the space wherein Icelanders live and embody a world that is both pastness and presentness, both nature and culture, both individualism and collectivity. I have not aimed at 'mere' description; rather I have aimed at a 'graphic theory' (Okely 1996: 16). In accordance with my view of the anthropological practice I have used an imaginative attention to detail in order to arrive at a general theoretical understanding that resounds with my experience. In the process of attending to the themes and practices of Icelandicness, I have also found that the three axes resonate with one another. Time, space, and people form a simultaneity in the Icelandic world.

Within this simultaneity, certain themes of directive force were identified as ideology, memory, and honour. They were seen as mainly grounded in tradition, landscape, and community respectively, but in practice they work together and makes things happen. They inform social experience and motivate action. Thus they become embodied and are indistinguishable elements in the practical and moral horizon within which people respond to circumstances on a global scale. A place apart, the Icelandic world is deeply implicated in the modern world order, as these notes will have indicated. It remains to clarify the remarkably sensual quality of the world of the Icelanders.

Times of Telling

From the basic silence, Icelandicness stands out as *told*. The Icelandic world is 'said', and the Icelandic language therefore to a remarkable degree pulls the local images towards a centre of understanding, alienating the margins. Images are recycled in stories, *sögur*, that are shared reminiscences of life in Iceland. As in many other places of the world, people tell stories to each other—and to visitors— either in the form of traditional narratives or in the form of constructed biographies, such as obituaries for instance; this is a means of giving cognitive coherence to experience (Baumann 1986: 113). In storytelling, the narrated event and the narrative event, in Roman Jakobson's terms, tend to fuse. Although temporally distinct, the two events become united, and in the process of telling itself, the experience is one of wholeness (Bakhtin 1981: 255). Thus, by being told and retold, the simultaneity of the Icelandic world becomes transformed into a homogeneous sensation of an all-embracing 'time', which, like myth, fuses the story time and the lived time. In the time of telling, Icelandicness is recreated.

As Walther Benjamin has suggested for storytelling in general, it is based on the ability to exchange experiences: the storyteller draws on experience and in narrating turns that experience into the experience of the listener (see A. Benjamin 1991). When one can no longer exchange experience, storytelling ends. By ending, the narrative—like music—is remembered as belonging to a separate time. By being continued, as in the Icelandic case, the epic remembrance continues to unite people in a space between the told and the lived, or again between pastness and presentness. As we have said before, the poetic imagery of tradition serves as a charter for a sense of a transcendent collectivity.

The epic remembrance is tied to themes of directive force that are told within a particular field of resonance. We have seen the truth of this claim for the Icelandic world. History in the ordinary sense of the word grinds itself on to particular spaces; there would be no dynamics in history were it not for the resistance made by what had already taken place. Matters of both time and space are vital to the sense of history. Part of the vitality is owing to the storyteller, who seems to live within every Icelander.

The poetics of language is matched by a poetics of space, a notion of the landscape connecting people to each other and to the past. If storytelling is vital to Icelandicness, memorizing the landscape is no less so. Due to the feeling of compression of the Icelandic world within the larger historical context, the local territory must be intensified, as it were. The historical position of remoteness is transgressed by way of a hypersignification of the landscape. Selves and others are mutually implicated also in this respect.

The times of telling in Iceland suspend the world between past and present, between nature and society, and between story and history. Ultimately, telling reverses the normal order of things, because it subordinates time to the mythical nature of what must be 'said' and repeated.

Sounds of Silence

Early on in this work I argued that Icelandic was a language of silences. There is a way in which the attention to silence may make us retrace the story told so far, just like the story of music in general may subvert the history of modernity told until now, by retracing the repressed possibilities of individuality (Bowie 1991: 84).

Stories and sounds are only in action. The music of Icelandicness only exists by virtue of its victory over that silence which it embraces in order always to conquer anew the fragile and immaterial being of sounds, to paraphrase Brelet (1961: 103). Sound is an event, which obliges the listener to participate in its action. The desire for duration, which we identified in a previous chapter, is immanent in the re-sounding nature of the subarctic symphony. It is incarnate in time, yet is not to be confused with time.

There are two kinds of silence in music. One is integrated in the musical form, where it works by creating instants of suspension between the sounds. The other is the original silence from which the musical form emerges, and it works by marking the boundary of music itself. Within Iceland, silences of the first kind were part of the sense of community. They replaced absent sounds, and made a world of possibilities felt, between the words; they were integrated in the form of Icelandicness. Beyond the sounds was a larger silence which escaped the form, but which nevertheless protected it from the noises of the exterior world.

In music, the time experienced and the time contemplated is the same; in the sound of silence there is no past and no future, only suspended present or pure potentiality. While a few sounds may spur a whole set of concrete expectations, silences point to abstract possibilities. Such is also the nature of silence in Iceland. On the back of the 'said' is a space of potentiality, which is acutely felt once inside the music of Icelandicness, existing by virtue of repetition and duration.

If words pull people towards the centre of a particular moral world, deeds and practices may have the opposite effect. In the domain of potentiality there is ample room for eccentricities or cultural counterpoints. 'Others' are silent accomplices to selves, declaring their singularity and integrity. If words and conversation are what make summaries possible, locally and anthropologically, practices may provide silent contestations of such summaries. The point to remember, whenever we summarize or generalize in words, is that conversation does not exalt consensus at the expense of contestation (cf. Daniel 1996*b*: 361). There may be disagreement or silent disclaimers, yet contestation takes place on shared grounds, as established in language. This applies both to the Icelandic and the anthropological conversation.

FIG. 11. Return to silence.

Dealing in words with worlds of experience that are largely silent, we are bound to rely on summaries that are inherently 'centralizing' on the one hand, and 'marginalizing' on the other. Yet in the feel for the contexture of the world, both of these propensities are embraced; the tension between them is a dynamic zone in the orchestration of duration. Culture contains its own counterpoints as language contains its own silences.

Relapse to Rock

Approaching the final tone, it is tempting to revert to the poetical mode by which we began. This time we shall listen to W. H. Auden's travel companion, Louis MacNeice, whose poem about Iceland from 1937 cuts to the hard rock of what we have until now described as the sensational feel of the Icelandic world.

> No shields now
>   Cross the knoll,
> The hills are dull
>   With leaden shale,
> Whose arms could squeeze
>   The breath from time
> And the climb is long
>   From cairn to cairn.

Houses are few
  But decorous
In a ruined land
  Of sphagnum moss;
Corrugated iron
  Farms inherit
The spirit and phrase
  Of ancient sagas

Men have forgotten
  Anger and ambush,
To make ends meet
  Their only business:
The lover riding
  In the lonely dale
Hears the plover's
  Single pipe

And feels perhaps
  But undefined
The drift of death
  In the sombre wind
Deflating the trim
  Balloon of lust
In a grey storm
  Of dust and grit.

So we who have come
  As trippers North
Have minds no match
  For this land's girth;
The glacier's licking
  Tongues deride
Our pride of life,
  Our flashy songs.

But the people themselves
  Who live here
Ignore the brooding
  Fear, the sphinx;
And the radio
  With tags of tune
Defies their pillared
  Basalt crags.

Whose ancestors
  Thought that at last
The end would come
  To a blast of horns
And gods would face
  The worst in fight,

Vanish in the night
  The last, the first

Night which began
  Without device
In ice and rocks,
  No shade or shape;
Grass and blood,
  The strife of life,
Were an interlude
  Which soon must pass

And all go back
  Relapse to rock
Under the shawl
  Of the ice-caps,
The cape which night
  Will spread to cover
The world when the living
  Flags are furled.

        Louis MacNeice, 1936

This poem provides us with a counterpoint to Auden's with which we started. A world devoid of people, and with sentiments frozen. The poem need not reflect the fate of Iceland, of course. If the ice-caps spread further and everything else relapses to rock, I am certain that the Icelandic world will remain. Ice may cover old notions of history, and tradition may fossilize, but there will be a new world melting its way; the forces inherent in the story of Icelandicness are not readily tamed.

Possibly, there will be less stress on continuousness in the future, yet as remote islanders in the world order, Icelanders are likely to go on stressing their singularity. In such stress lies an access to a domain of freedom that will allow people to go on orchestrating their lives in their own way. While so far, it seems that the domains of freedom that have been open to the Icelanders since the first loss of autonomy have been only their myths and their nature, the future may reshape even those. The Icelanders may find themselves in new histories, yet even by being new they will still imply the old ones.

What will relapse to rock, then, is not the Icelandic world. The reason for introducing the idea is another. What will stop here is my story about that world. Just as Auden's poem at the beginning of this book gave a sense of the magnitude ahead of us in our approach to this world apart, now MacNeice, who has so far been a mute travel companion, helps me towards the recognition that I, too, must now fall silent.

REFERENCES

Alþingisbækur Íslands (1912–1982), 15 vols, Reykjavík: Sögufélagið.

Anderson, Benedict (1991), *Imagined Communities*, revd. edn., London: Verso.

Anderson, Johann (1746), *Nachtrichten von Island*, Hamburg: G. C. Grund.

Andersson, Theodore M., and Miller, William Ian (1989), *Law and Literature in Medieval Iceland*, Stanford, Calif.: Stanford University Press.

Annálar Íslands 1400–1800. Annales Islandici. Posteriorum saeculorum, i–iv, Reykjavík 1922–42: Hið íslenzka bókmenntafélag.

Ardener, Edwin (1971), 'The Historicity of Historical Linguistics', in E. Ardener (ed.), *Social Anthropology and Language*, London: Tavistock (ASA Monographs 10).

——(1982), 'Social Anthropology, Language and Reality', in David Parkin (ed.), *Semantic Anthropology*, London: Academic Press (ASA Monographs 22).

——(1987), 'Remote Areas: Some Theoretical Considerations', in Anthony Jackson (ed.), *Anthropology at Home*, London: Routledge (ASA Monographs 25).

——(1989*a*), *The Voice of Prophecy and Other Essays*, ed. by Malcolm Chapman, Oxford: Blackwell.

——(1989*b*), 'The Construction of History: "Vestiges of Creation"', in Tonkin, McDonald, and Chapman (1989).

——(1993), 'Ritual og Socialt Rum', *Tidsskriftet Antropologi*, 25: 23–8.

Ardener, Shirley (1984), 'Gender Orientations in Fieldwork', in Ellen (1984).

Árnason, Jón (1860), *Íslenzkar þjóðsögur og ævintýri*, i–vi, Reykjavík: Bókaútgafan þjóðsaga.

Auden, W. H., and MacNeice, Louis (1985), *Letters from Iceland*, London: Faber & Faber.

Bakhtin, Mikhail M. (1981), *The Dialogic Imagination*, Austin, Tex: University of Texas Press.

Barth, Fredrik (1992), 'Towards Greater Naturalism in Conceptualizing Societies', in Adam Kuper (ed.), *Conceptualizing Society*, London: Routledge.

Bateson, Gregory (1972), *Steps to an Ecology of Mind*, New York: Ballantine Books.

Baumann, Richard (1986), *Story, Performance, and Event: Contextual Studies of Oral Narrative*, Cambridge: Cambridge University Press.

Bekker-Nielsen, Hans, and Widding, Ole (1972), *Arne Magnusson: The Manuscript Collector*, Odense: Odense Universitetsforlag.

Bender, Barbara (1993*a*), 'Introduction—Meaning and Action', in Barbara Bender (ed.), *Landscape. Politics and Perspectives*, Providence and Oxford: Berg.

——(1993*b*), 'Stonehenge—Contested Landscapes (Medieval to Present-Day)', in Bender, (1993*a*).

Benediktsson, Jakob (ed.) (1968), *Íslendingabók, Landnámabók*, Reykjavík: Hið íslenzka fornritafélag (Íslenzk fornrit, 1).

——(1964), 'Þættir úr sögu íslenzks orðaforða', in Halldór Halldórsson (ed.), *Þættir um íslenzk mál*, Reykjavík: Almenna bókfélagið.

Benediktsson, Jakob(ed.) (1985), *Crymogæa: Þættir úr sögu Íslands*, by Arngrímur Jónsson (1609), Reykjavík: Sögufélagið.

Benjamin, Andrew (1991), 'Tradition and Experience: Walther Benjamin's "On some Motifs in Baudelaire"', in Andrew Benjamin (ed.), *The Problems of Modernity. Adorno and Benjamin*, London: Routledge.

Bjarnadóttir, Kristín (1986), 'Drepsóttir á 15. öld', *Sagnir*, 7: 57–64.

Björnsdóttir, Inga Dóra (1989), 'Public View and Private Voices', in Durrenberger and Pálsson (1989).

——(1996), 'The Mountain Woman and the Presidency', in Pálsson and Durrenberger (1996).

Björnsson, Árni (1986), *Þorrablót á Íslandi*, Reykjavík: Örn og Örlygur.

Björnsson, Lýður (1972), *Saga sveitarstjórnar á Íslandi*, i, Reykjavík: Almenna bókfélagið.

——(1979), *Saga sveitarstjórnar á Íslandi*, ii, Reykjavík: Almenna bókfélagið.

Blau, Herbert (1992), *To All Appearances: Ideology and Performance*, London: Routledge.

Bloch, Marc (1979), *The Historian's Craft*, Manchester: Manchester University Press.

Boon, James (1982), *Other Tribes Other Scribes*, Cambridge: Cambridge University Press.

——(1986), 'Between the Wars—Bali: Rereading the Relics', in George Stocking (ed.), *Malinowski, Rivers, Benedict, and Others: Essays on Culture and Personality*, Madison: University of Wisconsin Press.

Bourdieu, Pierre (1977), *Outline of a Theory of Practice*, Cambridge: Cambridge University Press.

——(1986), *Distinction*, Cambridge: Polity Press.

——(1990), *The Logic of Practice*, Cambridge: Polity Press.

——(1991), *Language and the Symbolic Order*, Cambridge: Polity Press.

Bowie, Andrew (1991), 'Music, Language, and Modernity', in Benjamin (1991).

Brelet, Gisèle (1961), 'Music and Silence', in Susanne K. Langer (ed.), *Reflections on Art: A Sourcebook of Writings by Artists, Critics, and Philosophers*, New York: Oxford University Press.

Bruner, Edward M. (1986), 'Experience and its Expressions', in Victor Turner and Edward Bruner (eds.), *The Anthropology of Experience*, Urbana, Ill.: University of Illinois Press.

Brydon, Anne (1996), 'Whale-Siting: Spatiality in Icelandic Nationalism', in Pálsson and Durrenberger (1996).

Búalög (1915–53), *Búalög um verðlag og allskonar venjur í viðskiptum og búskap á Íslandi*, i–iii, Reykjavík: Sögufélagið.

Burguière, André (1982), 'The Fate of the History of Mentalités in the Annales', *Comparative Studies in Society and History*, 24: 424–37.

Byock, Jesse L. (1990–1), 'Modern Nationalism and the Medieval Sagas', *Yearbook of Comparative and General Literature*, 39: 62–74.

——(1992), 'History and the Sagas: The Effect of Nationalism', in Gísli Pálsson (ed.), *From Sagas to Society. Comparative Approaches to Early Iceland*, Middlesex: Hisarlik Press.

Callaway, Helen (1992), 'Ethnography and Experience: Gender Implications in Fieldwork and Texts', in Okely and Callaway (1992).

Casey, Edward S. (1987), *Remembering: A Phenomenological Study*, Bloomington, Ind.: University of Indiana Press.

Certeau, Michel de (1984), *The Practice of Everyday Life*, Berkeley and Los Angeles: University of California Press.

Chadwick, Nora K. (1946), 'Norse Ghosts: A Study in the *Draugr* and the *Haugbúi*', *Folklore*, 57.

Chapman, Malcolm (1992), *The Celts: The Construction of a Myth*, New York: St Martin's Press.

Charlsley, S. (1987), 'Interpretation and Custom: The Case of the Wedding-Cake', *Man*, 22: 93–110.

Ciklamini, Marlene (1966), 'Grettir and Ketill Hængr, the Giant-Killers', *Arv*, 22.

Clausen, Oscar (1967), *Sögur og sagnir af Snæfellsnesi*, i, Reykjavík: Skuggsjá.

——(1968), *Sögur og sagnir af Snæfellsnesi*, ii, Reykjavík: Skuggsjá.

Clifford, James (1988), *The Predicament of Culture: Twentieth Century Ethnography, Literature and Art*, Cambridge, Mass.: Harvard University Press.

——and Marcus, George (1986), *Writing Culture: The Politics and Poetics of Ethnography*, Berkeley and Los Angeles: University of California Press.

Cohen, Anthony (1987), *Whalsay: Symbol, Segment and Boundaries in a Shetland Island Community*, Manchester: Manchester University Press.

——(1989), *The Symbolic Construction of Community*, London: Routledge.

——(1994), *Self-Consciousness: An Alternative Anthropology of Identity*, London: Routledge.

Collingwood, R. G. (1945), *The Idea of Nature*, Oxford: Clarendon Press.

Comaroff, John, and Comaroff, Jean (1992), *Ethnography and the Historical Imagination*, Boulder, Colo.: Westview Press.

Connerton, Paul (1989), *How Societies Remember*, Cambridge: Cambridge University Press.

Crapanzano, Vincent (1992), *Hermes' Dilemma and Hamlet's Desire. On the Epistemology of Interpretation*, Cambridge, Mass.: Harvard University Press.

D'Andrade, Roy (1992), 'Schemas and Motivation', in Roy D'Andrade and Claudia Strauss (eds.), *Human Motives and Cultural Models*, Cambridge: Cambridge University Press.

Daniel, E. Valentine (1985), 'A Crack in the Mirror: Reflexive Perspectives in Anthropology', *Urban Life*, 14/2: 240–8.

——(1996*a*), ' From an Anthropologist's Point of View: The Literary', in Daniel and Peck (1996).

——(1996*b*), 'Crushed Glass, or, Is There a Counterpoint to Culture?', in Daniel and Peck (1996).

—— and Peck, Jeffrey M. (eds.) (1996) *Culture/Contexture. Explorations in Anthropology and Literary Studies*, Berkeley and Los Angeles: University of California Press.

Davidson, Donald (1980), *Essays on Actions and Events*, Oxford: Clarendon Press.

——(1984), *Inquiries into Truth and Interpretation*, Oxford: Clarendon Press.

Davis, John (1992), 'History and the People without Europe', in Kirsten Hastrup (ed.), *Other Histories*, London: Routledge.

Dening, Greg (1993), 'The Theatricality of History Making and the Paradoxes of Acting', *Cultural Anthropology*, 8: 73–95.

Diplomataricum Islandicum, I–XVI, Copenhagen and Reykjavík 1857–1972: Hið íslenzka bókmenntafélag.

Douglas, Mary (1966), *Purity and Danger*, Harmondsworth: Penguin.

——(1975), 'Deciphering a Meal', *Implicit Meanings*, London: Routledge & Kegan Paul.

——(1977), 'Introduction', in Jessica Kuper (ed.), *The Anthropologist's Cookbook*, London: Routledge.

Dumézil, Georges (1959), *Les Dieux des Germains*, Paris 1957: PUF.

Durkheim, Emile (1938), *Rules of the Sociological Method*, Chicago: Chicago University Press.

Durrenberger, E. Paul (1996), 'Every Icelander a Special Case', in Pálsson and Durrenberger (1996).

——and Pálsson, Gísli (eds.) (1989), *The Anthropology of Iceland*, Iowa: University of Iowa Press.

Dyrvik, Ståle *et al.* (1979), *Norsk økonomisk historie 1500–1970. I: 1500–1850.* Oslo: Universitetsforlaget.

Eggers, C. U. D. (1786), *Philosophische Schilderung der Gegenwärtigen Verfassung von Islands*, Altona: J. D. U. Echhardt.

Einarsson, Magnús (1996), 'The Wandering Semioticians: Tourism and the Image of Modern Iceland', in Pálsson and Durrenberger (1996).

Einarsson, Níels (1990), 'From the Native's Point of View—Some Comments on the Anthropology of Iceland', *Antropologiska Studier*, 46/47: 69–77.

——(1996), 'A Sea of Images: Fishers, Whalers, and Environmentalists', in Pálsson and Durrenberger (1996).

Einarsson, Oddur (1971), *Íslandslýsing: Qualiscunque descriptio Islandiae* (1589), ed. Jakob Benediktsson, Reykjavík: Bókútgafa menningarsjóðs.

Einarsson, Stefán (1957), *A History of Icelandic Literature*, Baltimore: Johns Hopkins University Press.

Ellen, Roy (ed.) (1984), *Ethnographic Research. A Guide to General Conduct*, London: Academic Press.

Ellis Davidson, Hilda R. (1964), *Gods and Myths of Northern Europe*, Harmondsworth: Penguin.

——(1967), *Pagan Scandinavia*, London: Thames & Hudson.

——(1973), 'Hostile Magic in the Icelandic Sagas', in V. Newall (ed.), *The Witch Figure*, London: Routledge & Kegan Paul.

Evans-Pritchard, Edward E. (1962), *Social Anthropology and Other Essays*, New York: Free Press.

——(1973), 'Some Reminiscences and Reflections on Fieldwork', *Journal of the Anthropological Society of Oxford*, 4: 1–12.

Fabian, Johannes (1983), *Time and the Other: How Anthropology Makes its Object*, New York: Columbia University Press.

——(1991), 'Dilemmas of Critical Anthropology', in Lorraine Nencel and Peter Pels (eds.), *Constructing Knowledge: Authority and Critique in Social Science*, London: Sage.

——(1996), *Time and the Work of Anthropology. Critical Essays 1971–1991*, 2nd edn., Amsterdam: Harwood Academic Press.

Fernandez, James (1986), *Persuasions and Performances: The Play of Tropes in Culture*, Bloomington, Ind.: Indiana University Press.

Finsson, Hannes (1796), *Mannfækkun af hallærum*, Reykjavík 1970: Almenna bókfélagið.

First Grammatical Treatise, Hreinn Benediktsson (ed.), Reykjavík 1972: Institute of Nordic Linguistics.

Foote, Peter, and Wilson, David (1970), *The Viking Achievement: The Society and Culture in Early Medieval Scandinavia*, London: Sidgwick & Jackson.

Friedrich, Paul (1996), 'The Culture in Poetry and the Poetry in Culture', in Daniel and Peck (1996).

Geertz, Clifford (1970), *The Interpretation of Cultures*, New York: Basic Books.

——(1983), *Local Knowledge*, New York: Basic Books.

——(1988), *Works and Lives: The Anthropologist as Author*, Stanford, Calif.: Stanford University Press.

——(1995), *After the Fact*, Cambridge, Mass.: Harvard University Press.

Gell, Alfred (1992), *The Anthropology of Time*, Oxford: Berg.

——(1995), 'The Language of the Forest: Landscape and Phonological Iconism in Umeda', in Hirsch and O'Hanlon (1995).

Gellner, Ernest (1985), 'No Haute Cuisine in Africa', *Relativism and the Social Sciences*, Cambridge: Cambridge University Press.

Giddens, Anthony (1991), *Modernity and Self-Identity: Self and Society in the Late Modern Age*, Cambridge: Polity Press.

Girard, René (1972), *Violence and the Sacred*, Baltimore and London.

Gíslason, Magnús (1977), *Kvällsvaka: En isländsk kulturtradition belyst genom studier i bondebefolkningens vardagsliv och miljö under senare hälften av 1800–talet och början af 1900–talet*, Uppsala: Acta Universitas Upsaliensis.

Goody, Jack (1982), *Cooking, Cuisine, and Class: A Study in Comparative Sociology*, Cambridge: Cambridge University Press.

Grágas (1974), repr. after Vilhjálmur Finnson's edn. 1852, Odense: Odense Universitetsforlag.

Greenway, John L. (1973), 'Paradigms of Heroism', in P. Foote, Hermann Pálsson, and D. Slay (eds.), *Papers of the First International Saga Conference at Edinburgh 1971*, London: The Viking Society.

Grettis saga Ásmundarsonar, ed. by Guðni Jónsson, Reykjavík 1936: Hið íslenzka fornritafélag (Íslenzk fornrit, 7).

Gunnarsson, Gísli (1983), *Monopoly Trade and Economic Stagnation. Studies in the Foreign Trade of Iceland 1602–1787*, Lund: Studentlitteratur.

Gurdin, Julie E. (1996), 'Motherhood, Patriarchy, and the Nation: Domestic Violence in Iceland', in Pálsson and Durrenberger (1996).

Gurevich, A. Ya. (1969), 'Space and Time in the *Weltmodell* of the Old Scandinavian Peoples', *Mediaeval Scandinavia*, 2.

Guttormsson, Loftur (1983), *Bernska, ungdómur og uppeldi á Einveldisöld*. Reykjavík: Ritsafn sagnfræðistofnunar, 10.

Hænsa-Þóris saga, ed. by Sigurður Nordal and Guðni Jónsson (1938), Íslenzk fornrit, 3, Reykjavík: Hið íslenzka fornritafélage.

Halldórsson, Halldór (1971), 'Allt er mér leyfilegt: Þátturinn Daglegt mál', *Morgunblaðið*, 28 Nov., Reykjavík.

Hanks, William (1996), 'Communicative Practice in the Corporeal Field', Paper given at the Institute of Anthropology, University of Copenhagen, Spring 1996.

Hannerz, Ulf (1980), *Exploring the City*, New York: Columbia University Press.

——(1992), 'The Global Ecumene as a Network of Networks', in Adam Kuper (ed.), *Conceptualizing Society*, London: Routledge.

Harré, Rom (1978), 'Architectonic Man: On the Structuring of Lived Experience', in R. H. Brown and S. M. Lyman (eds.), *Structure, Consciousness, History*, Cambridge: Cambridge University Press.

Harris, Marvin (1977), *Cannibals and Kings*, New York: Fontana/Collins.

Hastrup, Kirsten (1981), 'Cosmology and Society in Medieval Iceland: A Social Anthropological Perspective on World-view', *Ethnologia Scandinavica*, (repr. in Hastrup 1990*b*).

Hastrup, Kirsten (1982), 'Establishing an Ethnicity: The Emergence of the "Icelanders" in the Early Middle Ages', in David Parkin (ed.), *Semantic Anthropology*, London: Academic Press (ASA Monographs 22).

——(1985*a*), *Culture and History in Medieval Iceland: An Anthropological Analysis of Structure and Change*, Oxford: Clarendon Press.

——(1985*b*), 'Male and Female in Icelandic Culture', *Folk*, 27: 49–64.

——(1986), 'Tracing Tradition: An Anthropological Perspective on Grettis saga Ásmundarsonar', in J. Lindow, L. Lönnroth, and G. W. Weber (eds.), *Structure and Meaning in Old Norse Literature: New Approaches to Textual Analysis and Literary Criticism*, Odense: Odense University Press.

——(1987*a*), 'Fieldwork among Friends', in Anthony Jackson (ed.), *Anthropology at Home*, London: Routledge (ASA Monographs 25).

——(1987*b*), 'Presenting the Past: Reflections on Myth and History', *Folk*, 29: 257–69.

——(1990*a*), *Nature and Policy in Iceland 1400–1800: An Anthropological Analysis of History and Mentality*, Oxford: Clarendon Press.

——(1990*b*), *Island of Anthropology: Studies in Icelandic Past and Present*, Odense: Odense Universitetsforlag.

——(1990*c*), 'The Ethnographic Present: A Reinvention', *Cultural Anthropology*, 5: 45–61.

——(1990*d*), 'Studying a Remote Island: Inside and Outside Icelandic Culture', *Island of Anthropology. Studies of Past and Present in Iceland*, Odense: Odense University Press.

——(1990*e*), 'The Anthropological Vision—Comments to Níels Einarsson', *Antropologiska Studier*, 46/47: 78–84.

——(1991), 'Eating the Past: Some Notes on an Icelandic Food Ritual', *Folk*, 33: 229–43.

——(ed). (1992*a*), *Other Histories*, London: Routledge.

——(1992*b*), 'Uchronia and the Two Histories of Iceland', in Hastrup (1992*a*).

——(1992*c*), 'Writing Ethnography: State of the Art', in Okely and Callaway (1992).

——(1992*d*), 'Out of Anthropology: The Anthropologist as an Object of Dramatic Representation', *Cultural Anthropology*, 7, 327–45.

——(1994), 'Othello's Dance: Cultural Creativity and Human Agency', paper presented to the workshop on 'Locating Cultural Creativity', University of Copenhagen.

——(1995*a*), *A Passage to Anthropology: Between Experience and Theory*, London: Routledge.

——(1995*b*), 'The Inarticulate Mind: The Place of Awareness in Social Action', in Anthony Cohen and Nigel Rapport (eds.), *Questions of Consciousness*, London: Routledge (ASA Monographs 33).

——(1996), 'Anthropological Theory as Practice', *Social Anthropology*, 4: 75–82.

——and Hervik, Peter (eds.) (1994), *Social Experience and Anthropological Knowledge*, London: Routledge.

Haugen, Einar (1957), 'The Semantics of Icelandic Orientation', *Word*, 13/3.

——(1970) 'The Mythical Structure of the Ancient Scandinavians', in M. Lane (ed.), *Structuralism: A Reader*, New York: Basic Books.

——(1976), *The Scandinavian Languages: An Introduction to their History*, New York: Faber & Faber.

Hermanns-Auðardóttir, Margrét (1989), *Islands Tidiga Bosättning*, Umeå: University of Umeå (Studia Archaelogica Universitatis Umensis 1).

Hermannsson, Halldór (ed.) (1917), 'Annalium in Islandia farrago' and 'De mirabilius Islandia' by Gísli Oddson, Bishop of Skálholt, *Islandia*, x.

Herzfeld, Michael (1987), *Anthropology through the Looking-Glass: Critical Ethnography in the Margins of Europe*, Cambridge: Cambridge University Press.

——(1995), 'Hellenism and Occidentalism: The Permutations of Performance in Greek Bourgeois Identity', in James G. Carrier (ed.), *Occidentalism: Images of the West*, Oxford: Clarendon Press.

Hirsch, Eric (1995), 'Landscape: Between Place and Space', in Hirsch and O'Hanlon (1995).

——and O'Hanlon, Michael (eds.) (1995), *The Anthropology of Landscape: Perspectives on Place and Space*, Oxford: Clarendon Press.

Hjelmslev, Louis (ed.) (1941), *Breve til og fra Rasmus Rask*, København: Einar Munksgaards Forlag.

Hobsbawm, Eric (1969), *Bandits*, London: Weidenfeld & Nicholson.

——and Ranger, Terence (eds.) (1983), *The Invention of Tradition*, Cambridge: Cambridge University Press.

Hólmarsson, Sverrir (1989), 'Túlkar för mannfræðings til Íslands', *Þjóðlíf*, 5/10: 54–6.

Hubert, H., and Mauss, Marcel (1964), *Sacrifice: Its Nature and Function*, Chicago: University of Chicago Press.

Hume, Kathryn (1974), 'The Thematic Design of *Grettis Saga*', *Journal of English and Germanic Philology*, 73/3.

Ingold, Tim (1992), 'Culture and the Perception of the Environment', in Elisabeth Croll and David Parkin (eds.), *Bush Base, Forest Farm: Culture, Environment, and Development*, London: Routledge.

Íslendingabók, ed. by Jakob Benediktsson, Reykjavík: Hið íslenzka fornritafélag (Íslenzk fornrit, 1).

Jackson, Þorleifur Jóakimsson (1919), *Landnámssaga Nýja Íslands í Canada*, Winnipeg: Columbia Press.

Jochumssen, Matthias (1977), *Anmerkninger ofver Island og dessen indbyggere. Inberetning efter reser på Island i årene 1729–31*, ed. by O. Vassveit, Oslo: Universitetsbiblioteket.

Jochumsson, Matthías (1936), 'Grettisljóð', *Ljóðmæli*, Reykjavík.

Johnson, Mark (1993), *Moral Imagination. Implications of Cognitive Science for Ethics*, Chicago: Chicago University Press.

Jónsbók, Kong Magnus Hakonssons Lovbog for Island. Vedtaget på Altinget 1281, ed. Ólafur Halldórsson, Copenhagen 1904: S. L. Möllers bogtrykkeri.

Jónsson, Arngrímur (1609), *Crymogæa*, in Jakob Benediktsson (ed.), Reykjavík 1985: Sögufélagið.

Jónsson, Baldur (1978), *Íslenzk málvöndun*, Reykjavík: mimeo.

Jónsson, Finnur (ed.) (1931), *Edda Snorra Sturlusonar*, Copenhagen.

Jónsson, Guðni (ed.) (1936), *Grettis saga Ásmundarsonar*, Reykjavík: Hið íslenzka fornritafélag (Íslenzk fornrit, 7).

Jósephsson, Þorsteinn (1967), *Landið þitt*, Reykjavík: Mál og menning.

Karlsson, Stefán (ed.) (1983), *Guðmundar sögur biskups*, i, Copenhagen: C. A. Reitzels forlag (Editiones Arnamagnæanæ, Series B, vol. 6).

Ker, W. P. (1923), *The Dark Ages*, Edinburgh: Blackwood.

Koester, David (1990), *Historical Consciousness in Iceland*, Doctoral diss., Dept. of Anthropology, University of Chicago.

——(1995a), 'The Social and Cultural Dimensions of Icelandic Obituarial Discourse', *Journal of Linguistic Anthropology*, 5: 157–82.

Kaster, David (1995*b*), 'Gender Ideology and Nationalism in the Culture and Politics of Iceland', *American Ethnologist*, 22: 572–88.

Kohn, Tamara (1994), 'Incomers and Fieldworkers: A Comparative Study of Social Experience', in Hastrup and Hervik (1994).

Kristjánsson, Haukur (1982), 'Lýsing Snæfellsnes frá Löngufjörum að Ólafsvíkurenni', *Árbók Ferðafélag Íslands 1982*.

Kristjánsson, Jónas (1988), *Eddas and Sagas. Iceland's Medieval Literature*, transl. by Peter Foote, Reykjavík: Hið íslenska bókmenntafélag.

Kristjánsson, Lúðvík (1980), *Íslenzkir sjávarhættir*, i, Reykjavík: Menningarsjóður.

——(1982), *Íslenzkir sjávarhættir*, ii, Reykjavík: Menningarsjóður.

——(1983), *Íslenzkir sjávarhættir*, iii, Reykjavík: Menningarsjóður.

Kristmundsdóttir, Sigríður Dúna (1989), 'Outside, Muted, and Different: Icelandic Women's Movements and their Notions of Authority and Cultural Separateness', in Durrenberger and Pálsson (1989).

Kulturhistorisk Leksikon for Nordisk Middelalder, i–xxii, Copenhagen, Stockholm, Oslo 1956–1978: Rosenkilde og Bagger.

Küchler, Susanne (1993), 'Landscape as Memory: The Mapping of Process and its Representation in Melanesian Society', in Bender (1993*a*).

Ladurie, Emmanuel Le Roy (1981), 'A Concept: The Unification of the Globe by Disease', *The Mind and Method of the Historian*, Chicago: University of Chicago Press.

Lakoff, George (1987), *Women, Fire, and Dangerous Things*, Chicago: Chicago University Press.

Landnámabók, ed. by Jakob Benediktsson, Íslenzk fornrit, 1, Reykjavík: Hið íslenzka fornritefélag.

Lárusson, Ólafur (1944), *Byggð og saga*, Reykjavík: Ísafold.

Laxdæla saga (1934), ed. Einar Ó. Sveinsson, Reykjavík: Hið íslenzka fornritafélag (Íslenzk fornrit, 5).

Layton, Robert (1995), 'Relating to the Country in the Western Desert', in Hirsch and O'Hanlon (1995).

Leach, Edmund (1989), 'Tribal Ethnography: Past, Present, Future', in Tonkin, McDonald, and Chapman (1989).

Lévi-Strauss, Claude (1992), *La pensée sauvage*, Paris: Plon.

——(1964), *Le cru et le cuit*, Paris: Plon.

——(1968), *L'origine des manières à table*, Paris: Plon.

Lid, Niels (1934), 'Altnorwegisches Þorri', *Norsk Tidsskrift for Sprogvidenskab*, 7.

Liep, John (1987), 'Kannibaler og kulier. Antropofagiske scener fra en Sydhavsø', *Stofskifte*, 15.

Linger, Daniel (1994), 'Has Culture Theory Lost Its Minds?', *Ethos*, 22: 284–315.

Löfgren, Orvar (1990), 'Consuming Interests', *Culture and History*, 7: 7–36.

Lönnroth, Lars (1976), *Njáls saga: A Critical Introduction*, Berkeley and Los Angeles: University of California Press.

Lovsamling for Island (1853–89), ed. O. Stephensen and Jón Sigurðsson, Copenhagen: Høst og søn.

Lowenthal, David (1985), *The Past is a Foreign Country*, Cambridge: Cambridge University Press.

Lutz, Catherine, and Abu-Lughod, Lila (eds.) (1992), *Language and the Politics of Emotion*, Cambridge: Cambridge University Press.

Lyman, Stanford, M. (1978), 'The Acceptance, Rejection, and Reconstruction of Histories: On Some Controversies in the Study of Social and Cultural Change', in Richard Harvey Brown and Stanford M. Lyman (eds.), *Structure, Consciousness and History*, Cambridge: Cambridge University Press.

McDonald, Maryon (1989), *We are not French! Language, Culture, and Identity in Brittany*, London: Routledge.

——(1993), 'The Construction of Difference: An Anthropological Approach to Stereotypes', in Macdonald (1993).

Macdonald, Sharon (1993), 'Identity Complexes in Western Europe: Social Anthropological Perspectives', in Sharon Macdonald (ed.), *Inside European Identities*, Oxford: Berg.

Magnússon, Finnur (1989), 'Work and the Identity of the Poor: Work Load, Work Discipline, and Self-Respect', in Durrenberger and Pálsson (1989).

——(1990), *The Hidden Class: Culture and Class in a Maritime Setting, Iceland 1880–1942*, Aarhus: Aarhus University Press (North Atlantic Monographs, 1).

Magnússon, Skúli (1944*a*), *Beskrivelse af Gullbringu og Kjósar syslur* (1785), ed. Jón Helgason, Copenhagen: Munksgård (Bibliotheca Arnamagnæana, 4).

——(1944*b*), *Forsog til en kort beskrivelse af Island* (1786), ed. Jón Helgason, Copenhagen: Munksgård (Bibliotheca Arnamagnæana, 5).

Malinowski, Bronislaw (1922), *Argonauts of the Western Pacific*, London: Routledge.

Marcus, George E., and Fischer, Michael J. (1986), *Anthropology as Cultural Critique*, Chicago: University of Chicago Press.

Mauss, Marcel (1950), *Essai sur le don*, Paris: Presses universitaires de France.

Mead, George Henry (1934), *Mind, Self, and Society*, Chicago: Chicago University Press.

Meletinskij, E. (1973), 'Scandinavian Mythology as a System', *Journal of Symbolic Anthropology*. 1/2.

Middleton, David, and Edwards, Derek (eds.) (1990), 'Introduction', *Collective Remembering*, London: Sage.

Morphy, Howard (1995), 'Landscape and the Reproduction of the Ancestral Past', in Hirsch and O'Hanlon (1995).

Motz, Lotte (1973), 'Withdrawal and Return: A Ritual Pattern in Grettis Saga', *Arkiv for Nordisk Filologi*, 88.

Mullaney, Steven (1992), 'Civic Rites, City Sites: The Place of the Stage', in David Scott Kastan and Peter Stallybrass (eds.), *Staging the Renaissance: Reinterpretations of Elizabethan and Jacobean Drama*, London: Routledge.

Nordal, Sigurður (1931), *Íslenzk lestrarbók*, Reykjavík: Mál og menning.

——(1938), 'Sturla Þórðarson og *Grettis saga*', *Studia Islandica*, 4.

——(1942), *Íslenzk menning*, Reykjavík: Mál og menning.

Okely, Judith (1975), 'Gypsy Women: Models in Conflict', in Shirley Ardener (ed.), *Perceiving Women*, London: Croom Helm.

——(1978), 'Privileged, Schooled, and Finished: Boarding Education for Girls', in Shirley Ardener, *Defining Females: The Nature of Women in Society*, London: Croom Helm.

——(1984), 'Fieldwork in Home Countries', *RAIN*, 61: 4–6.

——(1992), 'Anthropology and Autobiography: Participatory Experience and Embodied Knowledge', in Okely and Callaway (1992).

——(1994), 'Vicarious and Sensory Knowledge of Chronology and Change: Ageing in Rural France', in Hastrup and Hervik (1994).

——(1996), *Own or Other Culture*, London: Routledge.

Okely, Judith and Callaway, Helen (eds.) (1992), *Anthropology and Autobiography*, London: Routledge (ASA Monographs 29).

Ólafsson, Eggert (1772), *Reise igiennem Island*, Sorøe: Det Kongelige Vidensskabsakademi.

Olavius, Olafur (1780), *Oeconomisk Reise igiennem Island*, Copenhagen: Gyldendals Forlag.

Olwig, Karen Fog, and Hastrup, Kirsten (eds.) (1996), *Siting Culture*, London: Routledge.

Olwig, Kenneth R. (1993), 'Sexual Cosmology: Nation and Landscape at the Conceptual Interstices of Nature and Culture; or What does Landscape Really Mean?', in Bender (1993*a*).

Orkneyinga saga, ed. by Finnur Guðmundsson (1965), Reykjavík: Hið íslenzka fornritafélag (Íslenzk fornrit, 34).

Ottenberg, Simon (1990), 'Thirty Years of Fieldnotes: Changing Relationships to the Text', in Sanjek (1990).

Paine, Robert (1995), 'Columbus and the Anthropology of the Unknown', *Journal of the Royal Anthropological Institute (incorporating MAN)*, 1: 47–65.

Pálsson, Gísli (1979), 'Vont mál og vond málfræði', *Skírnir*, 153: 175–201.

——(1982), 'Territoriality among Icelandic Fishermen', *Acta Sociologica*, 25, Suppl.: 5–13.

——(1987), *Sambúð manns og sjávar*, Reykjavík: Svart á hvítu.

——(1988), 'Models for Fishing and Models of Success', *Maritime Anthropological Studies*, 1: 15–28.

——(1989), 'Language and Society: The Ethnolinguistics of Icelanders', in Durrenberger and Pálsson (1989).

——(1990), 'The Idea of Fish: Land and Sea in the Icelandic World-view', in Roy Willis (ed.), *Signifying Animals: Human Meaning in the Natural World*, London: Unwin Hyman, 119–33.

——(1991), *Coastal Economies, Cultural Accounts: Human Ecology and Icelandic Discourse*, Manchester: Manchester University Press.

——(1995), *The Textual Life of Savants*, New York: Harwood Academic Press.

——and Durrenberger, E. Paul (1982), 'To Dream of Fish: The Causes of Icelandic Skippers' Fishing Success', *Journal of Anthropological Research*, 38: 227–42.

———(1990), 'Systems of Production and Social Discourse: The Skipper Effect Revisited', *American Anthropologist*, 92: 130–41.

———(eds.) (1996), *Images of Contemporary Iceland*, Iowa: University of Iowa Press.

——and Helgason, Agnar (1996), 'The Politics of Production: Enclosure, Equity, and Efficiency', in Pálsson and Durrenberger (1996).

Pálsson, Hermann (1962), *Sagnaskemmtan Íslendinga*, Reykjavík: Mál og menning.

Pinson, Ann (1979), 'Kinship and Economy in Modern Iceland: A Study in Social Continuity', *Ethnology*, 18: 183–97.

——(1985), 'The Institution of Friendship and Drinking Patterns in Iceland', *Anthropological Quarterly*, 58: 75–82.

Pratt, Mary Louise (1992), *Imperial Eyes: Travel Writing and Transculturation*, London: Routledge.

Putnam, Hilary (1990), *Realism with a Human Face*, Cambridge, Mass.: Harvard University Press.

Quine, W. V. (1992), *Pursuit of Truth*, revd. edn., Cambridge, Mass.: Harvard University Press.

Rabinow, Paul (1977), *Reflections on Fieldwork in Morocco*, Berkeley and Los Angeles: University of California Press.

Radley, Alan (1990), 'Artefacts, Memory and a Sense of the Past', in Middleton and Edwards (1990).

Rafnsson, Sveinbjörn (1974), *Studier in Landnámabók: Kritiska bidrag til den isländska fristatstidens historia*, Lund: Gleerup (Bibliotheca Historica Lundensis, 31).

——(ed.) (1983), *Frásögur um Fornaldarleifar 1817–1823*, i and ii, Reykjavík: Stofnun Árna Magnússonar.

Rappaport, Roy A. (1968), *Pigs for Ancestors: Ritual in the Ecology of a New Guinea People*, Yale: Yale University Press.

Rapport, Nigel (1994), *The Prose and the Passion: Anthropology, Literature, and the Writing of E. M. Forster*, Manchester: Manchester University Press.

Rasmussen, Knud (1929), *Intellectual Culture of the Iglulik Eskimos*, Copenhagen: Gyldendalske Boghandel (Report of the Fifth Thule Expedition 1921–4, 7/1).

Rich, George W. (1989), 'Problems and Prospects in the Study of Icelandic Kinship', in Durrenberger and Pálsson (1989).

Ricoeur, Paul (1992), *Oneself as Another*, Chicago: Chicago University Press.

Rosaldo, Renato (1980), *Ilongot Headhunting, 1883–1974: A Study in History and Society*, Stanford, Calif.: Stanford University Press.

Rosch, Eleanor (1978), 'Principles of Categorization', in Eleanor Rosch and B. B. Lloyd (eds.), *Cognition and Categorization*, Hillsdale, NJ: Lawrence Erlbaum.

Rotberg, R. I., and Rabb, T. K. (eds.) (1981), *Climate and History*, Princeton: Princeton University Press.

Rudie, Ingrid (1994), 'Making Sense of New Experience', in Hastrup and Hervik (1994).

Sahlins, Marshall D. (1974), *Stone Age Economics*, London: Tavistock.

——(1985), *Islands of History*, Chicago: University of Chicago Press.

——(1993), 'Goodbye to Tristes Tropes: Ethnography in the Context of Modern World History', *Journal of Modern History*, 65/1: 1–25.

Said, Edward W. (1978), *Orientalism*, London: Vintage.

——(1992), *Musical Elaborations*, London: Vintage.

——(1993), *Culture and Imperialism*, London: Vintage.

——(1994), *Representations of the Intellectual. The 1993 Reith Lectures*, London: Vintage.

Samuel, Raphael, and Thompson, Paul (1990), 'Introduction', in R. Samuel and P. Thompson (eds.), *The Myths We Live By*, London: Routledge.

Sanjek, Roger (ed.) (1990), *Fieldnotes: The Makings of Anthropology*, Ithaca, NY: Cornell University Press.

Schier, Kurt (1975), 'Iceland and the Rise of Literature in "Terra Nova": Some Comparative Reflections', *Grípla*, 1.

Scholte, Bob (1974), 'Toward a Reflexive and Critical Anthropology', in Dell Hymes (ed.), *Reinventing Anthropology*, New York: Vintage Books.

Schutz, Alfred (1951), 'Making Music Together: A Study in Social Relationship', *Social Research*, 18: 76–97.

Selincourt, Basil de (1961), 'Music and Duration', in Susanne K. Langer (ed.), *Reflections on Art: A Sourcebook of Writings by Artists, Critics, and Philosophers*, New York: Oxford University Press.

Shotter, John (1990), 'The Social Construction of Remembering and Forgetting', in Middleton and Edwards (1990).

Sigurðsson, Jón (1951), *Hugvekja til íslendinga*, ed. by Sverri Kristjánsson, Reykjavík: Mál og menning.

Sjørslev, Inger (1987), 'At æde eller blive ædt', *Stofskifte*, 15.

Skaptadóttir, Unnur Dís (1996), 'Housework and Wage Work: Gender in Icelandic Fishing Communities', in Pálsson and Durrenberger (1996).

Steffensen, Jón (1975), *Menning og meinsemdir: Ritgerðasafn um mótunarsögu íslenzkrar þjóðar og baráttu hennar við hungur og sóttir*, Reykjavík: Sögufélagið.

Stokes, Martin (1994), 'Introduction: Ethnicity, Identity and Music', in Martin Stokes (ed.), *Ethnicity, Identity and Music: The Musical Construction of Place*, Oxford: Berg.

Storm, Gustav (ed.) (1888), *Islandske Annaler indtil 1578*. Kristiania 1888: Det Norske Historiske Kildeskriftfond.

Strathern, Marilyn (1995), 'Foreword: Shifting Contexts', in Marilyn Strathern (ed.), *Shifting Contexts: Transformations in Anthropological Knowledge*, London: Routledge (ASA Decennial Conference Series).

Svavarsdóttir, Ásta (1982), ' "Þágufallssýki" ', *Íslenzk mál*, 6: 33–55.

Sveinsson, Einar Ó. (ed.) (1934), *Laxdæla saga*, Reykjavík: Hið íslenzka fornritafélag. Íslenzk fornrit, 5.

——(1959), *Handritamálið*, Reykjavík: Hiðíslenzka bókmenntafélag.

Sørensen, Preben Meulengracht (1977), *Saga og samfund*, København: Berlingske.

——(1993), *Fortælling og ære. Studier i islændingesagaerne*, Aarhus: Aarhus Universitetsforlag.

Taylor, Charles (1985*a*), 'Social Theory as Practice', in Charles Taylor, *Philosophy and the Human Sciences*, Cambridge: Cambridge University Press.

——(1985*b*), 'Understanding and Ethnocentricity', in Taylor (1985*c*).

——(1985*c*), *Philosophy and the Human Sciences*, Philosophical Papers 2, Cambridge: Cambridge University Press.

——(1989), *Sources of the Self*, Cambridge: Cambridge University Press.

Tedlock, Dennis (1983) 'The Analogical Tradition and the Emergence of Dialogical Anthropology', *The Spoken Word and the Work of Interpretation*, Philadelphia: University of Pennsylvania Press.

Tilley, Christopher (1993*a*), 'Art, Architecture, Landscape [Neolithic Sweden]', in Bender (1993*a*).

——(1993*b*), 'Introduction: Interpretation and a Poetics of the Past', in Christopher Tilley (ed.), *Interpretative Archaeology*, Oxford: Berg.

——(1994), *A Phenomenology of Landscape. Places, Paths and Monuments*, Oxford: Berg.

Tonkin, Elizabeth (1990), 'History and the Myth of Realism', in Samuel and Thompson (1990).

——McDonald, Maryon, and Chapman, Malcolm (1989) (eds.), *History and Ethnicity*, London: Routledge (ASA Monographs 27).

Troil, Uno von (1780), *Letters on Iceland*, London (1980): J. Robson.

Trouillot, Michel-Rolph (1991), 'Anthropology and the Savage Slot', in Richard Fox, (ed.), *Recapturing Anthropology*, Washington: American School of Research.

Turner, Victor (1971), 'An Anthropological Approach to the Icelandic Saga', in T. O. Beidelman (ed.), *The Translation of Culture: Essays to E. E. Evans-Pritchard*, London: Tavistock.

——(1986), 'Dewey, Dilthey, and Drama: An Essay in the Anthropology of Experience', in Victor Turner and Edward Bruner (eds.), *The Anthropology of Experience*, Chicago: University of Illinois Press.

Turville-Petre, Gabriel (1964), *Myth and Religion of the North: The Religion of Ancient Scandinavia*. London: Weidenfeld & Nicholson.

Vansina, Jan (1985), *Oral Tradition as History*, Madison: University of Wisconsin Press.

Vasey, Dan (1996), 'Premodern and Modern Constructions of Population Regimes', in Pálsson and Durrenberger (1996).

Vendler, Zeno (1984), 'Understanding People', in Richard A. Shweder and Robert A. LeVine (eds.), *Culture Theory: Essays on Mind, Self, and Emotion*, Cambridge: Cambridge University Press.

Vetter, Daniel (1640), *Islandia*, ed. by B. Hórak, Brno 1931: Vydárá Filoficka Fakulta.

Wagner, Roy (1975), *The Invention of Culture*, Englewood Cliffs, NJ: Prentice-Hall.

Weber, Gerd Wolfgang (1981), 'Irreligiosität und Heldenzeitalder: Zum Mythencharacter der altisländischen Literatur', in Ursula Dronke *et al.* (eds.), *Speculum Norroenum. Norse Studies in Memory of Gabriel Turville-Petre*, Odense: Odense University Press.

Wieland, Daryll (1989), 'The Idea of Mystical Power in Modern Iceland', in Durrenberger and Pálsson (1989).

Wolf, Eric (1982), *Europe and the People without History*, Berkeley and Los Angeles: University of California Press.

Yates, Frances (1992), *The Art of Memory*, London: Pimlico.

Þórðarson, Þórbergur (1981), *Suðursveit*, Reykjavík: Mál og menning.

Þorsteinsson, Björn (1976), *Tíu þorskastríð 1415–1976*, Reykjavík: Sögufélagið.

INDEX

RARITAN VALLEY COMMUNITY COLLEGE

3 3666 50095 8698

DL 375 .H37 1998

Hastrup, Kirsten.

A place apart

**RARITAN VALLEY COMMUNITY
COLLEGE LIBRARY
ROUTE 28
NORTH BRANCH, NJ   08876-1265**